Fundamentalists
in the City

Recent titles in
RELIGION IN AMERICA SERIES
Harry S. Stout, General Editor

Fundamentalists in the City

Conflict and Division in Boston's Churches, 1885–1950

MARGARET LAMBERTS BENDROTH

OXFORD

UNIVERSITY PRESS

2005

OXFORD
UNIVERSITY PRESS

Oxford University Press, Inc., publishes works that further
Oxford University's objective of excellence
in research, scholarship, and education.

Oxford   New York
Auckland   Cape Town   Dar es Salaam   Hong Kong   Karachi
Kuala Lumpur   Madrid   Melbourne   Mexico City   Nairobi
New Delhi   Shanghai   Taipei   Toronto

With offices in
Argentina   Austria   Brazil   Chile   Czech Republic   France   Greece
Guatemala   Hungary   Italy   Japan   Poland   Portugal   Singapore
South Korea   Switzerland   Thailand   Turkey   Ukraine   Vietnam

Copyright © 2005 by Oxford University Press, Inc.

Published by Oxford University Press, Inc.
198 Madison Avenue, New York, New York 10016

www.oup.com

Oxford is a registered trademark of Oxford University Press

Library of Congress Cataloging-in-Publication Data
Bendroth, Margaret Lamberts, 1954–
    Fundamentalists in the city : conflict and division in Boston's churches, 1885–1950/
Margaret Lamberts Bendroth.
        p. cm.— (Religion in America series)
    Includes bibliographical references and index.
    ISBN-13 978-0-19-517390-1
    ISBN 0-19-517390-2
        1. Fundamentalism—Massachusetts—Boston—History—19th century.   2. Boston
(Mass.)—Church history—19th century.   3. Fundamentalism—Massachusetts—Boston—
History—20th century.   4. Boston (Mass.)—Church history—20th century.
I. Title.   II. Religion in America series (Oxford University Press)

BR560.B73B46 2005
277.44'61081–dc22   2005040555

9 8 7 6 5 4 3 2 1

Printed in the United States of America
on acid-free paper

To Anna, who loves Boston,
and to Ginny Brereton,
irreplaceable colleague and friend

Acknowledgments

This book began under a grant from the Pew Charitable Trusts. Many thanks to Pew and to Joel Carpenter, who provided the original inspiration for the grant and continued encouragement for this project. An Individual Research Assistance Grant from the American Academy of Religion provided badly needed funding for summer work on membership records at Tremont Temple Baptist Church.

Many people assisted along the way. Pam Greenberg and Brenda VanderLinde typed and fiddled for many hours with the Tremont Temple membership data. Joan MacDonald and Bill Salter provided kind hospitality, including access to air conditioning and the latest Red Sox scores during long summer days in the church offices. Hal Worthley, at the Congregational Library, guided me through the intricacies of the Park Street Church records. Sharon Taylor opened her home to me, listened to me talk about the project, shared her own work, and provided gracious access to the Andover-Newton Library. Doug Koopman, director of the Center for Social Research at Calvin College, gave good advice about spreadsheets and, even better, provided funding to help pay for competent help. I am also indebted to the staff in the Microfilm Room at the Boston Public Library, and the tireless help of Kathleen Struck and the interlibrary loan staff in the Hekman Library at Calvin College.

Many friends and colleagues read all or part of the manuscript in its various incarnations, including Virginia Brereton, Paul Kemeny, Kristin Farmelant, Michael Hamilton, and Bill Trollinger. My colleagues in the history department at Calvin College listened to many garbled versions of the final product, in lunchtime conversations and seminars, and lent expertise on every possible subject: Canadian Baptists, occupational categories in census reports, and the follies of revivalism.

As always, my husband Norman and children Nathan and Anna surrounded me with warmth, good humor, and plenty of distractions along the way. Though they have yet to edit any prose or proofread any pages, they have made themselves indispensable to me in plenty of other less practical, but equally wonderful ways.

Long ago, I promised Anna that I would dedicate this book to her because it is about Boston, a city that has always been her home, even when she lived in other places. I also dedicate this work to my dear friend Ginny Brereton, who knew about this project from its very beginning, read and commented on almost every page, but did not live to see it finally in print. Very simply, this book would not have been possible without her; I will always be deeply indebted to her wisdom, humor, and irreplaceable friendship.

Contents

Fundamentalists in the City

I

Introduction

This was supposed to be a book about religious protest—certainly with a subject like fundamentalism and a city like Boston, that seemed a more-than-likely outcome. What better example of cultural opposition than American Protestant fundamentalism, a movement famous for splitting denominations, staging heresy trials, and offering dire predictions of the End Times? And what better setting than Boston, a city renowned for its brusque incivility and epic social clashes? The very unlikeliness of fundamentalism finding a home along the banks of the Charles, in the very citadel of urbane liberalism, made the idea all the more compelling. Indeed, putting the two together seemed a worthy project in every respect: not only would they make a great story, but they would provide a new perspective on the murky social origins of an important, and often misunderstood, cultural movement. It is one thing to chart the rise of fundamentalism from books, periodicals, and sermons; a truly local history of the movement was bound to offer a far more dramatic, human tale.

But as is true of most historical accounts, the picture that emerged was a bit messier—and far more interesting—than the original. Boston certainly had its share of fundamentalists, including two large, nationally known churches and a long roster of colorful, combative spokesmen. Many of them, including Tremont Temple's J. C. Massee and Park Street Church's Harold Ockenga, were undisputed leaders in the national movement. Others were simply fun to write about: W. H. Davis, the ill-fated Boston Common evangelist; Margaret Shepherd, the shady "converted nun"; Joel Wright, the pentecostal visionary from New Hampshire; Arcturus Zodiac Conrad, the pugnacious Congregationalist, and Cortland Myers, his equally aggressive counterpart at Tremont Temple. The story of conservative Protestants in Boston is worth knowing about for many reasons, not least for introducing a new cast of odd and fascinating people, largely wiped from historical memory by the customary focus on Irish Catholics and elite Yankee Protestants. Bringing to light these unknown Protestants opens up new layers of division and conflict in the city's past, not just between Catholics and Protestants but also within a socially and theologically diverse Protestant world.

But Boston's story is also important for the perspective it provides on American fundamentalism. Almost all historical accounts have dealt with the movement as a broadly national phenomenon, and have concentrated primarily on leaders and issues.[1] As a result, historians know surprisingly little about the people who filled the pews in fundamentalist churches.[2] Nor can they really explain how the welter of social tensions in the late nineteenth century gave rise to fundamentalist militancy; most often historians simply invoke the problems around urbanization and immigration without delving into them much further.[3] But to paraphrase a famous Bostonian, all religion is, in the end, local. Though a close retelling of Boston's story can't be simply enlarged into a blanket explanation for the rise of American fundamentalism, it does offer valuable contextual clues about why and how Protestants began to divide from each other a century ago.

A closer focus is not a simpler one, however. For one thing, at close range the problem of definition becomes extraordinarily difficult. The term "fundamentalism" did not become common usage until the 1920s, after it was suggested by the publication of the twelve-volume series of theological arguments entitled *The Fundamentals* between 1911 and 1915, and coined by Curtis Lee Laws, the editor of the *Watchman-Examiner*. By then, the term usually referred to separatist Protestants who embraced a strict rendering of the doctrine of biblical inspiration—often referred to as "inerrancy"—or subscribed to some form of dispensational premillennialism. This was a system of interpreting human history since Adam as a series of dispensations, or periods of time, in which divine providence repeatedly trumped sinful disobedence. Premillennialists also believed that the world would end catastrophically and perhaps soon, depending on their reading of biblical prophecies.

In Boston, before the movement coalesced, no one was properly a fundamentalist, or even a "protofundamentalist"; people were simply different types of evangelical Protestants. On one end of the spectrum were liberals, in Boston primarily Unitarians; the rest differed from each other mostly in what they chose to emphasize. New England Baptists, for example, tended to be more zealous about revivals, Congregationalists talked endlessly about church polity matters, and Methodists rallied around the temperance banner.

But in the 1880s, some of them—though certainly not all—became militant. They began to see themselves as a beleaguered minority in a hostile world, and began to move in opposition to their religious rivals and the city's political power structure. Because "fundamentalist"—most often employed as a theologically descriptive term—unnecessarily narrows the scope of this social process, I have used it somewhat sparingly, especially in the early chapters of the book. A neologism like "oppositional Protestant" might have been an appropriate substitute, but it is simply too awkward. So to avoid putting too much construction on the past, I have most often chosen to refer to my subjects as *conservative evangelicals* or *conservative Protestants*, to distinguish them from their more liberal cousins or from Protestants who remained content with a simple denominational label.

Any term, however, is problematic. Although the Protestants described in this book shared common aims, and in many cases, common church pews, they hardly walked in lock step. They came together in several noteworthy instances to protest an unjust law or organize a mass revival but did not share a single leader, a doctrinal statement, or a social program. They do not, in other words, fit the scholarly picture of fundamentalism as a sheltered, separatist "enclave culture."[4] Leading conservative churches like Tremont Temple and Park Street tended to be some of the largest in the city, with hundreds, eventually thousands, of members. They attracted a steady stream of hardworking, middling social sorts from around the city and suburbs, not the angry or alienated few.

Under the right circumstances, of course, they were certainly capable of militant opposition; what's interesting, however, is the relative unimportance of theological liberalism in motivating them to action. Unitarians and heretical seminary professors—of which Boston had no small supply—rarely found mention in a Tremont Temple sermon; attacks on orthodox doctrine never sent conservative Protestants out onto the streets in protest.

But Catholics genuinely alarmed them. Evangelicals in Boston worried far more about Catholic presence than just about anything else; in the late nineteenth century, the threat of "Romanism" created new bonds of Protestant unity, unending fodder for sermons, and even an agenda for political action. Though overt hostilities declined in ensuing decades, conservative Protestants continued to define themselves in opposition to Catholics, whom they saw as the embodiment of cynical authoritarianism and spiritual indifference. Students of fundamentalism might recognize these as categories that, in the pitched denominational battles of the 1920s, conservative Presbyterians and Baptists used to attack their liberal opponents. Without drawing the point too strongly, I do think the coincidence is noteworthy: the link between doctrinal orthodoxy and righteous individualism—a construction that led many Protestants out of their denominations in the twentieth century—had been established much earlier, in evangelical Protestant confrontations with Roman Catholics.

Opposition to Catholics shaped conservative Protestant identity in interesting ways. In Boston, an alliance of convenience between Irish Catholic and elite Yankee politicians meant that, especially when it came to the prohibition of alcohol, middle-class evangelicals felt betrayed by fellow Protestants, perceived as both wealthier and more theologically liberal than they. But anti-Catholicism also set limits on evangelical alienation. Because most Americans agreed that the aims of "Romanists" were fundamentally undemocratic, evangelical opponents could mount angry protest against local government authorities, and still insist that they were their country's truest defenders.

In this respect, the Catholic presence is an important, though often overlooked, source of fundamentalist militance. Religious scholars have generally assumed that American fundamentalism was, until the 1970s, primarily a religious movement, far less political than other types of conservative faith in other parts of the world. But, as this book argues, in its local context American fundamentalism could be deeply political. Moreover, the commonly accepted picture of fundamentalist movements as inherently opposed to free expression does not hold here either.[5] As the following chapters demonstrate, Boston's Protestant minority first united around a passionate campaign to preserve free speech and equal access to the city's public spaces, rights they worried about losing if Catholic political and numerical dominance were allowed to continue.

Gender also played an important role in defining fundamentalism. One of the original purposes of this book was to test some of the broader narratives about masculinity and conservative religion that have shaped a great deal of recent scholarship, including my own.[6] The goal was to see how the rhetoric about godly manhood and feminine submission, a staple of fundamentalist books and periodicals, really "worked" in daily congregational life. Here too the picture was less clear than I had originally expected: in most cases my subjects seemed blissfully unaware of larger battles being waged on paper above their heads. But in a larger sense, the narrative of fundamentalism as a "masculinizing" movement did hold true. In the first phase of organization, women supplied most of the moral indignation and tactical political leadership for the conservative Protestant cause—this by virtue of their relative distance from institutional power. Already trained in the temperance movement, women were quick to mobilize and relatively heedless of traditions when these impeded greater moral goals. But in the early twentieth century, masculine leadership shaped moral indignation into a more permanent public presence. Nowhere was this more evident than in the large-scale, cooperatively organized urban revival campaigns that Bostonians pursued with enthusiasm and success. The vividly masculine rhetoric of revival preachers was not, as is often assumed, simply intended to marginalize women or to resist feminization. In a larger sense, the assertion that religion was "men's business" instead of women's signaled the arrival of a broader public agenda among conservative Protestants. Fundamentalism was a women's movement in its most moralistic, confrontational stage; and a men's movement as it moved toward consolidation and, in many ways, accommodation to the rules of secular urban life.

But how typical was Boston? Certainly not all evangelicals encountered Boston's type of Catholic community, which was, by the late nineteenth century, one of the most homogeneous and politically powerful in the country. Moreover, as an old and geographically small city, Boston hosted more than the usual share of religious turf battles and endured more attempts to regulate public space; the civic temperature has generally run a few degrees hotter in the Hub than in larger, newer, and more spacious cities. Boston's story is not meant to explain all others, not do I mean to suggest that anti-Catholicism lies at the bottom of all fundamentalist resistance. But the broader principle behind this story will, I believe, hold true for all other cases, that fundamentalism's diverse appeal to individual men and women emerges most clearly when set in a particular time and place.

In Boston, the history of fundamentalism has two main phases, one beginning in 1885 and the other in 1909. In both of those years, Boston changed its city charter, and in doing so directly and indirectly affected the status of conservative Protestants. In 1885, a shakeup of the police department and the mayor's office brought evangelicals into bitter conflict with governing authorities. In 1909 a Progressive-era reform of the city's traditional machine politics ushered in an era of vividly populist leadership, paralleling a golden age of citywide evangelistic campaigns and conservative Protestant folk heroes.

Part I of this book, covering a period from the mid-1880s to the turn of the century, features intense political and religious conflict. The discord began with the surprise arrest of three clergymen engaged in open-air preaching on Boston Common, and quickly branched out into a battle for control of other public spaces, including parks, street corners, and eventually the entire city school system. That complex narrative has several installments, and begins with a walking tour of Protestant Boston, section by section and in some cases street by street, as a pedestrian would have encountered it in 1885. This opening chapter provides some important contextual cues for understanding the contentious events of that spring, as well as clarifying the importance of geography for Protestant churches. Protestants did not, of course, literally sacralize city space, but they were nonetheless territorial after their own fashion. Knowing who worshiped where and near whom is key to understanding the religious sensitivities of the 1880s and 1890s.

Boston Common is another central motif in this book; a famous city park with deep spiritual and civic significance for Protestants, it was, not by accident, the spot where city police arrested three clergymen in late May 1885. That event and its consequences unfold in the next three chapters; chapter 3 details the arrests, chapter 4 describes the militant coalition that assembled in their wake, and chapter 5 analyzes the evangelical institutions that formed as a result. Chapter 6 is a history of Tremont Temple, the city's largest Baptist church and a pillar of Protestant resistance in the late nineteenth century. That story completes the picture of militant evangelicalism, with a closer look at the people who were attracted by Tremont Temple's intriguing mixture of theatrical showmanship, cultural politics, and simple, heartfelt gospel preaching.

Part II deals with three city-wide revivals. The first, in 1909, was a coordinated simultaneous campaign led by the scholarly Presbyterian J. Wilbur Chapman; the second, in the winter of 1916–17, headlined the famous baseball evangelist Billy Sunday. Though the revivals do not provide a tight narrative of religious growth, they do offer a revealing glimpse of the ways that conservative Protestants were coming to terms with their role in the city. Both of these revivals dealt with urban sin and corruption but, especially in comparison with previous decades, in an increasingly abstract sense. By the early twentieth century, evangelicals were less local than they had been before; most Protestant churches had already relocated to Boston's streetcar suburbs by the time Billy Sunday tried to rally a no-license vote in 1916. The exceptions, of course, were the two downtown monoliths, Tremont Temple and Park Street Church. The history of Park Street Church, told in chapter 8, dramatizes some of the growing tensions between evangelicals and their urban environment. This congregation narrowly avoided closing its doors in the years before the Chapman revival, just managing to reinvent itself as an urban congregation by forging new ties to a larger world of evangelicals in rural New England. By the 1940s, Park Street had not only outstripped Tremont Temple in popular appeal but was taking a leading role in the neoevangelical revival sweeping the United States after World War II.

The undisputed central figure in that movement was Billy Graham; the story of his revival tour of Boston and New England in early 1950 constitutes this book's final chapter. In one sense, the Graham crusade demonstrates evangelical detachment from the city—he and his associates were far more interested in saving the nation and the world than Boston in particular. But it also shows the continuing power of local attachments: Graham held his last, most emotionally charged meeting on Boston Common. But this book does not end, as it began, with a pedestrian's-eye view of Boston. Evangelicals were far less embedded in the city at midcentury than they were in 1885; their secularization, if it can be called such, consisted in an increasingly generalized attachment to Boston, less as a place and more as a symbolic launching site for worldwide revival.

It is easy to assume that oppositional movements like fundamentalism do not succeed because American culture simply refuses to fight back. Religious passions run a bit cooler in the United States, the argument goes, because instead of battling against religious dissidents, American pluralism simply flattens out differences and in the end absorbs them. Certainly the stories on the following pages demonstrate how difficult it is to establish an alternative religious presence. The clashes were real: evangelicals persevered through hostility from city hall, the intellectual scorn of theological opponents, wrenching demographic transitions, and difficult financial choices. But these repeated confrontations were not always enough to sustain a permanent split. Evangelicals in Boston, and in the larger Protestant world, looked long and hard for an opponent willing to put up a decent, long-term fight. Nowhere was their task more complicated than in Boston, a city that by the early twentieth century had long since lost its taste for religious certainties.

2

A Protestant on Foot

Imagine a Sunday afternoon walk through late nineteenth-century Boston, or more exactly, in the spring of 1885—that time of year when spring has finally established itself and winter is over. The ocean breeze is still clean and chilly, carrying a hint of salt. After the interminable gray of winter, sunlight on one's face forces an uncomfortable squint but feels almost gentle on skin normally bundled against the cold. The long humid weeks of summer lie ahead, and the threat of a few more dreary days is not completely past. It's a rare day, and a good one for walking.

The beginning point is the busy corner where Park and Tremont Streets intersect at Boston Common. Once dotted with Puritans' cows and sheep, by the late nineteenth century the Common was a vibrant city park, a maze of crisscrossing walkways lined by tall rows of elm trees. On a Sunday afternoon in early spring, the bustle of traffic at the Park Street corner might be broken by the sharp crack of a bat—the workingmen from the South End and the boys from Beacon Hill are playing baseball on the flats near Charles Street—or the insistent rant of the street preachers working hard to drum up an audience. Over toward Tremont Street, where narrow side alleys lead into a maze of shops and offices, all is quiet. On a Victorian Sunday afternoon, Massachusetts's blue laws would have closed this district up tight—according to one contemporary description, "as silent and deserted as a section of Pompeii."[1] Given the choice of destinations, either down the hill toward the business section or up into Beacon Hill, the genteel brownstones lining Park Street would look far more inviting.

This is no random stroll, of course. The sidewalks covered in this chapter are meant to provide an overview of congregational life in late nineteenth-century Boston, and, for reasons that will become clearer as the walk progresses, a unique perspective on the rise of American Protestant fundamentalism. It was once common for historians to view the late nineteenth century as an era of upheaval for American churches, brought on by the unsettling social effects of large-scale immigration and urbanization. Following Arthur Schlesinger's description of the "spiritual crisis" of religious faith at the turn of the century, generations of historians envisioned the churchgoing faithful as deeply unsettled by the strange new notions of scientists and the strange new ways of foreign people. Under this older paradigm of secularization, urban Protestants were the most beleaguered of all, fending off a huge descending wave of Catholic immigrants, often depicted as uneducated, united, and militant.[2]

More recently, historians and sociologists have taken a different tack, playing down the rhetoric of decline in order to demonstrate the long-term survivability of religion in modern commercial culture. Newer analyses of census returns and congregational records find that, far from wilting under the press of urban diversity, churches flourished as religious competition escalated. By providing a "mediating space" for religious people to adjust to secular trends, turn-of-the-century urban life spurred a "profound transformation, even flowering," of traditional belief and behavior. The city was not the nemesis of religious faith but the site of its continual rebirth.[3]

There is truth in both descriptions, but neither does justice to American Protestant fundamentalism, a movement notorious for its sharp, ungainly edges and defiance of neat scholarly categories. In the first case, the framework is too narrow. Assuming that all Protestants tilted toward the defensive during the Gilded Age, Schlesinger's heirs understood fundamentalism as the most reactionary form of a generally dysfunctional set of religious responses. Within this line of interpretation, the reemergence of a conservative evangelical movement in the 1970s was all but inexplicable. But it would be equally misleading to assume that fundamentalism was only a colorful form of adjustment to an open religious market. It is, by definition, a movement that resents the imperatives of adjustment; it has often failed because its unwillingness or inability to empathize with changing times.

Understanding oppositional faith requires a sensitive set of conceptual tools, for, as many recent books have shown, being fundamentalist in a modernizing American culture is not a simple, straightforward task. Not surprisingly, perhaps, the following pages contain many stories of forgotten political rivalries and once-thriving congregations, unfolding within the larger narrative of Boston's complex fortunes in the late nineteenth and early twentieth centuries. As this chapter attempts to show, Protestant reaction was first a local and then a regional and national movement; it took shape most powerfully within the vicissitudes of daily church life, quite literally at street level.

Boston is not, of course, a neutral backdrop for a story about religion or about change. Despite its liberal image, over the past hundred years the city has been notorious for mounting stubborn resistance to change, from the antibusing crisis of the 1970s to the inexplicable survival of Fenway Park's famous "Green Monster." As the journalist Alan Lupo has observed, "Perhaps the biggest cliché this city has had to bear is that it is a liberal city." Despite the famous tradition of liberal politics, Lupo writes, Boston is

> and always has been, a city torn apart by the extremes, a city both liberal and conservative, both enlightened and parochial and stifling. At times in history it has been very hard to be an Irishman in Boston, or an Italian, or a Jew, or a black, or, lately, a Yankee. It has *always* been hard to be a moderate.[4]

The same might be true in regard to religion, where several centuries of history and a cramped geography have continually sharpened awareness of the costs and the finality of congregational upheaval. In Boston, perhaps more than in some newer cities, churches did not sit on vast undifferentiated space but quite consciously held possession of hard-won urban turf.

Admittedly, Boston is a specific case, but perhaps also a finer lens through which to view a complex process of religious change. The dailiness of church life in late nineteenth-century Boston demonstrates on the one hand the innovative possibilities of religion in a large city and on the other the limited options for change. White native-born conservative Protestants were hardly a beleaguered group and proved themselves remarkably resilient in the face of challenges. But they were not uniformly successful. Fundamentalism took root in Boston, as this book suggests, in shallow, often rocky ground.

Boston, 1885

First, some background.

In 1885 Boston was, as it is today, a geographically compact city, famous for its narrow cobbled streets and ancient red-brick buildings. Most late nineteenth-century tourist guidebooks divided the immediate metropolitan area, known as "Boston proper," into several discrete sections: the business district or downtown, the Back Bay, and then the North, South, and West Ends (see fig. 2.1).

Of course, like most urban boundaries, these were somewhat fictional: the North and West Ends were almost parallel to each other on a map, and the South End was technically north of another section, South Boston. Moreover, in the mid- to late nineteenth century, Boston's contours were changing constantly, eventually encompassing some six hundred acres of reclaimed ocean land at its southern flanks. By the 1880s, the city also included vast

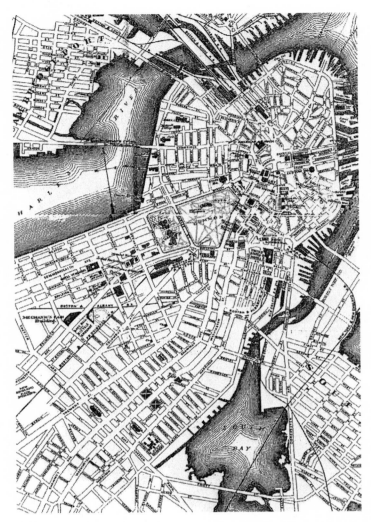

FIGURE 2.1. Boston in 1885. From Moses King, ed., *King's Handbook of Boston* (Boston: Rand, Avery, 1885).

stretches of newly annexed suburban towns stretching from Charlestown to Roxbury, some thirty-seven square miles in all. The core area of Boston proper remained small, however, and was still largely traversible on foot, horsecar, or trolley.[5]

According to the national census of 1890, Boston's population stood at nearly half a million, making it the sixth largest city in the United States. Though far behind New York and Chicago, each with more than double Boston's population, Boston still dwarfed newer upstarts like San Francisco,

Detroit, and Minneapolis.[6] But numerical rank or physical size had never captured Boston's own sense of itself. In the decades before the Civil War, the "Hub" was not only the capital of New England but renowned as the "Athens of America," the national center of learning, literary culture, and moral reform. Of course, by the late nineteenth century, this description was also a bit of a fiction: Boston kept its hold on American elite culture, but its economic power and intellectual hegemony were perceptibly slipping.

Urban disaster played a role in the transition. In early November 1872 a fire leveled large sections of the city's commercial district all the way down to the harbor, taking an undetermined number of lives, as well as sixty-five acres of warehouses, banks, and churches. The fire destroyed not only the Boston, Hartford and Erie Railroad depot but the offices of several leading newspapers. The worst damage was done to the dry goods and wholesale clothing trade in the city; some twenty thousand shop girls were "thrown out of employment" in the weeks and months that followed.[7] Rebuilding began quickly but temporarily slowed during the nationwide economic depression of the mid-1870s. In following decades, the effects of the fire permanently altered the shape of Boston, accelerating a process already underway in the years after the Civil War. The old downtown became less central as residential buildings and cultural landmarks migrated to surrounding districts, especially the new growth areas of the Back Bay and South End.[8]

Then, of course, there were the Irish. Though still sequestered in the city's North, South, and West End neighborhoods, Irish Catholics were a formidable presence. In 1885, only 39 percent of Boston's population were native born; another 27 percent were first-generation immigrants, predominantly Irish, and the rest the children of a previous immigrant generation.[9] These are not an unusually high percentages for the time period—in some midwestern cities like Chicago and Milwaukee the proportion of first and second generation immigrants rose as high as 90 percent—but Boston's Irish were unusually visible. The city's Catholic parishes, concentrated in a few areas of the city, were some of the most ethnically homogeneous in the nation. The first visible sign of success was the election of Hugh O'Brien as the city's first Irish-born mayor in 1885. Though Protestants accepted him as an Irishman of "the better sort" who kept property taxes low and widened the streets, they certainly realized that larger changes were in the offing.[10] O'Brien appeased his critics by overseeing the construction of the Boston Public Library in Copley Square and Frederick Law Olmsted's park system, but the day was not far off when Boston's Protestants would be reduced to, as one wag put it, "a fringe of piety surrounding the Irish."[11]

Despite O'Brien's electoral triumph, 1885 was not a peaceful year in Boston. As the following chapters will relate in more detail, the entire decade was marked by tense political conflict that pitted the state legislature against the city government, with the policing of the liquor trade at the center of contention. In 1885, a state bill to reorganize Boston's police department set the Irish Catholic Democrats in city hall directly against the Yankee Protestant Republicans in the Massachusetts state legislature. The so-called Police Bill, passed in June 1885, was a bitterly contested Protestant victory, inspiring some of the most heated name-calling in the history of the city's common council.[12]

The religious and political disputes were in many ways defined by geography. In the late nineteenth century, both Catholics and Protestants placed enormous stock in their physical hold on Boston's soil. The Catholic parish system, with its theological understanding of church land as literally sacred, necessitated long-term investment in neighborhoods; even if the population changed, a Catholic church could not simply pick up and follow its congregation to the suburbs. In the rite of consecration the bishop walked around the building, sprinkling Gregorian water and chanting a psalm; inside, he anointed the twelve consecration crosses positioned around the sanctuary and then sacralized the altar with oil and incense in preparation for Mass. Not surprisingly, Catholic churches tended to stay put even when the odds shifted against them; moving a church would require desacralizing the spot on which it had been built.[13] But Protestants also placed immense store in physical place; by the late nineteenth century, some churches had inhabited the same geographic spot for three centuries or more. Leaving was perhaps theologically possible, but financially and emotionally difficult. Moreover, Protestants contended not just with encroaching Catholics but with competitive upstarts of their own faith, always eager to take a shot at Puritan hegemony.

Even so, Protestants moved constantly. Stephan Thernstrom's landmark study of the city as a whole found that during the 1880s, twice the number of families moved into Boston as had lived there at the beginning of the decade; nearly the same number left the city during that time.[14] Protestants were no exception; indeed, nothing illustrates the fluid, dynamic quality of nineteenth-century urban Protestantism better than an overview of church life in three sections of the city. The first stage is a look around "old Boston," which included Beacon Hill and the original downtown; the second, the wealthy Back Bay; and the third the busy, transient neighborhoods of the South End.

Old Boston

The intersection of Park and Tremont was home to one of the city's most venerable Protestant institutions, the Park Street Church. The congregation was established in 1809 under the shadow of the growing theological divide between Congregationalists and Unitarians, and it quickly achieved a reputation for conservative orthodoxy. In fact, according to local legend, the Park and Tremont intersection was known as "brimstone corner" because of the fiery sermons emanating from the Park Street pulpit. Edward Dorr Griffin,

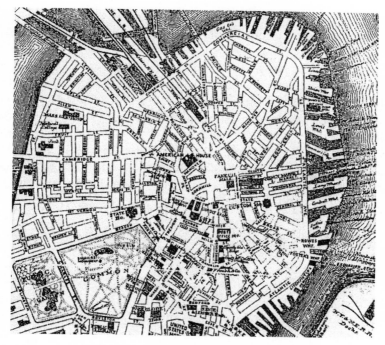

FIGURE 2.2. Old Boston. From Moses King, ed., *King's Handbook of Boston*
(Boston: Rand, Avery, 1885).

the church's first pastor, was famous for a descriptive homily entitled "On the
Use of Real Fire in Hell." Whatever the reason, the spot had a certain moral
reputation within the larger city: in 1926 the young H. L. Mencken marched
defiantly over to the Park and Tremont corner to sell copies of the *American
Mercury*, a publication "banned in Boston" for its salacious content. The
Watch and Ward Society promptly called for his arrest, but of course by then
they were too late: Mencken had already assumed a place in the long line of
Park Street's martyrs of free speech.[15]

By the time of the Civil War, the Park Street congregation had established
a firm reputation for evangelical piety. Home to an impressive list of missionary and benevolent organizations, the church grew steadily, though not
remarkably, for most of the century. By 1885, under the steady pastorship of
John Withrow, it listed over nine hundred members on its books.[16]

Most Bostonians admired the church not for its theology but its distinctive colonial brick architecture, especially the Christopher Wren spire. The
steeple, by conscious intent, rose ten feet higher than the nearest landmark,
the State House dome. Described by a visitor's guidebook as a "heaven-
pointing finger at the very center of Boston life," the Park Street spire visually
dominated the Common and the busiest sections of Tremont Street.[17]

Up the Park Street rise, past the dignified façades of the Woman's Club and the Union Club-house, stood the Massachusetts State House, the highest point in "old Boston." Henry James described this walk as one of "indefinable perfection," the shops and private clubs along the way "a syllable in the word Respectable several times repeated."[18] The State House rested appropriately at the summit, with the Common spreading out as a large front lawn. Behind and to the west of the State House the narrow streets and aging brownstones of Beacon Hill, the city's historic "Brahmin" district, wound down toward the harbor. Within the building's Doric columns and gilded dome, the past confronted visitors at every turn: busts of presidents, tattered battle flags, replicas of ancestral tombstones, and even the ancient wooden codfish taken from the original State House, built in 1711.

A few steps down the hill to the right of the capitol sat the Congregational House, a "vast hive of benevolent industry" at the corner of Beacon and Bowdoin Streets.[19] The building's geographic situation was apt. In 1885 Congregationalists were the second largest Protestant group in the city (behind the Baptists), numbering some ten thousand in the 1890 census and representing a broadly middle-class constituency spread across the surrounding suburbs.[20] This brown, granite-faced building, a stone's throw from the Boston Athenaeum and the Massachusetts Bible Society, served as a denominational headquarters as well as the physical and spiritual home of many famous Yankee institutions: the American Board of Commissioners for Foreign Missions, the American Missionary Association, the New West Educational Society, the Woman's Home Missionary Association, the American Peace Society, and the City Mission Society. It also housed the editorial rooms of the *Congregationalist,* and on Mondays the city's Congregational clergy met there for mutual edification in a large airy hall on the third floor.

Of course, even the Congregational House had to find a way to pay the rent. The bottom level of the building was a wooden storefront with large glass display windows. As the city's Congregational clergy wound their way up to their quarters, they would have walked past three commercial establishments occupied by the Roxbury Carpet Company, Thomas Todd's printing business, and Professor Robert R. Raymond's School of Oratory and Elocution.

From their upstairs windows, Congregationalists would also have had a good view of the new Unitarian denominational headquarters, a brown sandstone fortress under construction also near the corner of Beacon and Bowdoin Streets. (The building would be dedicated in June 1886.) In Boston, Unitarians took third place in the Protestant pecking order, numbering some 9,652 in the 1890 census. According to one account, their churches were "numerous" and "in a very prosperous condition" in post–Civil War Boston. Indeed, the census reported church property assets valued at nearly two and a half million dollars, far beyond those of any other Protestant body.[21] Though in the late nineteenth century Unitarians worried about declining numbers, they continued to enjoy a measure of cultural prestige. The "unusual social charm" of the Unitarian clergymen who shaped Henry Adams's early years persisted in the post–Civil War generation. In the salons of Beacon Hill and Cambridge, and in Brookline and West Roxbury's gracious suburban homes, Adams's self-described "mild deism" was respectably typical.[22]

Unitarians boasted a grand church structure just a block below their new headquarters on Beacon Street. King's Chapel, at the corner of Tremont and School Streets, was "one of the most cherished of Boston's antiquities." Organized as an Anglican church in 1686 at the orders of the famous nemesis of the Puritans, Governor Edmund Andros, it became a Unitarian congregation under James Freeman in 1787. The mix of traditions continued, however—hence George Santayana's description of the church as "High Church Unitarian," with nothing "either to discourage a believer or to encourage an unbeliever."[23] But the building's high-backed pews and tall pulpit belied even the illusion of change. Its ancient churchyard contained the mortal remains of the Puritan notables John Winthrop, Governor William Shirley, and John Cotton, as well as a distinguished array of lesser Congregational clergy. Described somewhat condescendingly by one guidebook as an "interesting relic," King's Chapel sat just around the corner from Boston's new City Hall, built during the Civil War, a fitting statement of its social and political prestige.[24]

The front doors of King's Chapel were only a few steps from the heart of Boston's business district. This old and busy part of town extended from the harbor north and west toward the Common and sat sandwiched between the immigrant neighborhoods of the city's North and South Ends. Quiet on a Sunday, this section would be filled with street traffic at every time of the day during the week, the sidewalks busy with rushing newspapermen and clerks in bowler hats and dark suits. During the 1880s, "newspaper row" on Washington Street was home to nearly all of Boston's local papers, from the elegant halls of the respectable *Evening Transcript* to the crowded warrens of the Democratic *Boston Post*.[25] During the daytime hours, downtown was also full of factory workers, manual laborers, and teamsters, since that district was also the center of the shoe and leather industry, as well as the wool and paper trades, in the 1880s. Even on a Sunday afternoon, a mix of weekday smells would still linger: freshly caught fish, ripening fruit, sweating horses, and salt breezes off the harbor. Not far from the factory and office districts were the open-air markets supplied by New Hampshire farmers, South American plantations, British merchants, and North Atlantic fishermen. The warehouses and stalls offered a rotating inventory of flour, grain, produce, foreign fruit, tea, coffee, sugar, and fish.[26]

But commerce had not yet visibly overtaken religion, and even in 1885 a casual walk through Boston's old downtown provided ample evidence of Protestant hegemony. The Old South Church still occupied the same corner of Washington and Milk Streets as had its original sanctuary, built in 1669. The plain square building, erected in 1729, had witnessed some major events in Boston's history: the anguished confession of the famous "witch judge" Samuel Sewall in 1696, the fiery sermons of the evangelist George Whitefield, and the planning of the Boston Tea Party. The infamous skeptic Benjamin Franklin had been baptized there. Though the church structure survived the fire of 1872, the congregation decided soon afterward that they had experienced enough of the rigors of their downtown location; like many upscale Boston Protestants, they moved to the Back Bay as the new land opened in the 1880s. After a brief stint as a local post office and being auctioned off as "junk," the eighteenth-century building quite fittingly stayed on as a historic monument, renowned as one of Boston's most famous landmarks. In 1885, "Old South" was literally a museum; funds for preserving the old building came from paid admissions to exhibits of new inventions and "colonial antiquities."[27]

Back on busy Tremont Street, physically below the Congregational and Unitarian citadels on Beacon Street, other denominations competed more aggressively for space. One of Boston's most famous Baptist churches, Tremont Temple (at the time still known as Union Baptist), sat "sandwiched between marts of trade" and facing the handsome granite facade of the Horticultural Hall, its large granite statue of the Greek goddess Ceres staring down across the way.[28] As chapter 4 explains in more detail, Tremont Temple was an unusual place, part theater and part church. In 1885, the building was only four years old but, because of recurring fire damage, the congregation's third on that site. Tremont Temple did not look at all like a traditional New England church: the bottom floor consisted of rented storefronts, topped by two rows of tall Palladian windows. Inside, on Sunday mornings the Reverend Emory Haynes preached in a large ornate auditorium, pacing back and forth across the platform, pulling on his long, pointed beard. Arrayed in theater seats before him, the congregation was thriving mix of working-class families and young men and women living all around the Boston area. Popularly known as the "stranger's Sabbath home," in the late nineteenth century Tremont Temple was fast becoming one of the largest Baptist churches in the country.

Tremont Temple was busy every day of the week. Because the original congregation was opposed to Boston's pew-rent system, the church supported itself by renting out space to shops and businesses and by allowing regular access to its auditorium, which was one of the largest in the city at the time. On any given day of the week, the crowds on Tremont Street might be waiting to attend a political rally, a magic show, or an edifying moral lecture. Tremont Temple's building was also the unofficial headquarters for Boston Baptists, housing an array of missionary societies, charitable organizations, and denominational publications.

New England Baptists were an entrepreneurial lot. Unlike Congregationalists and Unitarians, they could not claim a direct Puritan lineage, and they fought a bit harder to attain the respectability that these other Protestants took for granted. For many, memories of their seventeenth-century origins as a persecuted sect still lingered, despite the fact that in terms of numbers, by the early nineteenth century Baptists nationwide had far outstripped all rivals and ascended to the first rank of American denominations. In Boston, all Baptists combined (three separate bodies totaling 11,626) slightly outnumbered Congregationalists; however, they fell significantly behind in the value of their church properties, some twenty-eight churches assessed at $1,502,000. Both Congregationalists and Unitarians, with a comparable number of church buildings, owned properties valued at nearly a million dollars more.[29]

Methodists occupied slightly more marginal space down a few blocks on Bromfield Street, a narrow lane off Tremont Street. The first Methodists had not arrived in Boston until 1790—relatively late by New England standards. Out in the rest of the country, the nineteenth century had become known as the "Methodist Age," in reference to the denomination's enormous numerical and cultural dominance; New England, however, presented a different story. In 1890, the census put Methodists at a distant fifth among Boston's Protestants, their total number at 5,963, with twenty-four churches and total assets slightly over a million dollars. Their own First Church was not organized until 1795; it was built on Bromfield Street in 1806, where it stood until it was sold and torn down in 1913. Despite the denominations' relative youth, Boston's Methodists were just as busy as their Congregational and Baptist peers in building a vigorous organizational infrastructure. The Wesleyan Association Building, also on Bromfield Street, which was erected in 1870, housed the Methodist Historical Society, the Book Depository, the Women's Foreign Missionary Society, and the Women's Home Missionary Society. Two interdenominational groups, the Massachusetts Woman's Christian Temperance Union and the Total Abstinence Society, also maintained headquarters there. The Boston Theological Seminary stayed in the Bromfield Street site until 1886, when it joined the other major Methodist site in the old downtown, Boston University. Founded in 1869, the seminary was housed in a tall brownstone on Mt. Vernon Street on the opposite side of Beacon Hill. All told, however, Methodists had a rather slim purchase on downtown real estate. The vast majority of their churches listed in the 1885 city directory were in outlying sections of town: Allston, East and South Boston, Dorchester, Revere, Winthrop, and Charlestown. In 1914, Methodist headquarters would move to the new site of Boston University, further west in Copley Square.[30]

Three or four blocks further down Tremont Street, the gray Ionic portico of St. Paul's Episcopal Church faced the Common, between Winter and Temple Streets. Built in 1820, St. Paul was a quiet presence in Boston's central district, a testament to the wealth and power of its congregation and to the healthy presence of the denomination in the city. Episcopalians were one of the few Protestant denominations in Boston to enjoy strong and consistent growth from the late nineteenth century to the early decades of the twentieth century. The census of 1890 put them at 8,167, not far behind Congregationalists, Baptists, and Unitarians. Episcopalians were also among the wealthiest of Boston's Protestants, with twenty-seven buildings valued at over two million dollars.[31]

Protestant respectability was in many ways a function of geography. There were no Roman Catholic churches or Jewish synagogues anywhere near "old Boston." Nor, for that matter, were there any Lutherans, Universalists, German Reformed, Presbyterians, or Adventists. These were mostly decamped to the west and south.[32] At least in its older sections, Boston was hardly a free religious market for spiritual entrepreneurs. History rewarded those who arrived first—primarily Congregationalists, Unitarians, and Episcopalians—with physical priority of place.

But in the 1880s, Protestant hegemony was fraying a bit at the margins. If Beacon Hill was "the boundary line between the old and the new Boston," one did not have to walk far to discover this.[33] Back at the Congregational House on Beacon Street, the pedestrian might have caught a glimpse of the New Jerusalem Society just around the corner on Bowdoin Street. This church, on the less prestigious "back side" of Beacon Hill, was part of the mystical sect begun by Emmanuel Swedenborg in the eighteenth century, and for a long time was the only Swedenborgian church in the city. By 1885, however, the members had established new congregations in the outlying suburbs of Roxbury, Brookline, Newton, and Waltham.[34]

The back side of Beacon Hill also housed Boston's small but influential African American population. The African Meeting House was organized the same year as Park Street, in 1809, and functioned as a church as well as a social and cultural center for the several thousand mostly free African Americans in the city. Except for some tumultuous times during the Civil War era—highlighted by the formation of an all-black regiment, the Massachusetts Fifty-fourth—this population was mostly stable and self-contained. By the 1890s, however, pressures of European immigration forced African Americans increasingly out of the old West End and into newer neighborhoods further south along Tremont Street, and eventually into Roxbury and Dorchester. By the turn of the century, Boston's Twelfth Baptist Church in the South End had become one of the city's premier African American congregations.[35]

Beacon Hill also housed a series of healing establishments run by Dr. Charles Cullis. Although in a decade or so most Bostonians would associate spiritual healing with Mary Baker Eddy and the Christian Scientists, local interest in healing was already strong in the 1880s. By that time Cullis had established a Faith Training College for healers, a Willard Tract Repository to promote evangelism, and a Beacon Hill Church, dedicated in 1883. Down toward Roxbury, in Grove Hall, Cullis also maintained a Consumptives Home, where his faith cure was put into practice. The dignified, kindly Dr. Cullis represented not just evangelical religion on Beacon Hill but a particularly intense form of late nineteenth-century piety. Holiness believers held fast to the promise that absolute consecration to God would bring eventual freedom from sin; many, though not all, also believed that this freedom included deliverance from physical disease. Cullis, a former homeopathic physician, was an influential figure in what was by the 1880s a growing national network of "faith homes" and specialized hospitals.

Though the holiness movement was not large in Boston, it was well represented in New England, especially with the formation of the Christian and Missionary Alliance in eastern New York state in the 1890s.[36] Bostonians might have had at least a passing acquaintance with the movement's legendary fervor: in the spring of 1885, a group of evangelists from the Salvation Army branch in Augusta, Maine, were arrested for holding a "tumultuous assembly" on Boston Common, in which, said the Boston Globe, they descended each night to "march and howl and beat their drums."[37] In 1901 Park Street Church ousted one particularly enthusiastic sect with considerable difficulty from its sanctuary.[38]

Cullis was not, of course, the only Bostonian interested in spiritual remedies for disease. Other firmly respectable Protestants, including the Boston pastor A. J. Gordon, openly believed in the possibility of healing through divine grace. The Emmanuel movement and, more famously, Mary Baker Eddy's Christian Science church were growing rapidly in the late nineteenth century. In 1882, the Church of Christ (Scientist) consisted of only one small congregation; by 1890, it included 20 churches, 90 societies, and some 250 practitioners. The Christian Science Monitor, founded in 1883, boasted a circulation of ten thousand.[39]

Not all Protestants viewed Christian Science in the same way. In their April meeting in 1885, the Congregational clergy of the Suffolk North Association heard an address on the rise of the Christian Science movement and concluded that "the matter promises to be short-lived." They decided to take no action. Other liberal clergy, including the Unitarians Cyrus Bartol and Andrew Preston Peabody, were openly supportive of Mrs. Eddy, recognizing in her teachings on "mind cure" echoes of the ideas of Ralph Waldo Emerson.[40] But a few months earlier, in February 1885, popular lecturer Joseph Cook had used his Tremont Temple platform to attack Christian Science as a false religion. He was buttressed by other leading conservative voices, including the Boston University professor Luther Townsend and even Gordon, who denounced "the Boston craze" as occult nonsense and fundamentally "anti-Christian."[41]

Even old Boston, therefore, presented the orthodox with an unnerving mix of sacred and secular. When the members of Park Street Church descended the front steps of their building after Sunday service, they stood face to face with the Boston Music Hall, which in April 1885 was hosting the New England Kennel Club. Though originally intended for concerts of "high character," the Music Hall was slipping a bit in the 1880s, booking entertainments "not entirely in keeping with the high designs of those who planned the hall: fairs, public meetings, cat-shows, dog-shows, balls, foot-races, walking-matches, [and] a summer beer-garden with orchestral accompaniment."[42]

Not too far off, on the far end of Washington Street, was the heart of the theater trade in Boston, and what would soon become a center of vaudeville entertainment. Though reportedly still "clean and decent" in the early 1880s, not all of it was terribly respectable. In 1883, B. F. Keith and Edward Albee opened a Barnum-style museum in Boston, featuring a baby midget, a mermaid, a chicken with a human face, and the nation's largest hog. By 1885, the theater was holding continuous performances, from ten in the morning to ten at night.[43] Religion and entertainment jostled visibly for place in other ways as well. In 1885, entrepreneurs demolished the venerable Hollis Street Congregational Church (founded in 1732 but decamped to the Back Bay in 1882) and constructed the Hollis Street Theater in its place.[44]

The Tremont Temple faithful were also within walking distance of Scollay Square, Boston's old "red light" district, a few blocks to the northeast. There the entertainment did not even aspire toward refinement; the Austin and Stones Dime Museum, opened in 1881, offered a mix of musical acts and carnival freaks. One of Boston's most famous burlesque theaters was the Old Howard, built on the site of an old Adventist church but now ministering to a different crowd of faithful with a brewery on the first floor and a regular parade of sensational acts: the Human Fly, Buffalo Bill, and Boston's pugilist extraordinaire, John L. Sullivan. By the turn of the century, the fare was also becoming more bawdy, and by the 1920s, the Old Howard was a notorious landmark, famous for its seedy stripshows.[45]

Beyond Scollay Square lay the North End, at the time a stretch of rooming houses that, according to one Protestant, visibly displayed "the seedy and degraded air of those who inhabit them."[46] Certainly the North End had its share of Yankee Protestant history: Paul Revere had hung his famous lanterns from the spire of the old Christ Church on Hull Street. But to most Protestants, the North End's poor Irish Catholic population had rendered it almost physically inaccessible. "There is more romance and glory in going to Africa to convert the heathen, than there is in visiting the North End of Boston for the same purpose," one erstwhile missionary observed ruefully in 1887. "But . . . there is no less danger."[47]

The Back Bay

The corner of Beacon and Charles Streets, connecting Beacon Hill to the Back Bay, was a "sort of isthmus," George Santayana once observed, connecting "the two islands of respectability composing socially habitable Boston." To the north and south—the "vulgar directions"—were black and Irish

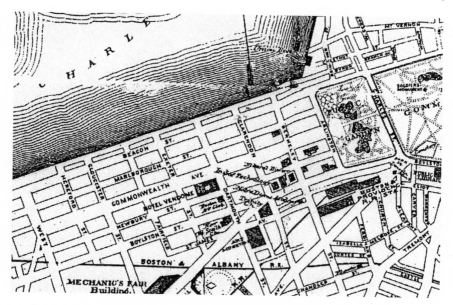

FIGURE 2.3. The Back Bay. From Moses King, ed., *King's Handbook of Boston* (Boston: Rand, Avery, 1885).

neighborhoods in the North, West, and South Ends of the city. Respectable pedestrians looked straight ahead and crossed the street with "the right-minded file," carefully observing the proper marked crossing. "If anywhere in Boston," Santayana remarked, "you scurried across a street at an unmarked place and at a rash angle, like a dog or a child chasing a stray ball, you would set all the heads in all the windows wondering why you did it."[48]

In the post–Civil War era, the Back Bay emerged as one of the most elegant sections of the city. "Volumes might be written descriptive of its magnificent thoroughfares," one guidebook exulted, "its architectural splendor, its palatial mansions and hostelries, its public institutions, and its creation out of the sea into one of the most attractive and beautiful habited spots the world can show."[49] In 1885, the Back Bay was still quite new, a tract of reclaimed land built up out of the marshy salt flats of the Charles River. Begun in the late 1850s, by all accounts the project was a testimony to engineering prowess and the growing value of city real estate. The trains had just finished hauling in landfill from the outlying suburbs two and half decades later. But even by then, the elegant brick rowhouses and broad avenues of the Back Bay exhibited its special character. An 1859 ruling from the state legislature mandated that profits from sale of the land be used for civic purposes— for schools, museums, and academies of higher education.[50]

Boston's "new West End" was wealthy and geographically isolated. Bordered by the Public Garden on one side and the Charles River on the next, the

Back Bay was also cut off from the rest of the city by the Boston and Albany Railroad tracks to the southeast. Only three streets—Berkeley, Dartmouth, and Massachusetts Avenue—crossed the tracks. As a result, the Back Bay developed as a "well-defined unit" with a well-deserved reputation for "social homogeneity."[51] Indeed, when Baptists conducted a door-to-door survey of 806 families in the Back Bay in 1912, they found, to their great disappointment, only 26 fellow communicants, two fewer than the total number of Roman Catholics. Over half the canvassed households in the Back Bay reported in as Episcopalian (279) or Unitarian (190).[52]

The Back Bay's tall church spires, irregularly piercing its low line of red-brick and brownstone rooftops, immediately became one of that district's most distinctive features. Even today, especially from the Cambridge side, the church steeples—a jagged row of Italianate, medieval, and colonial—stand in sharp relief against the modern horizon line. A hundred or more years ago, the sight was just as compelling to someone looking westward from the Common in the early spring. "The bare limbs of the trees form a network against the glowing evening sky," one visitor enthused, "and behind this network rise in the distant background the towers and spires of the Back Bay churches," "all the more beautiful" as one approached.[53]

Religion of a particular sort was clearly part of the Back Bay's early development. To be sure, Roman Catholics, Jews, Lutherans, Presbyterians, Adventists, and the like did not manage to stake out much territory there. The archbishop John J. Williams was, according to one account, "long hesitant" about planting a Catholic church in the Back Bay. The chief virtue of the site he finally selected in 1887 was its inconspicuous location, a stone's throw from the railroad tracks. And not surprisingly, St. Cecilia's attracted few wealthy residents; its primary constituents were Irish maids from Back Bay households.[54] But the mid–nineteenth century did see a rapid influx of new Unitarian, Congregational, and Episcopalian churches, each one more elegant and influential than the next, most relocating from the city's older quarters.

A walk four or five blocks west down Newbury Street in 1885 would have allowed a glimpse of at least six new churches and quickly affirmed the impression of a religious monopoly. "Almost on the wheels of the gravel cars," one historian writes, "came the Unitarians of the Federal Street Church," who in 1859 began building on Arlington Street, across the street from the Public Garden.[55] Just a block beyond, the elegant gothic exterior of Emmanuel Church, built in 1862, announced the presence of Episcopalians in the Back Bay. Emmanuel's first pastor was Frederick Dan Huntington, who arrived there after famously converting from Unitarianism and resigning his Harvard post as Plummer Professor of Christian Morals. Central Congregational, completed in 1867 after moving from older quarters back downtown on Winter Street, sat on the next block at the corner of Berkeley Street and Newbury. And just a few blocks to the north on Berkeley Street was First Church Unitarian.

Further down Newbury Street to the next intersection at Clarendon, he or she would encounter another congregation of Unitarians, this group from the Brattle Street Church, one of the very oldest in the city organized in Boston in 1698. In 1871, these migrants to the Back Bay raised an elegant new Romanesque structure designed by the architect Henry H. Richardson. But they did not prosper. Irreverent passersby nicknamed their building the "Church of the Holy Bean Blowers," after the trumpeting angels on the frieze; to make matters worse, the new congregation soon ran into financial trouble. In 1882 they sold their edifice to the First Baptist Church, which was looking to move from the South End into more respectable quarters.[56]

Nowhere, however, was the cultural power of religious institutions more powerfully displayed than in Copley Square. At the corner of Dartmouth and Boylston Streets, the "new Old South" Congregational church, a monument in Italianate style, was completed in 1875; it was "one of the most costly and most conspicuous of the many noteworthy buildings" in that part of the city.[57] In 1885, George A. Gordon had just been installed as pastor, having survived a fairly intense grilling by his fellow Congregationalists John H. Withrow at Park Street and Albert H. Plumb from the Walnut Avenue Church in Roxbury. A leading proponent of the "New Theology," the witty Scotsman held his post at Old South for the next twenty years and became well known for his liberal views on Christian doctrine, in Boston and across the country.[58]

Theology was an important topic in Boston in the spring of 1885. Conservatives worried about the "New Creed" emanating from Andover Seminary, though much of the talk by then was about the doctrine of future probation. The general tenets of the new theology—the humanness of Christ and the fallibility of the Bible—had been hard enough for the orthodox to swallow. The latest Andover idea, that sinners would have an opportunity to repent and be saved even after death, seemed outright heresy. As Joseph Cook had warned an indignant crowd in the spring of 1884, the orthodox churches were in peril; indeed, "their very survival was at stake."[59]

But these fears seemed far removed from the massive church buildings in Copley Square. Even Old South's glory dimmed a bit in the shadow of Trinity Church, built for its Episcopal congregation after their original structure on Summer Street was destroyed in the fire of 1872. Trinity was consecrated in 1877 and forever associated with the commanding pulpit presence of its famous pastor Phillips Brooks. At six foot four and three hundred pounds, Brooks was a celebrated figure in Gilded Age Boston, renowned for his warm piety and rapid-fire sermon delivery—estimated at 213 words a minute. His church was no less famous. Designed in French Romanesque style by the renowned Boston architect Henry H. Richardson, Trinity was both massive and exquisite. Its great central tower rose some 211 feet above an enormous tripartite gallery, enclosed in black walnut and stained-glass windows created by John La Farge. There were simply not enough superlatives in contemporary guidebooks to describe its presence in the city. As one architect put it, "Trinity Church has made Copley Square."[60]

This was no small achievement. In 1885, Copley Square housed some of Boston's leading cultural and educational institutions: the Harvard Medical School, the Massachusetts Institute of Technology, the Boston Society of Natural History, the Museum of Fine Arts. The Boston Public Library, with its classical portico facing directly onto Trinity Church, would be completed in 1895. Some of Boston's finest hotels also congregated in or near the square, including the Vendome, the Victoria, and the Brunswick, a favorite of visiting English nobility.[61]

But, like old Boston, the Back Bay also admitted a spiritual nonconformist now and then, a fact that led the *Congregationalist* to complain about the craze for "Oriental theism" in the "elegant drawing rooms" of the "truly cultured."[62] In the heart of that district, at the intersection of Exeter and Newbury Streets, the new Hollis Street Congregational Church sat right next to the First Spiritual Temple, a "curious, costly edifice" just being completed in 1885. This was an interesting juxtaposition for the Hollis Street group, whose original building had become a vaudeville venue back in the theater district: the Spiritual Temple would become the Exeter Street Theater in 1914. Generously funded by the local merchant Marcellus J. Ayer, the Romanesque building included a hall that seated fifteen hundred and the headquarters of the Working Union of Progressive Spiritualists, a group that soon numbered over a thousand. According to Ayer, the idea for the temple came from several of his deceased family members who instructed him to erect a building to herald the coming of a new spiritual dispensation. Though a bit unorthodox in the Protestant scheme of things, the Spiritual Temple followed a fairly conventional Christian format, holding regular Sunday morning and evening services, as well as an afternoon Sunday school.[63]

The vast open spaces of Copley Square, ringed by costly church spires and bastions of Protestant culture, offered eloquent testimony to the general vitality of religious life in Boston. Even on a spring evening, scores of congregants across the city would be returning to church for a second service. When an enterprising journalist at the *Boston Advertiser* conducted a head count of Protestant and Catholic churchgoers in April 1882, he tallied reports of over seventy-seven thousand people present for morning services around the city and almost forty-eight thousand back for church in the evening. Indeed, though Protestants might have worried about being outnumbered by Catholics on Boston's census rolls, they were not being jostled off the sidewalks by Rome's legions on Sunday mornings. The *Advertiser* also reported that some 60 percent of Boston's churchgoers were Protestants, with the largest numbers among Congregationalists and Baptists (with twenty-five and twenty-three churches, respectively, and both totaling around fifteen thousand), Episcopalians (twenty churches with 12,040 in attendance), Methodists (twenty-five churches and 11,394 in the pews) and Unitarians (twenty-six churches totaling 9,202). According to these figures, nearly one-third of Boston's population was in church that Sunday in 1882, an even higher proportion than in previous years.[64] In his magisterial study *Christianity in the United States*, published in 1888, Daniel Dorchester found similar reason for optimism. Charting New England's alarming increase in "foreign elements," he nonetheless found evangelical churches at least keeping pace with the influx. Whereas in 1820 Boston had had only one evangelical church for every 3,248 inhabitants, by 1880 the ratio had been reduced to one church for every 2,656 Bostonians.[65]

The expensive churches ringing Copley Square reinforced a sense of religious stability. When Bostonians wrote about religion in commemorative volumes, census reports, guidebooks, and city directories, they always referred to visible institutions. Indeed, the guidebook shorthand for "religion" was a listing of church buildings and the prominent men associated with them; the section in *King's Handbook* entitled "The Soul of the City" offered little more than a description of expensive building exteriors. A church without a recognizable denominational label was all but invisible to the public eye, except as an oddity—the Congregational response to Mary Baker Eddy is yet another case in point. Thus the city directory for 1885 listed only ten churches outside the usual denominational categories, roughly 5 percent of the total. The proportion climbed slowly over the ensuing decades, reaching 11 percent by 1915 and 16 percent by 1935.[66] The apparent durability of old-line Protestant denominations is hardly surprising: by 1885 most of Boston's major denominations had stood alongside each other in the city for more than 250 years. During that time they had weathered intense theological controversy and some powerful personalities and still managed to maintain a common civility, though not without occasional strain. According to Congregational polity, even the orthodox folk at Park Street were expected to make an appearance when the liberals at Old South installed a new pastor—but that didn't always mean either group enjoyed themselves much.

Yet in many ways the staid, expensive churches of Copley Square are tangential to Protestant history in Boston. The central story of religious growth and transformation was unfolding not in the ordered, tree-lined streets of the Back Bay but in the noisy, crowded South End. Geographically, the two sections were just a few blocks apart, but in many other ways they were many miles distant.

The South End

Crossing from the Back Bay to the South End was no easy stroll in 1885. Two sets of railroad tracks separated the two sections, and the best way across

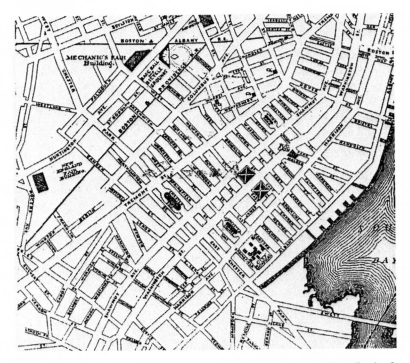

FIGURE 2.4. The South End. From Moses King, ed., *King's Handbook of Boston* (Boston: Rand, Avery, 1885).

would have been Dartmouth Street, running roughly south from Copley Square. But getting one's bearings at that point might be difficult: the South End's main thoroughfares, Washington, Tremont, Shawmut, Harrison, and Columbus Streets, began at a forty-five-degree angle to the streets of the Back Bay and gradually swung around to become more or less parallel. The unwary newcomer would find it difficult to know whether these streets were headed south or west out of the city.

In the late nineteenth century, the South End was constantly changing. Because land reclamation projects continued in stages from the seventeenth century on to the mid–nineteenth century, the borders of the South End shifted regularly; at one point an extension of the downtown area, by the late nineteenth century this "moveable designation" extended several miles south toward the Roxbury and Dorchester suburbs.[67]

But there were other reasons why a Protestant might feel a bit anxious venturing into the South End in 1885. Though the original inhabitants of that section had been white, middle-class, and Protestant, they had not stayed there long. Falling real estate prices during the depression of the 1870s, paralleled by the completion of the Back Bay project, spurred a rapid exodus.

When Albert Wolfe wrote *The Lodging House Problem in Boston* in 1906, he described the South End's white population fleeing "like rats." The exodus, he said, "began in the seventies, gained momentum during the early eighties, and was practically finished before 1890."[68] By that time, native-born Protestants could commute from the city's nether regions on an electric streetcar line that passed through the South End into Scollay Square. Consequently, in 1885 the South End was fast becoming a lodging-house section dotted with saloons and small shops. These housed a poor and working-class Irish population, as well as new arrivals from rural New England and the Canadian Maritimes.

The South End was also a point of uneasy intersection between Protestants and Catholics. The Cathedral of the Holy Cross sat on Washington Street, a busy thoroughfare that served as an unofficial dividing line between the two groups. Completed in 1875, it covered nearly an acre of ground and stood almost as large as Notre Dame cathedral in Paris. The interior was furnished on a lavish scale, with a seating capacity of thirty-five hundred for a parish of some ten thousand adult members.[69] Without any equivocation, the cathedral was a powerful statement of Catholic memory: the bricks across the arch of the vestibule were taken from the Ursuline convent in Charlestown that had been burned down by anti-Catholic rioters in 1834.[70]

In many ways, the cathedral and its adjacent bishop's house functioned as a Catholic parallel to the various Protestant denominational headquarters downtown. But its presence did not necessarily indicate Catholic hegemony in the South End, where there were still a relatively small number of parishes. The Cathedral's nearest neighbor was the Church of the Immaculate Conception on Harrison Avenue, built by the Jesuit Fathers in 1861 and adjoining the original campus of Boston College. Most of Boston's thirty-odd Roman Catholic churches were, like some of the lesser Protestant denominations, dispersed around the city, in outlying areas like East and South Boston, and in the suburban districts of Roxbury and Dorchester.[71]

But that situation was changing rapidly. By the turn of the century the South End would house three Roman Catholic churches and was fast becoming first in size and importance for the denomination. Similarly, in the mid-1880s, most of Boston's Jewish congregations were located in the South End, all within a few blocks of each other in the Park Square area. Ohabei Shalom was built by Jewish immigrants from northeastern (Polish) Germany on Warren Street in 1852; Adath Israel, a breakaway congregation of southwestern German Jews, was built on Pleasant Street the following year. Although Boston's relatively small Jewish population (about six thousand in 1885) gradually left the South End for better quarters, the 1885 city directory listed eight Jewish congregations, seven of which were still in their original neighborhoods. Like the city's other religious groups, Jews established a network of social clubs, charitable societies, and educational institutions. But more change lay ahead. A much larger influx of Russian Jews, a group far more impoverished and unskilled than the first arrivals, was only just beginning in 1885.[72]

The seventeen Protestant congregations in the South End were situated to the north and west of the Washington Street dividing line. Their diversity would have been evident the minute one crossed the railroad tracks on the Dartmouth Street overpass and stood in front of the First Reformed Episcopal Church. In Boston, this congregation was the sole representative of a small new denomination, formed in 1877 in reaction to "High Church" tendencies in the larger Protestant Episcopal body. From 1880 to 1892, the pastor of the South End congregation was James M. Gray, a protégé of Bishop William Rufus Nicholson, the leading advocate of dispensational teaching among Reformed Episcopalians. In 1904, Gray went on to became the first dean, and later president, of Chicago's Moody Bible Institute, the educational epicenter of the fundamentalist movement in the early twentieth century. After leaving Boston, Gray made his mark on the national movement as one of the seven editors of the *Scofield Reference Bible*, first published in 1909, and as a contributor to *The Fundamentals*, the twelve-volume series of articles on Protestant orthodoxy published between 1910 and 1915.[73]

In marked contrast, the Ruggles Street Baptist Church, situated on the outer reaches of the South End, exhibited both Social Gospel and fundamentalist tendencies. The humanitarian emphasis came from a bequest of one-and-a-quarter million dollars left by Daniel Sharp Ford to the Boston Baptist Social Union, with a large share specifically earmarked for Ruggles, Ford's own childhood congregation. By 1901 Ruggles had seventeen paid staff members who ran an employment bureau, an industrial school, a relief department of church missionaries who canvassed their neighborhood for people in need, and a medical dispensary that included a maternity department that distributed sterilized milk for young children. The church also had its own "gospel wagon" and two very popular workingmen's Bible classes.[74]

But the arrival of Amzi Clarence Dixon as pastor in 1901 immediately led to problems. Although sympathetic in principle to the church's social outreach, Dixon wanted to establish a local reputation as an evangelist. In 1902 he rented the National League baseball park in the South End and held a well-planned but poorly attended revival meeting there. Dixon also led a huge parade of some two thousand adherents of Gospel Temperance through the streets of Roxbury, visiting every saloon and stopping for services on street corners. The Baptist pastor was also fond of stirring up controversy, publicly denouncing Boston's three great sins, "yellow journalism, rum, and the pagan doctrine of Christian Science," which he dismissed in the local papers as "humbuggery."[75] But he did not stay in Boston long. Dixon thought that he deserved more control of the use of the Ford legacy; according to the terms of the bequest, the Boston Baptist Social Union was charged with administering the funds toward the "religious, moral and intellectual improvement of the working people of Boston." In his view, this goal required a largely "spiritual" program of evangelistic preaching, and a few years after his arrival, he had created an impasse in his congregation. At issue was a sum of $350,000 that was designated for a facility for Social Union's activities, which Dixon believed should go toward constructing a new tabernacle on the Tremont Temple scale, emphasizing evangelism and gospel preaching and, no doubt, showcasing his skill behind a pulpit. The controversy led to Dixon's resignation in 1906 and subsequent pastorates at the prestigious Moody Church in Chicago and the famous Spurgeon Tabernacle in London. From those two posts, Dixon established himself as a leading spokesman for the fundamentalist movement, something he had been unable to do in Boston. In the years following his departure, Ruggles quietly continued on its unconventional course, successfully joining evangelism and Social Gospel work.[76]

Half a block from James M. Gray's Reformed Episcopal congregation, down Dartmouth Street and to the left, sat the Columbus Avenue (Second) Universalist Church, one of two churches from that denomination in the South End. The guidebook described its traditional Gothic design, elegant steeple, and painted windows as "exceedingly cheerful and pleasant," perhaps in keeping with the Universalists' rejection of hellfire theology. The Columbus Avenue congregation was a relative newcomer to the South End, arriving there just after the fire in 1872, but it had a long history in the city. Hosea Ballou, the leader of the Universalist movement in New England, had established the original congregation downtown on School Street in 1817.[77]

The story of the Universalists in Boston illustrates the city's unique religious blend. Although the denomination was small, it was well represented in New England: Boston alone listed ten Universalist churches with some 1,228 members, ranking them before both Presbyterians and Lutherans.[78] They were difficult to categorize as either liberal or conservative. In Daniel Dorchester's classification scheme, the Universalists' rejection of eternal damnation and the doctrine of the Trinity put them in a "nonevangelical" category, alongside Unitarians and Freethinkers, but the denomination's origins as a dissenting sect gave rise to decidedly populist leanings.[79] The pastor of the Columbus Avenue church, Alonzo Ames Miner, was a case in point. Miner was a prominent, educated man; he served as president of Tufts University from 1862 to 1874 and on the state board of education for many years afterward. A fervent apostle of temperance, he also shared the anti-Catholic sentiments of most other South End pastors. Indeed, according to one admiring account, "'the air was blue'" when Miner became aroused on the topic of "Romanism," "and every syllable was a missile that struck home." As one Catholic author summed him up, Miner was "sensible enough in all other respects" but under the spell of religious prejudice, "[cast] off all reason and sanity."[80]

Animosities aside, however, Universalists and Catholics shared a certain reverence for sacred space. When the Second Church moved from its original spot on School Street to the South End in 1872, the congregation spent a week saying farewell to their old building. On the final Sunday, they met three times—morning, afternoon, and evening—each time "tenderly mindful of what has been described as 'sacred sentiment'—the affections of a people inwrought with every brick and timber and furnishing of the historic temple." After hours of baptisms, sermons, and commemorative hymns, and amid a profusion of flowers spilling across the altar and communion table to the side aisles of the sanctuary, the people tearfully agreed to "take up 'the ark of God' and bear it to another place." "And now, Ancient Temple," Reverend H. I. Cushman addressed the beloved building, "with all our hearts we salute thee, while we pronounce the hardest word of all, FAREWELL!" "Members of the School Street parish! we yield to law! we yield to the behests of Progress. The growth of our beloved Boston bids us 'go hence.'"[81]

Universalists were not the only homesick Protestants in the South End. A few blocks further down, where Warren Avenue intersected Brookline Street, sat Boston's First Presbyterian Church. Though predominant elsewhere (the third-largest denomination nationwide in 1890), Presbyterians were outsiders in Boston and in New England. In 1801 they had adopted a Plan of Union with the Congregationalists, promising to share assets in the joint task of bringing churches to the western territories. Within a few decades, however, both denominations were ruing their ecumenical impulse. The Presbyterians withdrew in 1837, under pressure by conservatives worried about the lax doctrine of their Calvinist cousins. Suspicious Congregationalists pointed out that nearly all of the new western churches were becoming Presbyterians. ("They have milked our Congregational cows," one critic moaned, "but have made nothing but Presbyterian butter and cheese.") But if it was any consolation to Congregationalists, Presbyterian expansion permanently weakened their presence in New England. The 1890 census listed only about fifteen hundred Presbyterians in Boston, with only seven churches in the city directory.[82]

The First Church was also a largely immigrant congregation, organized in 1846 by a "homesick Scot" yearning for native preaching. In the late nineteenth century, the church attracted large numbers of Canadians from Cape Breton County in Nova Scotia; between 1895 and 1919, all of First Church's pastors were Nova Scotians who offered regular services in Gaelic. Another small Scottish Presbyterian Church, its members from neighboring Richmond County in Nova Scotia, sat just a block away. On Sunday afternoons, as people from both congregations gathered for evening services, passersby would hear Gaelic conversation carrying up and down the block, in an area commonly known as "Scotch corner."[83]

By now the impression would be firm: the Protestant churches in the South End were considerably more variegated than their counterparts in old Boston and the Back Bay. In 1885, the list included Unitarians and Congregationalists, as well as Presbyterians, Universalists, Methodists, Baptists, Reformed Episcopalians, and Adventists. In the 1870s two black Baptist churches, the Ebenezer and Day Star, had also settled in the South End. A few churches defied categorization. The People's Church was a Methodist congregation but aimed at a wide clientele, and its building was designed to seat four thousand people. The Church of the Unity was organized in 1857 to promote "the cause of Liberal Christianity." Housed in a building designed to resemble a Greek temple, the congregation was officially Unitarian but certainly eclectic, headed by radical preacher-poet Minot J. Savage.[84]

The South End churches were also, on the whole, a fairly nimble group. Berkeley Temple, situated just a block or so away from First Presbyterian, at the corner of Berkeley and Tremont Streets, provides a case in point. The church's first home was on Pine Street, on the edge of old Boston. Built in 1827, it was intended as a Congregational mission in what was then a poor area of the city, and though the first members struggled financially, they committed themselves to keeping pew rents affordable for their unchurched neighbors. Eventually, however, the congregation decided to throw in its fortunes with the city's rising middle class. In 1860, the struggling Pine Street congregation made the risky decision to follow the wealthier populations to the new South End, despite the fact that their new sanctuary on Berkeley Street saddled them with many future years of debt. The experiment did not go well at first, for middle-class Protestants began to leave the South End in large numbers soon after the church arrived there, and by 1885, Berkeley Street was in perceptible decline. On the church rolls, membership stood at six hundred, but only half that number attended with any regularity. That same year, however, the congregation took another risk, transforming itself into a center of "institutional Christianity" in Boston. In 1888, the congregation called a dynamic new pastor, Charles Dickinson, and took on a new name, the Berkeley Temple. Within a few years the old Pine Street church had become a flourishing Social Gospel center, with a full array of social programs for the neighborhood's poor. By 1893 Berkeley Temple was also the largest Congregational church in Boston.[85]

At the Clarendon Street Baptist Church, just a block down Tremont Street from Berkeley Temple, the story was much the same. When A. J. Gordon became pastor in 1869, the church was staid, orderly, and fashionable. Within a few years, however, its character began to change, especially in the wake of the revival meetings led by the famed evangelist Dwight L. Moody in 1877. Moody's tent stood only three hundred feet from Gordon's church, and before long some of the revival's "reformed drunkards" began to drift inside during the Sunday service. Watching them in the pews, scattered among his comfortably middle-class church members, Gordon soon reached two important conclusions: first, the church could no longer dispense "the cup of dragons" in the communion service, and second, Clarendon Street had to offer more than sermons "to those whose stomachs are faint and empty."[86] Accordingly, Clarendon's worship services became simpler and the preaching more attuned to the unsaved. With the help of the aging abolitionist Wendell Phillips, Gordon organized the Boston Industrial Temporary Home to minister to the poor of the South End; just a few years later, he founded the Gordon School of Missions, an evangelistic institution that later became a major center of fundamentalist growth in New England. The church also developed a thriving mission to Chinese immigrants. In the short term, the changes were beneficial: in 1885, Clarendon boasted eight hundred members and the largest budget of Boston's Baptist churches, over $17,000 a year.[87]

But success in the South End was often short-lived. By the turn of the century, both Berkeley Street and Clarendon would fall on hard times. Clarendon found Gordon, who died in 1895, all but impossible to replace. In 1904, with "the drift of the members toward the suburban districts" a chronic problem, the once bustling congregation was without a pastor. From a peak of over twelve hundred in 1898, Clarendon's membership fell by more than half in the next ten years; from five hundred in 1908, the numbers drifted downward to around three hundred by 1920. Berkeley Temple declined even more suddenly. At its height, in 1894, the congregation was considering plans for an eleven-story building, fitted with a sanctuary to seat fifteen hundred, a gymnasium, and two hundred dormitory-style rooms. But the death of a key financial donor, the ill health of one pastor, and the absence of another led to a precipitous loss of members and resources. In 1901, the pastor formally resigned, marking the beginning of the end. By 1907, the church was failing so badly that it was forced to sell its building and merge with Union Church, another equally feeble Congregational church nearby. Predictably, the combining of two weak churches did not create a strong successor.[88] Clearly, church life in the South End was not for the faint of heart.

Late nineteenth-century Boston, for all its fabled skepticism, was a city of churches. Yet in many ways, the old Puritan worship-houses in the old downtown, the Victorian cathedrals in the Back Bay, and the transient congregations of the South End do not tell the whole story of religion in Boston. Most of the important events in this book, beginning with the next chapter, take place outdoors, in city parks, on courthouse steps, and on streets and sidewalks.

Boston, perhaps more than most, was an outdoor city. Since the days of the Revolution, its citizens had regularly resorted to riots, demonstrations, and public commotions to express personal as well as communal grievances.

Though in absolute numbers the frequency of outdoor uprisings slowed during the nineteenth century, Bostonians still distinguished themselves by their willingness to take to the streets if necessary.[89] It's fitting, therefore, that the next chapter begins in the same place this one did, on the ancient lawns of Boston Common.

PART I

Mobilizing

3

The Fight for
Boston Common

It is the right as well as the duty of all men in society, publicly
and at stated seasons to worship the SUPREME BEING, the Great
Creator and Preserver of the Universe. And no subject shall be
hurt, molested, or restrained, in his person, liberty, or estate, for
worshiping God in the manner and season most agreeable to the
dictates of his own conscience; or for his religious profession
or sentiments; provided he doth not disturb the public
peace, or obstruct others in their religious worship.

—Massachusetts Bill of Rights, article 2

On the morning of Wednesday, May 20, 1885, Boston police arrested
three Protestant clergymen for preaching on the Common. The
startling news spread rapidly across the city's evangelical Protestant
population, indignation gathering as the details emerged. The three
preachers—Adoniram Judson Gordon of Clarendon Baptist church,
Horace L. Hastings, editor of a widely read evangelical periodical,
the *Christian*, and William H. Davis, superintendent of a mission in
the North End—were hardly common criminals. When the three
arrived at the Municipal Criminal courthouse Thursday morning,
a crowd reported to number between four and five thousand,
"principally of the middle-class, well-dressed and well behaved,"
thronged the steps of the building.[1] It must have been a singular
sight. "Instead of drunkards and roughs," as Hastings later related,
"ministers of the gospel, prominent church members, officers of the
Y.M.C. Association, members of the Salvation Army, and prominent
business men, were striving to obtain admittance to the temple of

Justice," held back only by a lone police officer at the door. "It was clearly evident," he crowed, "that something unusual was going on in the police court of the city of Boston."[2]

Trouble was brewing. The case against the preachers rested on a city ordinance stipulating that "no person shall, except by permission of the appropriate committee, deliver a sermon, lecture, address or discourse on the Common or other public grounds." Strictly speaking, the three men were clearly guilty—all had preached on Sunday afternoon and none of them could produce a permit. But all were openly unrepentant. Gordon, according to one account, "looked disgusted," and "in a dignified manner entered a plea of 'not guilty.' "[3] All three refused to pay the ten-dollar fine and appealed the case to Superior Court, promising to test the constitutionality of the ordinance. Bail was furnished by one of Hastings's evangelistic associates, a Mrs. Cone, and two "prominent gentlemen," Leander Beal and George H. Quincy, who declared their desire that "the Common be as free for public worship...as it now is for band concerts on Sunday afternoon."[4]

The ministers' arrests and the events of the following weeks opened deep rifts in the religious life of late nineteenth-century Boston. Evangelical Protestant anger over the behavior of police and city government officials galvanized that community around old fears of Catholic conspiracy, touching off a period of religious strife that lasted well into the next decade. As the following several chapters demonstrate, anti-Catholicism proved to be a potent force for change, dividing liberal from conservative Protestants and generating new waves of religious zeal. Indeed, with only a slight risk of overstatement, one could trace the origins of fundamentalism in Boston to that Sunday afternoon in May 1885, and to a fateful convergence of politics, religion, and geography.

The Spiritual Geography of Boston Common

Situated deep within Protestant strongholds in the Back Bay and Beacon Hill, the Common embodied the city's Puritan and Yankee past. Memorial statues and patriotic plaques dotted its rolling, grassy hummocks, sober reminders of the sacrifices of Boston's citizens in the Revolution and the Civil War. The Common was no ordinary park. Legally, it belonged to all the citizens of Boston; until the 1830s they had grazed their cattle on its hills, and throughout the nineteenth century they had gathered there to celebrate important local events. Boston's city fathers maintained a firm commitment to this public legacy, for, as one of them declared, the Common was one of the few remaining "breathing spaces" left in the crowded city, and "the only place accessible to all the people."[5] In keeping with this goal, in 1875, city officials passed a Park Act to bring more land under city control, extending the Common's semirural spaces southward. Frederick Law Olmsted, the architect of Boston's famous "Emerald Necklace," designed a graceful string of glens and meadows that began at the Common and meandered south through the Fens and around Jamaica Pond and ended at Franklin Park in Dorchester.[6]

But for many of Boston's Protestant communities, the Common was also sacred space, ringed by venerable churches and replete with pious memories. Two of Boston's best-known conservative congregations, Park Street and Tremont Temple, sat on its eastern end. St. Paul's Episcopal Church faced the Common's south side on Tremont Street, and beyond the northwest end of the Common, between the newly landscaped Public Garden and the wealthy Back Bay, were some of Boston's most famous liberal congregations, including the Arlington Street Unitarian and First Baptist Churches. But the Common's religious legacy went beyond the presence of expensive church buildings. In the seventeenth century, Puritans hung Baptist and Quaker intruders there, and publicly punished their own offenders in the stocks. The Common also had a long association with open-air preaching. In 1740 George Whitefield stoked the fires of the First Great Awakening before an astonishing crowd of fifteen thousand; New England Methodists traced their beginnings to a sermon preached by Jesse Lee under an elm tree in 1790.[7]

By the 1880s, however, the Common's spiritual future was cloudy. Massive land reclamation projects in the Back Bay and South End had shifted Boston's geographic center south and west, leaving the Common cramped into the far northeast corner of the city. Although its north and upper side faced Beacon Hill and the State House, gambling dens and grog shops had sprung up along the lower side that bordered the South End.[8] Boylston and Tremont Streets were regularly clogged with horsecar and pedestrian traffic, prompting a controversial campaign by private developers to widen the streets by paving over ancient sidewalks. The Common also began to take on the signs of urban congestion and poverty. By the 1880s, the Boylston Street corner had become a dumping ground for trash and the once elegant lawns home to transients and the unemployed.

The Common was also primary recreational space for two of Boston's most two densely populated and poorest neighborhoods, the West and South Ends. Though children from wealthy Beacon Hill neighborhoods had long coasted its hills in winter and swam in its shallow ponds during the summer, by the late nineteenth century they could not easily claim the land as their own.[9] Indeed, Olmsted's genteel moral vision of parks as places of quiet, refined amusement was fast giving way to the needs of working men and women for Sunday recreation and amusement.[10] Beginning in the 1870s, the city's aldermen regularly debated the morality and propriety of public baseball games on the Common, as well as the growing array of commercial amusements—Sunday concerts, puppet shows, open-air dances, a Buffalo Bill show—that brought large crowds to the city's Protestant center on its holiest of days.[11]

Harangues on the Common also raised darker fears of anarchism and labor violence. The mid-1880s also saw a huge upsurge in work stoppages— eleven in the spring of 1886 alone—and an unsuccessful bid for mayor by the labor organizer George McNeill that same year. During the spring of 1886, the Knights of Labor campaigned vigorously, holding rallies in Faneuil Hall and bringing in some ten thousand Boston workers; in just thirteen weeks, the organization nearly quadrupled its membership. In 1885, disgruntled workingmen would have been a familiar sight on the Common; striking workers often took up temporary residence there or gathered to hear incendiary speeches.[12]

The Common's complex religious and social history explains some of the reasons why the arrests of the three preachers resonated so powerfully. The decision to preach in public there brought Gordon, Hastings, and Davis into contested space, and subjected them to hostile public scrutiny. Although Gordon was a highly respected Baptist minister, in the eyes of the park commissioners his sermon was only one more of the "orations, harangues or loud outcries" they were attempting to ban for the sake of civil order.[13] Under city law, open-air preaching was an amusement, on the level of a Buffalo Bill show.

FIGURE 3.1. A Summer Sunday: Boating, Baseball, and "Salvation on the Common" (A Summer Sunday," *Boston Sunday Globe*, 24 May 1885).

If that were not bad enough, Hastings and Davis also endured being labeled "cranks" by the Boston press—a term most often applied to the rowdy fans who filled the bleachers at baseball games.[14] Still, as subsequent events would illustrate even more vividly, new religious energies were gathering momentum in Boston in 1885 and made their first public appearance where Boston Common intersected rich and poor, new and old, immigrant and native-born (see fig. 3.1).

The Defendants

The three ministers crisscrossed social and religious boundaries within the city's evangelical Protestant community. Adoniram Judson Gordon, perhaps the most unlikely figure in the episode, was the revered pastor of the Clarendon Street Baptist Church.[15] A quiet, genial man with the dignified bearing of a Victorian clergyman, Gordon hardly fit the profile of a rabble-rousing street preacher, much less a budding fundamentalist upstart (see fig. 3.2). In fact, he was preaching on the Common that Sunday afternoon as a representative of the local YMCA, a well-established organization with impeccable Christian and middle-class credentials.

The other two men, W. F. Davis and H. L. Hastings, could not presume to Gordon's respectability. Neither could claim a prominent pulpit, nor was either man formally attached to any church through ordination. They claimed to be preaching on the Common more by accident than design, having run across each other in the course of a day spent preaching in city jails and other small religious gatherings.[16]

Davis was a former master at the Boston Latin Academy and superintendent of the North End Mission.[17] His father, J. B. Davis, had been a Finneyite abolitionist, educated at Oberlin and "radical in every line of reform."[18] The younger Davis was born in Attica, New York, in 1840; in the next ten years the family moved twice, first to Providence, Rhode Island, and then to Manchester, New Hampshire. Beginning at age twelve, he worked in the cotton mills in Manchester, Lowell, and South Carver, Massachusetts. By the time he was twenty-one, Davis had saved enough money for one year of schooling and was, by his own report, on the verge of a significant promotion when he received God's call came to preach the gospel. With money borrowed from friends, Davis began a remarkably thorough preparation for his chosen career on Boston's streets, entering Phillips Exeter Academy in 1861 and Harvard in 1864. Supporting himself as a teacher at the prestigious Boston Latin school, he married the daughter of an Exeter, New Hampshire, newspaper editor and briefly moved on to the postgraduate philosophy class at Harvard in 1869. Davis also studied for two years toward ordination at

FIGURE 3.2. Adoniram Judson Gordon. Frontispiece to Ernest Gordon,
Adoniram Judson Gordon: A Biography (New York: Fleming H. Revell, 1896).

Andover Seminary, but in the end he adamantly refused to avail himself of the economic security or social prestige his education might have afforded him. He would not answer to any honorific title—only "brother" or "neighbor"—and refused ordination as well as any denominational identity. When a Free Baptist church in Olneyville, New York, asked him to come and be their pastor, he announced instead that he would serve only as their traveling evangelist, a position he held for two and a half years. A well-educated and, by many accounts, "gentlemanly" figure, Davis espoused a radical humility that kept him close to his working-class origins. (Governor Oliver Ames reportedly labeled him a "crank" for refusing to buy milk on Sundays, which Davis claimed to do on behalf of workingmen.) On many occasions, he deliberately sought out marginal positions, returning to Boston in 1875 as superintendent of the North End Mission, and then moving on to evangelize lumberjacks in the Michigan woods. Forced to return East because of poor health, Davis still maintained a heavy schedule of itinerant preaching. "I am nothing but a Christian," he told a crowd of five thousand sympathizers in 1888; "I am merely a common man, and the only business I seem to have in this city is to preach to the common people on common land."[19]

Even before their paths crossed in April 1885, H. L. Hastings and Davis had much in common. Hastings was a well-known figure in the Advent Christian denomination, a group that had been formed in the aftermath of William Miller's failed prediction that the world would end in 1844; Hastings served as first president of its Christian Publication Society. After suffering considerable ill health and financial trials, Hastings came to Boston as an independent publisher. His first effort, a fervently revivalist periodical, the *Christian*, appeared in 1866, encapsulating three other small papers with names designed to advertise their populist leanings: the *Safeguard*, the *Common People*, and the *Armory*. Hastings's trials multiplied in the following years; in 1872 his publishing operation burned to the ground in the great fire, leaving him with debts he constantly struggled to repay. Through perseverance the circulation of the *Christian* had reached thirty-five thousand by 1876, which made it, according to the boast across the masthead, "the most widely circulated religious paper in New England."[20] Hastings filled his paper with "*true* stories, incidents, records of providences, answers to prayer, engravings, music, poetry, religion, and common sense. Sectarianism, controversy, politics, pills, patent medicines, pious novels and continued stories are excluded from its columns." But the paper carried no paid advertising either, and by May 1885, Hastings found himself over ten thousand dollars in debt.[21]

The arrest also netted a handful of street preachers and Salvation Army recruits, although these soon disappeared from press accounts.[22] In fact, at the time of the arrests, four different groups—Gordon and the YMCA, Davis and Hastings, the Salvation Army, and a group of "Brethren"—were all preaching to crowds on the Common. The Salvation Army, then very new in the United States, might have been a tempting target, for it had been attracting a run of bad press, stemming from a series of confrontations with police.[23] Very quickly, however, public interest focused on the fate of the three martyred preachers and, largely by virtue of Gordon's prestigious pulpit and Hastings's indefatigable printing press, these men willingly symbolized the fate of beleaguered Protestants everywhere.

All three could claim the right to speak for the broader evangelical Protestant community, since none was narrowly defined by sectarian boundaries, and all three traversed lines of social class, sometimes willingly and other times unwillingly. But the one line that they could and would not cross was the one separating immigrant Catholics from Yankee Protestants. As time went on, Gordon, Hastings, and Davis became standard-bearers for the evangelical Protestant minority in a city populated, and increasingly governed, by a Roman Catholic majority.

Protestants and Catholics

In December 1884 Boston elected its first Irish Catholic mayor, the Democrat Hugh O'Brien, by a margin of fifteen hundred votes, and reelected him a year later with the largest majority in any city-wide election to that point. On paper at least, the truth seemed clear: Boston was well on its way to being a Catholic, predominantly Irish, city.[24] But as in most city elections, the real story was a bit more complicated than the results implied. In late nineteenth-century Boston, politics did not split simply along class, religious, or ethnic lines but, as Geoffrey Blodgett explains, drew on "an incongruous, fragile alliance inside the Democratic party between an elite Yankee leadership minority and the leaders of a growing Irish working-class majority." This alliance between "Harvard College and the slums" became a "dominant force in the city's politics over the last quarter of the nineteenth century," bringing to power a new generation of Irish Catholic Democrats.[25]

Hugh O'Brien's political career is a good example of this alliance at work. His low tax rates and civic improvements won him the grudging respect of Boston's white Protestant leadership; O'Brien actively championed the Olmsted park system and the magnificent new Boston Public Library in Copley Square. Under the new city charter, passed just before his election in 1885, he also enjoyed far greater control over patronage jobs and the corresponding network of political favors that were fast becoming a staple of city hall. As the historian Thomas O'Connor writes, Boston Brahmins saw O'Brien as "a role model for his fellow immigrants, an example of what other serious, ambitious, and hard-working members of the Irish race could eventually achieve by abandoning their lazy, happy-go-lucky ways and adapting to the old Yankee principles of thrift, sobriety, and industry."[26] The *Congregationalist* agreed:

> Old residents of the city rub their eyes at the sight of an Irish Catholic mayor in Boston, vested with the largest powers of any municipal officer in the United States.... It is felt, however, that the power will be much safer in the hands of the mayor than in those of the council,

that is, the less respectable ward bosses and Irish Catholic politicians they hoped that O'Brien would somehow tame.[27]

Though Yankee elites preferred to downplay the revolutionary significance of O'Brien's election, it was an important symbolic milestone in the ethnic wards of the city, marking some hard-won economic and social successes. One Catholic author remembered with satisfaction that moment "at the beginning of 1887" when "the City government was organized with Irish Catholics in the position not only of Mayor but of Chairman of the Board of Aldermen, President of the Common Council, City Clerk, and Chairman of the School Committee." All this stood as proof, he said, "indeed, that times had changed."[28] When the Irish began to arrive in the 1830s and 1840s, they were poor and powerless; by the late nineteenth century they were guardians of a "separatist subculture" with its own canons of literary and cultural taste and a growing awareness of its political clout. By the 1880s, as O'Connor says, "the docility of the Irish in political matters was fast becoming a thing of the past."[29]

But the alliance between Yankee elites and Irish Catholics spelled political problems for evangelical Protestants. In particular it doomed to failure their moralistic political agenda, which centered around the prohibition of alcohol. As Maria Gordon concluded at the close of one failed license vote, "Beacon Street and the North End voted together."[30] In the late 1880s, conservative Protestants had few allies in the city government or in the Massachusetts statehouse. The strength of the Republican party was statewide and largely controlled by Brahmin elites who had not passed over into the Democratic party. Even a Republican governor and majority in the state legislature did not produce temperance legislation for the city of Boston.[31]

The liquor trade, more than any other issue, pitted Boston's evangelical Protestants against a new ruling class they perceived as hostile or indifferent to their moralistic concerns. Although Boston's Catholic community had its own thriving Total Abstinence Union, its leaders preferred to keep the matter out of politics: they had little to gain from pressing a controversial issue with a demonstrated capacity to ignite Protestant fanaticism.[32] Nor was the middle-class evangelical passion against alcohol shared by Yankee Protestant elites. As Blodgett notes, "the contrast of ambience between the saloon life of the Irish and the Back Bay card parties and club dinners favored by Yankee lawyers and their friends should not obscure a shared opposition to the dry ethic." Neither group looked with favor on the prospect of prohibition in the city of Boston.[33]

But by the mid-1880s, temperance had found its way to the center of an important political debate. Boston had had a variety of license and prohibition ordinances since 1852, but by the post–Civil War era, enforcement had declined. Though by some measures, the rate of intemperance was actually decreasing in the 1880s, to conservatives, the alcohol problem was becoming far more urgent than ever before.[34] Prohibition forces traced Boston's liquor problem to the chief of police, who was appointed by the city's aldermen and the mayor, all corrupt tools of a political machine owned by greedy distillers and saloonkeepers.[35] To make matters worse, the chief of police and his three-man police commission had unlimited power to grant liquor licenses and, according to Protestant critics, did so frequently.[36] Indeed, Boston's Protestants had long since concluded that the leaders of the existing police force were deep in the pockets of the city's liquor interests; no temperance legislation would pass without a thorough housecleaning among Boston's finest.

In the winter and spring of 1885, the state legislature vigorously debated a bill designed to create a metropolitan police force. Partisan politics, as well as high-minded rhetoric about administrative efficiency, figured prominently in the controversy, for the new force was to be administered by the Republican governor of Massachusetts, not the Democrat-controlled city of Boston. Supporters defended the police bill as a civil service reform, providing for better training and equipment, including Smith and Wesson .38 revolvers for every officer on the job. But the Irish Democratic opposition saw the reform as a purely partisan ploy of Republican "pseudoreformers" eager to take over the city.[37] And in many ways, they were right. When the police bill passed the House of Representatives on June 9, 1885, it granted Massachusetts Republicans far greater leverage over moral affairs in Boston and its freely imbibing citizens.[38]

During the spring of 1885 the police bill was a frontline issue in a looming culture war. The Baptist *Watchman* pronounced the tumult that followed the June vote a "disgraceful" example of lawlessness and disorder, as "representatives of Boston's rumsellers, gamblers and other law-breakers seemingly did all in their power to introduce indecorum and produce anarchy."[39] The city's Catholic leaders were no less eager to interpret the metropolitan police bill as a mean-spirited counterattack on their recent political success. According to the Boston *Pilot*, "the openly-expressed reason for this flagrant interference with Democratic right is that the Irish-American element has become the most numerous in Boston." In the spring of 1885, *Pilot* editor John Boyle O'Reilly was upbeat and defiant. "By the way," he declared, "the Irish-Americans of Massachusetts, and especially those of Boston, do not regard the future with fear on account of the Knownothing efforts of the Republicans."[40]

But perhaps they should have. In the highly charged moral and political atmosphere of early 1885, charges and countercharges flew. In mid-May, Patrick Maguire, the editor of the fervently Irish and passionately Democratic *Republic*, hinted publicly that the battle over the police bill was far from over. "It is apparent to all," he wrote, "who can look a little ahead into the future that there is a just retribution in store for its framers."[41] To Boston's evangelical Protestants, few of whom read Maguire's newspaper but who undoubtedly could read the signs of the times, the arrests of the three ministers could have only one explanation: the rumsellers were out for revenge.

The Conspiracy Emerges

Initial reaction to the arrests divided along religious lines. While evangelical Protestants were thronging the steps of the courthouse, the Roman Catholic *Pilot* granted Gordon, Davis, and Hastings only an inch or two of type, concluding that they "could have obtained permission to preach by applying for it, and one, at least, of the ministers expressed regret that leave had not been asked." O'Reilly blamed the Salvation Army ("a nuisance everywhere") for playing up religious persecution but happily noted that they "have not received much sympathy so far." The editors of the Democratic *Boston Globe* also dismissed the arrests as a simple bureaucratic misunderstanding.[42] Protestant elites tended to agree, at least initially. The *Boston Evening Transcript*, with a largely Brahmin readership, played down the incident as an instance of city officials protecting a newly seeded lawn from trampling by crowds.[43] The Unitarian *Christian Register* ignored the event except to offer the brief editorial epigram "Boston doesn't like Common preaching."[44]

But as local journalists began to grind out the particulars of the case, puzzling new details emerged. At the start, the circumstances were already a bit suspicious, since the Common was a well-known site for public speakers of all kinds, and few, if any, had ever faced arrest for practicing their freedom of speech. Laws governing public behavior were routinely ignored, for as one contemporary noted, "the volumes of statutes ruling Boston Common would fill a fair-size library."[45] Clearly, the arrests had not been random. The policeman who testified at the ministers' trial, Officer George F. Malcomb of Station 4, admitted that on Saturday, the day *before* the alleged infraction, he had been instructed by his superior, one Captain Hemmenway, to secure names and file warrants for any Sunday preachers on the Common. The warrants were then served the following Monday, all apparently according to a prearranged plan.

H. L. Hastings did what he could to fuel suspicion about his treatment. As he told the tale, in what was apparently an impromptu press conference, he had duly applied for a preaching permit immediately following his arraignment but received no response from the Committee on the Common. "After diligent inquiry," he announced with a flourish, "we have been unable to find any person who has at any time during the last few years been granted a permit to hold Sunday services. It would seem from this that the city officials regard Protestant services as illegal." In mocking defiance, he and his fellow defendant Davis led a service on the Common the following Sunday, May 24. Although they avoided breaking the law by reading Bible passages instead of preaching, Hastings still received a warrant, to his apparent delight. With a nearly audible wink for the Boston press, he announced that "our next performance is to appear in court tomorrow."[46]

Hastings's second arraignment proved to be front-page material. On Monday, May 28, Officer Malcomb repeated his testimony that he had never arrested any preachers before serving warrants to Hastings, Davis, and Gordon, and that he had done so on direct orders from his superior, Captain Hemmenway, who had told him to confront "any persons holding services of any kind" on the Common. Despite the fact that Davis and Hastings appeared to have been targeted for arrest, they received thirty-dollar fines for their infraction, which they promptly appealed.[47]

By then the Protestant community had become thoroughly aroused to the affront from city officials. Facing the annual middle-class exodus from the city during the hot summer months, Protestant churchmen were determined to keep the matter alive until September. On May 25, the Methodist Preachers' Association reported that it had applied for permits twice but received no word. They passed a resolution of solidarity with Gordon, Hastings, and Davis, declaring that

> the prohibition by the city government of Boston of the worship of God and the preaching of the gospel on the Common and other public grounds of the city . . . is directly opposed to the spirit of our institutions and thoroughly hostile to the highest interests of the public welfare.

The Methodist preachers also declared that it was the "duty of Christian people, and in particular the Christian ministers of Boston, to sustain religious services upon the Common and other public grounds."[48] On June 2, Boston's Baptist clergymen notified the Board of Aldermen that the offending ordinance was "clearly discriminating as to the purpose of preachers in complying with the higher law of Him who has commanded them 'to go out into the byways and compel men to come in.'"[49] On June 22, the Congregational Boston Ministers' Meeting issued a similar resolution calling for repeal of the ordinance in the name of religious liberty.[50] "One would not suppose it possible," the *Congregationalist* editorialized, "that in the nineteenth century, under the shadow of Bunker Hill, in the city that struck the first blow for independence, free speech can be a civil crime."[51]

In the weeks and years that followed, Boston had no shortage of religious intrigue. On May 28 an anonymous letter to the editor of the *Boston Evening Transcript* charged that when Davis and another associate had applied for preaching permits the previous summer, they had been ignored by city hall, even after repeated requests. The letter suggested that the three-person Committee responsible for granting permits may have acted on spite, in response to a summer of evangelistic meetings the YWCA had sponsored on the Common in 1880, led by Joseph Cook, Park Street's Reverend John Withrow, Hastings, and A. C. Earle, the pastor of Ruggles Baptist Church.[52]

Others located the conspiracy at an even deeper level. In October 1887 Davis published a lengthy, and bitterly angry, pamphlet describing his treatment by the courts and the "Rum-Jesuit conspiracy" in the city government, entitled *Christian Liberties in Boston: A Sketch of Recent Attempts to Destroy Them Through the Device of a Gag-By-Law for Gospel Preachers.* Hastings both published and distributed the diatribe; the author was serving a term in the Suffolk County jail for nonpayment of over two hundred dollars in fines incurred for his preaching exploits. According to Davis's account, which formed the bulk of his unsuccessful appeal to the Supreme Judicial Court in the fall of 1885, the battle over the Common had really begun in 1862, when the city council first passed a bylaw against public speaking there, hoping to silence the intemperate ravings of a temperance orator by the name of McClure. Other ordinances followed in 1876, 1883, and 1885, as revised continuances of the original. Davis and his lawyer, J. F. Pickering, argued that the entire process was illegal, and hinted at conspiracy, for, as they argued, the law had never become a matter of public record. As a bylaw buried in a pile of legislation, it had sat "silent and passive, like a dynamite bomb, ready to be exploded whenever the conspirators of the Vatican and of the saloon decided to act."[53]

As their notoriety grew, both Hastings and Davis began to depict themselves as heroic figures specifically targeted for harassment. In painstaking, fanatic detail, Davis's pamphlet outlined his own career preaching on the Common, beginning in 1882. He claimed that he had an agreement with the local police that as long as his crowds didn't obstruct sidewalks, he wouldn't be bothered. On the third Sunday of July in 1884, however, the police suddenly demanded a permit. Davis was arrested, "preaching to a moving audience of hundreds, all the way to the station house."[54] Undeterred, he held meetings on the Common for the rest of the summer, despite the constant threat of arrest.

Davis charged that his civil disobedience prompted the Committee on the Common's backroom decision to stop issuing preaching permits to those who asked. Notice of the new ordinance against preaching appeared only briefly, buried in a gossip section of the *Daily Advertiser* of August 4, 1884. But the Committee neither explained its actions nor warned any of the preachers on the Common of the new possibility for arrest and fine.[55]

Every setback only steeled evangelical resolve. In March 1886 the Superior Court rejected Hastings's appeal and levied a fine of forty dollars, which he was unable to pay. The aging street evangelist languished in the Charles Street Jail for a day, sputtering with indignation, until his family produced the money for his release. But Hastings put his brief incarceration to good use, writing his lengthy diatribe addressed to the Massachusetts state legislature. How could the city jail its ministers for preaching on the Common, he asked, "while at the same time the city authorities license Buffalo Bill to exhibit Indian Powwows, Pawnee war-dances and the like for money on the Lord's Day, in defiance of good order and State law"? The outrage against the God-fearing didn't even stop there, since the city taxed them in order to "to pay for Sunday Band Concerts, where sixty couples have been seen dancing at once on Boston Common on Sunday afternoon."[56]

The conspiracy only came to light, Davis and Hastings believed, when the police mistakenly hauled in Gordon, a well-known, highly respectable Baptist.

Hastings surmised that the real goal of city hall was to "haul in a few friend-less cranks, fine them, frighten others, and thus put an end to preaching on the public grounds." But when they also brought in Adoniram Judson Gordon, "they found that their net had more troublesome fish in it than they antici-pated; and it took more hauling than they expected."[57] Davis likewise opined that the authorities "didn't expect to catch Pastor Gordon," but when they found him along with Davis, Hastings, and the "despised Salvationists," their plot was forced into the open.[58]

By 1886, Hastings and Davis were intent on constructing their own version of the conspiracy; Gordon's role began to diminish accordingly, de-spite evidence that he had been, if anything, more intentional about provoking a conflict with city authorities than they were. In one earlier account, Davis had reported statements made by the YMCA secretary M. R. Deming on the Common on May 17. Deming is said to have announced: "We have come but here to make a test case" and "We have come to try whether Christian citizens can be robbed of their constitutional rights to worship God freely on common grounds of Boston, in this city which is the cradle of liberty, by a city ordi-nance."[59] But by early summer, Gordon had quietly disappeared from the case. The Committee on the Common attempted an awkward compromise by granting a permit to the YMCA, on condition that it quietly pay Gordon's fine and prevent an appeal. After waiting enough time to satisfy their dignity, YWCA leaders agreed, and the Baptist preacher no longer appeared in press accounts.[60]

Once the YMCA was out of the picture, only the most radical voices remained, and Boston faced serious religious polarization. The *Globe* pre-dicted a "wrangle of which no one can see the end." "Religious zeal when awakened is sure to be violent," the editors reminded their largely Democratic audience, "and there are many people in this city who would willingly pose as martyrs for causes of less moment than the one now involved."[61]

By the summer of 1886, evangelical Protestant indignation was only beginning to burn. Few seemed to care that, strictly speaking, the ordinance question was no longer a hindrance to public preaching. Under the new city charter, the mayor, not the Committee on the Common, had final power to grant preaching permits, and in July 1886, O'Brien publicly announced his intention to grant them to anyone endorsed by a reputable religious orga-nization. That proviso even included Hastings, who had procured a letter from the Methodist Preachers' Meeting of Boston. But by then, all this was pure technicality. During the elections of 1887, 1888, and 1889, Hastings blanketed the city with lurid caricatures of apish Irish Catholic politicians and besotted priests, plotting takeovers of the public schools, taking orders from the pope, and oppressing the Protestant citizens of Boston. "We do not in-terfere with politics," he noted a bit disingenuously, "but we do sometimes claim the Christian's privileges of telling a little truth."[62]

In his inaugural address in 1888, O'Brien devoted several pages to the subject of "preaching on the Common" and specifically complained about literature emanating from a "religious publishing-house on Cornhill." "My home was even invaded by these reptiles," he noted with obvious exasperation, "and day after day the door-bell was rung and packages of these papers were left to annoy my family."[63] In his address O'Brien intimated that much of the furor over preaching on the Common was being abetted by his political enemies, and protested his legal inability to repeal the offending law without support from the Committee on Ordinances. "As this matter is still being discussed by the public, the pulpit, and the religious press, and is giving rise to much unjust criticism of the executive branch of the government," O'Brien declared,

> I desire to say that if the City Council sees fit to abolish the ordinance referred to, it will meet with my approval now, as it would have met with my approval and signature in 1885. I have no fear that the people of Boston, who might be induced to visit the Common and public grounds on the Lord's day to hear religious instruction, will transgress the laws of order and propriety, or that a permit in the hands of a preacher is a necessity, even if such permit comes from the Mayor.

"The ordinance, however," O'Brien concluded, "as long as it stands, must be obeyed."[64]

When Davis finally emerged from jail on September 7, 1888, he entered into a thoroughly polarized religious and political situation, one he had played no small role in creating. In mid-February and through early March 1888, the Committee on Ordinances began public hearings to discuss repeal of the controversial law. Months passed with no word of a decision until August 1888, when the Committee announced a unanimous vote *against* repeal of the preaching ordinance.[65] Davis described the incident in lurid terms to a Tremont Temple audience: "At the close of these unprecedented hearings, one of the city council representatives of [the] Vatican sat on the table with hat on his head, and blew tobacco smoke into the faces of the ladies and ministers of the gospel who came to witness the final legal remonstrance against ranking Gospel ministers with dead dogs."[66]

Divine judgment loomed. That same summer, news broke that Jeremiah Mullane, the rumselling ringleader of the old Committee on the Common, had died—as had the district attorney who had sent Davis to jail and the judge who refused his appeal. Late that fall, O'Brien lost his bid for reelection. God had triumphantly entered Boston politics, and in the summer of 1888 the contest was far from over.

4

Militant Protestants

Politics, as a practice, whatever its professions, had always been the systematic organization of hatreds, and Massachusetts politics had been as harsh as the climate. The chief charm of New England was harshness of contrasts and extremes of sensibility—a cold that froze the blood and a heat that boiled it—so that the pleasure of hating—one's self if no better victim offered—was not its rarest amusement; but the charm was a true and natural child of the soil, not a cultivated weed of the ancients.

—Henry Adams, *The Education of Henry Adams*

In some ways, Boston's religious passions were unexceptional. By the time the police had made their arrests on the Common in 1885, mutual hostility between Protestants and Catholics had simmered across Europe and North America for almost four hundred years. In Puritan New England, Protestants celebrated Guy Fawkes Day, or "Pope Day," every November 5 by burning the Holy Father in effigy; schoolchildren played games like "Break the Pope's Neck" and, according to a ruling by the General Court in 1647, were forbidden to observe the "popish festival" of Christmas. Decades before the events in Boston, old antagonisms had erupted into violence as Protestants had rioted against Catholics up and down the East Coast during the "Know-Nothing" excitement of the 1840s. In the post–Civil War era, a second wave of anti-Catholicism swept the nation, spurred by heavy immigration of eastern and southern European Catholics into American urban centers. In 1884, the famous denunciation of the Democrats as the party of "Rum,

Romanism, and Rebellion" captured the concerns of many middle-class, native-born Americans. They worried a great deal about public education, especially that a Catholic parochial system would subvert the democratizing effect of American common schools. Rising labor violence, believed to be inspired by immigrant agitators, fueled what Richard Hofstadter once argued is a distinctly American tendency toward a conspiratorial, "paranoid style of rural politics."[1]

But Boston's conflicts were also unique. The concern over schooling was complicated by the city's particular religious configuration: not only did it array Catholics against Protestants but it set liberal Protestants against evangelicals, and Irish against British-Canadian immigrants.[2] The controversy also reawakened some old New England passions for anti-Masonry and Adventism, both of which found new expression in the conspiratorial logic of premillennial theology, fast becoming one of the staples of fundamentalist belief. And finally, the school controversy depended for energy and leadership on the growing network of Protestants directly affected by the events of 1885, especially evangelical women. Several women's organizations, including the Suffolk County affiliate of the Women's Christian Temperance Union—headed by "Boston's grand leader," Maria Gordon—helped evangelicals to articulate their growing sense of grievance against city hall and its Irish allies.[3]

The story of this rising militancy casts important light on fundamentalism from several angles. First, it demonstrates the important role women played in defining religious militancy. Although they were the majority constituency of Protestant churches in the late nineteenth century, women are somewhat tangential to most accounts of fundamentalism. To some degree, their absence reflects historians' tendency to focus on the movement's theological agenda, especially as it played out in colleges, seminaries, and national denominational meetings—all of which excluded women as a matter of course. Women's absence also seems to imply that fundamentalism was somehow out of character for the presumably more tolerant sex, even though the late nineteenth and early twentieth centuries witnessed a steady escalation of confrontational tactics in the suffrage and temperance campaigns. As Boston's story shows, Protestant women excelled at provoking conflict; at every turn in the story of rising religious confrontation, they were at the forefront. To a degree, women's leadership in anti-Catholic causes was a function of their secondary role in Protestant institutions; barred from ordained ministry and marginal to the city's ecclesiastical power structure, women had greater latitude to push the boundaries of religious civility. That their visibility in anti-Catholic rallies and political campaigns did not translate into larger institutional power should not be surprising. Women served the conservative Protestant cause best then, as they have often done since, as moral agitators, adept at defining but not necessarily resolving difficult social issues.

The Boston story also raises new questions about the public agenda of the emerging fundamentalist movement. Most historians' accounts of American Protestant fundamentalism ignore politics, in a sense rightly so. In contrast to the ardently nationalist rhetoric of other types of conservative religion, found today all around the world, from Northern Ireland to Iran, the American movement has tended to look mostly scholarly and pious.[4] Protestant fundamentalist leaders seemed to barely notice presidential campaigns and, because of their ardently millennial expectations, discouraged their followers from taking on political entanglements. But that should not be surprising: in the late nineteenth century, presidential elections were not always interesting. The ongoing sameness of party candidates in national contests rarely inspired the same kinds of ingenuity and passion that enflamed electoral contests on the state and city level. It was, in fact, within the local urban context that American fundamentalism was attuned to politics. Thus James M. Gray, a Reformed Episcopal pastor in Boston and later president of the Moody Bible Institute, urged a group of women in 1890 to vote because the act of voting was not just a "duty" but "a sacred thing, an act of worship, not of a political party, but of Almighty God."[5] Gray or A. J. Gordon may not have cared whether or not Grover Cleveland was president, but they would have worried a great deal about where the mayor or local alderman would enforce liquor laws or stand up for the public schools.

The other theme of this chapter is anti-Catholicism, an important, and often neglected, root of American fundamentalism. Admittedly, in this sense, Boston's story is exceptional; in few other places in the United States has the "systematic organization of hatreds" between the two branches of European Christendom been quite so central. But it would be wrong to conclude that anti-Catholicism was just an episodic passion of New Englanders. As the historian John Wolff argues, in the history of both American and British Protestantism, "antagonism to 'popery'" helped to "define evangelical identity."[6] In Boston, anti-Catholicism played a complex, sometimes contradictory role. It brought together an angry Protestant coalition, united in opposition to the growing political power of Catholics in the city government. But in the United States, anti-Catholic rhetoric was deeply tied to democratic national ideals; opponents of the Catholic Church saw themselves not as religious bigots but as defenders of individual rights and intellectual freedom—virtues supposedly endangered by the rising influence of European Catholics on American shores. To a degree, this nationalistic argument against Catholicism prevented conservative Protestants from following their alienation to its logical conclusion. The more they argued against "Romanism," the more they endorsed American ideals.[7] Indeed, as the next chapter demonstrates, anti-Catholicism energized Protestant institution-building; in the 1880s it spurred the creation of a network of churches, Bible institutes, and evangelistic organizations that would finally come to define conservative evangelical culture in twentieth-century New England.

Anti-Catholicism also played a role in Protestant division. Among conservatives, the crusades of the 1880s and 1890s deepened a growing social rift with liberal Protestants. Evangelical prejudice against Catholics, often situated among the less "respectable" sorts of Protestants, had resonated across social class divisions since the days of the Revolution. The public school battles of the late nineteenth century had a similar effect, inducing many liberals to take a stand for greater religious tolerance in the face of conservative prejudice. Thus, evangelicals who worried about "Romanism" quickly understood that this was only the tip of the proverbial iceberg. It is significant, I think, that the language they employed against "Romanists" in the 1880s proved adaptable to other situations, including their conflict with the forces of theological modernism in the 1920s. In both cases the enemy was a bureaucratically sophisticated foe, with a jaded attitude toward religion and an insiders' hold on positions of power. And in both cases, the opposition inspired conservative Protestants toward new affirmations of loyalty to individualism and fair play, and to redouble their efforts in evangelizing lost souls.

This chapter then charts the first part of this story, describing the ideas, alliances, and events that reawakened anti-Catholicism in Boston in the 1880s. The public school controversy provides the underlying narrative and a place to begin exploration of the rich subsoil of evangelical church culture in late nineteenth-century New England. Premillennial thinking made increasing sense in a social world shaped by British anti-Catholicism, the conspiratorial logic of anti-Masonry, tensions around gender roles, and passions for temperance. Unfortunately for some (and fortunately for others), the movement ended in an embarrassing scandal, but not before it left a permanent impact on people and churches in Boston.

Another Conspiracy Unearthed

In September 1885, just as Protestant indignation was reaching its peak over the arrests of Hastings, Davis, and Gordon, the denominational press broke more remarkable and mysterious news: Roman Catholic women were registering to vote. Protestant newspapers reported with growing alarm the efforts of Father James Supple, of the Frances de Sales Church in Charlestown, to mount a concerted political effort against the "bigoted men and strong-minded Protestant women" on the Boston school committee. Catholic women, normally noncombatants in the fray, were suddenly being pressed into service.[8]

But Protestants had their own forces in reserve. Women had been voting in Boston School Committee elections since 1879, though the turnout was usually small and concentrated in the upper- and middle-class Protestant wards of the city. They owed this right to the daughters and wives of Boston's Unitarian reformers, in particular the closely knit circle led by Theodore Parker, described by one historian as "a small group of Protestant middle and upper class women who came to a consensus about school politics by talking among themselves."[9] These women were primarily moral reformers and sought school suffrage as a way of introducing curriculum reforms that they believed would be of advantage to young women from the working classes. More concerned about moral uplift than equal rights, the New England Women's Club began campaigning for the vote in school elections in 1872, as a way of introducing a higher ethical and spiritual tone to public education. They had no intention—or means—of creating a grassroots political movement among the women of Boston: in 1879, the first contingent of female voters accounted for less than 1 percent of the city's female population.

But in the mid-1880s, a new group of evangelical Protestant female voters began to take a passionate interest in the Boston School Committee. In their case, temperance was the precipitating issue. Problems began in 1883, when officials closed an elementary school because it stood less than four hundred feet from a saloon and was thus in violation of a local ordinance. The decision to close a school and leave a saloon untouched infuriated the prohibition forces, who laid it at the feet of the sole Roman Catholic member of the school committee.[10]

The "school-house and the grog shop" issue quickly rallied a new and largely unpoliticized female constituency, particularly those connected with the local Women's Christian Temperance Union (WCTU). The Suffolk County WCTU, under the leadership of A. J. Gordon's wife Maria, played a central role in mobilizing them to action. In 1884 WCTU forces mapped out the territory they hoped to win by precincts, obtained voter registration lists, and sent out their members to reach each person "either by mail or personally" with temperance literature. In the 1884 school board election, the WCTU also pressed for the introduction of "scientific temperance" curriculum, warning students of the health risks of alcohol.[11] In response to the news from Charlestown, the Suffolk County WCTU raised the level of urgency, warning Protestant women that "a failure on your part to aid by your vote . . . will convict you of insincerity in your professions of interest in children's welfare, and put upon you the responsibility of keeping them in ignorance."[12]

Up to this point, Boston's evangelical Protestant women were not known for being politically radical. When the national woman suffrage movement split into two wings after the Civil War, Boston became home to the more conservative organization, the American Woman Suffrage Association, headed by Lucy Stone and Antoinette Brown Blackwell. The other, more radical branch, led by Elizabeth Cady Stanton and Susan B. Anthony, was the National Woman's Suffrage Association, headquartered in New York. Likewise, the

Massachusetts branch of the WCTU actively shunned the suffrage question, which had roiled the ranks of the national organization since Frances Willard assumed its presidency in 1874. As late as 1887, the Massachusetts branch president, Elizabeth Tobey, admitted that the vote was still "one of those 'opinions' on which we agree to differ" and pleaded with her members to consider an evangelist training course to help alleviate their "timidity in praying or speaking in the presence of others."[13]

In Boston, Maria Gordon played a pivotal role in guiding conservative women into action (see fig. 4.1). Mrs. Gordon, described by one who knew her well as "devout, vigorous, positive, militant, generous, tireless, prayerful, [and] warmhearted," was not one to back down easily. She was, in the words of this admirer, the kind of woman who "knew what people ought to do and

FIGURE 4.1. Maria Hale Gordon. From Scott M. Gibson, *A. J. Gordon: American Premillennialist* (University Press of America, 2001).

planned to see that they did it." Her temperance allies praised her as a "born leader" with "the skill of a general."[14] Though hardly radical on most matters, Gordon was convinced that women held the key to public morality. Speaking to a British audience during an overseas trip in 1888, Gordon declared that "in the contest between Emmanuel and the forces of evil, the reserves have been called into action; they are the women who form two-thirds of the members of the Christian church."[15]

Boston's Catholics were not likely to endure Protestant attacks in silence. Tridentine Catholicism, as Jay Dolan writes, "was riding a crest of popularity in Europe and enjoyed the support of a militant papacy." In Europe, as well as in much of the American Catholic hierarchy, the mood was "defensive, militant, and supremely confident."[16] Despite their recent experience as impoverished immigrants, Boston's upwardly mobile Catholics thoroughly enjoyed their rising political and cultural power. Indeed, one sign of their growing comfort was their relative reluctance to put money into parochial schools, at least compared to Catholics in other cities. It took a concerted effort by clergy in the early 1880s to increase the number of Catholic schools from sixteen in 1879 to thirty-five by 1884. In 1879, the Cambridge priest Thomas Scully provoked several years of controversy by threatening to deny Communion to parents who still used the public school system.[17]

The gathering confrontation between Irish Catholics and Protestant women first reached the secular press in a "School Suffrage Symposium" printed in the *Boston Post* in October 1885. John Boyle O'Reilly, the primary Roman Catholic contributor, opposed woman suffrage as a "humbug, a hypocrisy, a sentimental disease." "Women are better than men—and weaker," he declared. "They ought to rule, but they can't. They would make ideal laws, and men would break them with impunity." Elizabeth Tobey, representing the Massachusetts WCTU, denied being anti-Catholic but then declared that

> the present emergency makes it an imperative duty for every
> Protestant woman to use her right of school suffrage. It is not a
> question of privilege or choice, but one of stern duty, which every
> truly conscientious woman will recognize and act upon, whatever
> may be her views as to the expediency of extending further suffrage
> to women.

The Protestant figurehead Emory J. Haynes of Tremont Temple attempted to sound a more moderate tone in the symposium, promising that "the Protestant pastors will not descend to any egging on of the women in their congregations for a vulgar scramble at the election booths." Haynes declared that he would rather pay tuition for a private school—even if it meant he had to "dress in rags" to afford it—than send his wife "out to fight for the public schools with other women fired with fanatical zeal."[18]

Woman suffrage leaders had no religious stake in the school committee elections and at first welcomed the registration of Catholic women. Henry Blackwell reportedly commented: "[it] seems too good to be true."[19] The *Woman's Journal* reassured its readers that they had nothing to fear from an increase in "alien women" at the polls, since native-born women who could meet the literacy requirement for voting would outnumber them by a clear fifteen thousand votes. At any rate, the long-term benefits for women far outweighed any immediate risks to the Commonwealth. "The city is so evenly divided between Republicans and Democrats that a few thousand votes might very likely turn the scale," the *Journal* declared, noting that "the number of women voters in Boston has increased so largely during the past two years that the liquor-dealers and their friends have become alarmed." Suffrage leaders also played down the possibility that the women's vote would ignite religious antagonisms, and tried to sound a pacifying note of sisterhood. "Certain Democratic politicians," the *Woman's Journal* noted dismissively, "have accordingly exerted themselves to get up a scare among Catholic women, by representing to them that the Protestant women were making a crusade against Catholic members of the school committee."[20] The real issue for suffragists was voting rights, not religion. "Now let all women come forward who value the common schools," the *Woman's Journal* urged, "as well as all who are convinced of their equal rights as citizens, and enroll themselves as voters" in the school committee election.[21]

Women enthusiastically complied. In order to participate in the December school committee election, potential voters had to present a property assessment and pay a poll tax of one or two dollars; but even this requirement proved no deterrent. The 1885 contest recorded twice as many female voters as in the previous year. But, for Protestants at least, the election result was a mixed success. Most of the increase came from the Roman Catholic wards of the city, with the North End showing the highest female turnout of all. The two female candidates for school committee, the Unitarians Emily Fifield and Lucia Peabody, lost their bid for election but received more votes than any non-Democratic candidate in the field.[22]

Protestant leaders began to realize that their success depended on women. By 1887, even Emory Haynes had reconsidered his opposition to female voters and publicly lauded the WCTU for its "visionary" program. "The time will come," he predicted, "when rum-sucking libertines going about the streets of the city in the hunt for votes" will run into defeat. "There are women who would rather see every commonwealth racked to the core than have quiet under the present system. They have money, you politicians," Haynes warned, "and two dollars to your every dollar. You can't do anything but submit to her. The women fulfill all the conditions of prophecy. They are the very genius of Christianity."[23]

Anti-Catholic Theology

Of course, to many Protestants, the school board crisis was just the tip of a much larger iceberg. They worried far more about "Romanism," a term used to suggest a large and dangerous conspiracy. To Protestant critics, the Catholic Church loomed as a vast, unresponsive bureaucracy, its power wielded by invisible hands and manipulated by shrewd men for mysterious purposes—not unlike the Standard Oil trust or the Tweed Ring. Justin Dewey Fulton, Boston's leading anti-Catholic in the 1880s, entertained one lecture audience with the mysterious tale of two nuns walking the halls of the Capitol in Washington, D.C. According to Fulton, the sisters solicited donations from every new member of Congress and then recorded the names of all who refused in a "little black book." "Some wise, comprehensive intellect, has been at the back of all you see in Boston and in Washington," Fulton warned, "and our children's children will see that we have wrestled against more than flesh and blood, something that dominates, yet works outside."[24]

The larger problem with "Romanism," however, was theological: many Protestants doubted that Catholics were even fellow Christians. Rooted in ancient heresy and reduced to a hollow a ceremony presided over by a corrupt papacy, the Catholic Church, in their eyes, had long since veered from the true faith. If an "old pagan was to rise from the dead" and meet the modern-day pope, J. A. Wylie wrote in the fervently evangelical *Watchword*, "he would . . . conclude that the ancient Jove was still reigning, and was being worshiped by the same rites that were practiced in his honor two thousand years ago."[25] In a similar vein, Fulton charged that Romanism "claims to save without repentance. It offers salvation not by approach to Jesus through a holy God "but by a "human agency that is admitted to be sinful." Catholic doctrine was little more than a "mingling of scripture and philosophy, of piety and pleasure," easily deceiving the "ignorant or unthinking."[26]

H. L. Hastings's central role in the conflict with city hall injected a potent strain of theological pessimism into the political fray. His Adventist theology taught the certainty of Christ's Second Coming as a sudden, cataclysmic event putting a quick end to social and moral evil. In the post–Civil War decades, this apocalyptic premillennialism set Adventists apart from most other evangelical Protestants, who looked forward to Christ's return as the culmination of Christian progress in the world. Adventists were fundamentally pessimistic, not only about the future of secular society but also about the role of the Christian church as a force for change.[27]

Advent Christians were important theological precursors of fundamentalism in Boston. Though most Adventist churches were scattered across rural New England, most of the denomination's publishing enterprises, established by the entrepreneurial Joshua Himes in the 1830s and 1840s, were located in the city. Significantly, when John Nelson Darby, the British apostle of dispensational premillennial theology, traveled through the area in 1865 and then for longer periods in 1875 and 1876, he spent most of his time among Adventists. According to the historian Ernest Sandeen, some even converted to his particular biblical interpretation of End Times events.[28]

Clearly, even before his arrest, Hastings was theologically prepared to believe the worst about a world that he never accepted as his final home. "The Christian life is a warfare," he declared in 1882. "The world has many plans for unions, peace, and harmony, and is full of proposals for compromise and concession. It is the business of the Christian to reject all these, to stand for God, even if alone."[29] Hastings had good reason for pessimism, since after the fire of 1872 destroyed his printing press, he was always on the brink of financial ruin. Perhaps making a virtue of necessity, he chose to reject all of the trappings of capitalist success and the managerial values of American business culture. "Human ambition and love of the praise of men very poorly qualify any man to direct and control the affairs of a church," he declared; "and when the Holy Ghost makes men overseers to feed the flock of God, it selects men of a different stamp, more full of the divine spirit, and better fitted for the work than ambitious worldlings can ever hope to be until they are humbled, heart-broken, and truly converted to God."[30]

Hastings's theology of alienation also predisposed him to find the Roman Catholic hierarchy at the root of events surrounding his arrest. Like many Protestants, he was thoroughly prepared to believe that the Catholic Church was the great "whore of Babylon" who in the Book of Revelation joined forces with the Antichrist to make war on God's elect. But his arrest and imprisonment also focused his general resentment of wealth and power into a specific grievance against local Catholic authorities. "Why was it," he asked in 1887,

> that, when the Roman Catholic superintendent of the Common, whose name was on the complaint against a preacher as a government witness, saw that the case was coming, he *slipped away and could not be found* to testify? Why was it that when the Irish Roman Catholic wholesale and retail rumselling chairman of the committee on Commons was summoned, and was in court, that we were *not allowed to put him on the stand and get out of him the facts in the case?*. . . What say the Christians of Boston, and the ministers of the gospel, who dwell in ceiled houses, while W. F. Davis lies a prisoner in Charles street jail for preaching the gospel to the poor? [31]

Hastings was not, of course, the only one to see the arrests on the Common as a conspiracy engineered by Irish priests and politicians. Ernest

Gordon blamed his father's arrest on the machinations of a "Hibernicized" city government and a Roman Catholic canaille, led by the chief of police.[32] Upon hearing news of the arrest, Gordon's close friend Joseph Cook fired off a telegram issuing "congratulations on persecution" and declaring the defeat of "municipal misrule."[33]

As a leading premillennialist, A. J. Gordon played a central role in interpreting the signs of the times for his fellow evangelicals. His best-known book on eschatology, *Ecce Venit: Behold He Cometh,* was published in 1889, at the height of religious controversy in Boston.[34] *Ecce Venit* is essentially an historical narrative, designed to show modern-day Christians their place in the flow of divine time. Much of it is fairly standard interpretive lore: since the Reformation, the identification of the as the Antichrist of biblical prophecy and the Roman Catholic Church as the Great Harlot of Revelation had remained a staple of Protestant eschatology.[35] Gordon had no doubt that the pope was the Antichrist prophesied in 2 Thessalonians 2:3, "the man of sin," the "son of perdition." Nor did he doubt that Romanism was a perversion of true Christianity. "It is no exaggeration to say," Gordon wrote,

> that the Eucharistic cup which Rome now puts to the lips of her communicants, with its mixture of miracle and magic, resembles more nearly the chalice of the ancient Chaldean 'Mysteries' than it does the chaste and simple memorial cup which Christ left in the hands of His Bride, the Church.[36]

Indeed, in Gordon's view, the Catholic Church was an "abomination," "her worship corrupted with mixtures of heathen religion which the Scriptures call the worship of demons," more akin to the rites of "Babylonish sun-worshippers" than orthodox Christians.[37]

Gordon's views on Catholicism set him apart from the mainstream of premillennial interpretation during his time. John Nelson Darby and the majority of late nineteenth-century fundamentalists were "futurists," that is, they believed that most of the prophecies in the Book of Revelation, particularly those describing the Antichrist, had yet to transpire. Thus, futurist premillennialists departed from the traditional view that the biblical Antichrist was the pope. They spoke of him as a mysterious person yet unnamed but central to the violent consummation of human time at the time of time. As a "historicist," one who believed that biblical prophecy had already begun to be fulfilled within the unfolding of human history, Gordon was running against the majority view among premillennialists. For this, he was roundly and publicly criticized, most notably by James Brookes, the editor of a rival journal, *The Truth.*[38]

But Gordon's historicism did speak directly to the situation of Protestants in Boston, explaining their decline but offering a modicum of hope. The "true church," which Gordon described as God's "little flock," would always be beleaguered by "Pagans, Mohammedans, Infidels, and Apostates" and "branded with opprobrium, and torn by persecution, and beaten by hireling shepherds." It would be continually beset by religious counterfeits. "For when we study Satan's career in Scripture and in history," Gordon wrote, "we find that open infidelity is little in his line. His way has been to masquerade in the symbols and sacraments of the Church," not to oppose the truth head on.[39] Protestants, then, need not aspire to be outwardly successful. "That which is truly evangelical and evangelistic," Gordon wrote, "can never be fashionable."[40] Nor could they hope to triumph through direct, violent opposition. Though Gordon's brand of premillennialism certainly opened the door for conspiratorial speculation, it also rewarded patience. "Amid all the disheartenment, induced by the abounding iniquity of our times," he wrote in 1888, "amid the loss of faith . . . and the outbreaking of lawlessness, . . . this is the Lord's inspiring exhortation: 'Look up and lift up your heads; for your redemption draweth nigh.'"[41]

During the late 1880s, anti-Catholicism and prophetic speculation formed a powerful combination. In Tremont Temple rallies, speakers often invoked biblical prophecy in their denunciations of the Catholic Church. Hastings himself exegeted prophecies in Revelation and Daniel, and a Mrs. McKinstry, speaking on "Christian Patriotism, Prophetic Pictures," made a similar argument from the Book of Revelation.[42] James M. Gray, the Reformed Episcopal pastor and later president of fundamentalist Moody Bible Institute, told a packed house that though he still preferred Catholics to liberal Protestants, the "church of Rome was clearly the prejudiced enemy of God," supporting the claim with an extended exegesis of Daniel, 2 Thessalonians, and Revelation.[43] In 1888, a leading anti-Catholic James O'Connor related an account of a meeting at a premillennial Bible conference in Ocean Grove, N.J., in which Luther T. Townsend discussed the sad events in Boston with the dispensationalists Leander Munhall, George C. Needham, and William G. Moorehead. "The Church of Rome is so powerful in Boston," Townsend warned them, "and indeed in all of New England, that . . . not only is liberty in danger there, but life is rendered unendurable."[44]

But no one was as convinced as Hastings's codefendant, W. H. Davis, writing from his cell in the Suffolk County jail, that the Catholic Church, and its minions in city hall, was part of "a Satanic conspiracy against the highest weal of our Commonwealth."[45] Indeed, the dramatic events following the arrests on the Common stuck fast in the imagination of Boston's evangelical Protestants, and if they were ever tempted to forget, anti-Catholic agitators like Davis were quick to remind them, relentlessly pushing their own theory about the arrests as a "war measure" issued "at the bidding of the rumsellers of Boston" and their Jesuit allies.[46] Hastings, for example, pointed out that between May 1 and June 26, 1885, the city government had granted 2,579 liquor licenses and only two permits to preach on the Common. "Who is at the bottom of it all?" he demanded. "What influence *is* it that is moving for the suppression of free speech in old Boston? Are we coming under that power which in some countries excludes Bibles as demoralizing, and provides Sunday bull-fights for the edification and elevation of the people?"[47]

By the late summer of 1885, many Protestants were willing to believe that Hastings's interpretation of the events on the Common was the right one. The Congregationalist editor Austin Phelps warned his readers that "the grip of the Jesuit is hidden in the glove of the policeman." "We do not know what [the] future may have in store for us," he noted ominously, and warned of the "petty tyrannies of the possible 'O's' and 'Mc's'" in the Boston city government. Phelps appealed directly to his denomination's Puritan past, which he argued was fundamental to American rights of free speech. "From Queen Elizabeth on down," he declared, "the Puritan theory of liberty . . . has claimed the right to preach what and when and where the individual conscience shall dictate. The fathers came here for this more than for any other thing. Our history is full of it. We breathe it in the air. It runs in our blood."[48]

But in fact anti-Catholicism did not attract large numbers of Boston's old stock Puritans. Most of the movement's recruits were evangelical Baptists and Methodists—"low Protestants," according to one description. Deacon Bradbury, of Tremont Temple, declared in 1890 that "the Methodists predominated" at the Music Hall meetings, though "the Baptist sect was the one most hated by Rome." Congregationalists, he said, "have not been largely represented."[49] The *Pilot* tended to agree: "Our Baptist brethren, who used to be whipped at the cart's tail by the Boston Puritans, in the old days (and honestly deserved it, if their manners and morals were as bad as they are now), are foremost in the work of persecuting others for conscience sake today."[50] The oldest organization of the Protestant crusade was the Boston branch of the Evangelical Alliance, formed in 1867. Though its members deplored the overwrought goings-on in the Music Hall, they were pragmatic enough to recognize a power base when they saw one. "True, there may not have been as much broad-cloth there, or silk and bank-stock, as in some other places," one sympathetic observer wrote, "but there were souls and votes there."[51]

Allies

The anti-Catholic movement brought together an odd assortment of people. The chief beneficiary of the crusade against Rome was Justin Dewey Fulton, pastor of Baptist Tremont Temple from 1864 to 1873 (see fig. 4.2).

Beginning in August 1887, he occupied center stage at the Sunday afternoon rallies held at the Temple, and later the Music Hall. "Absolutely

FIGURE 4.2. Justin Dewey Fulton. From *Tremont Temple Baptist Church: A Light in the City for 150 Years* (Boston: Tremont Temple Baptist Church, 1989).

reckless as to truth or facts," a Catholic historian wrote, "ready to make the wildest assertions and the foulest insinuations, colloquial, picturesque, and dramatic in style, Fulton, above all, knew how to mingle piety, patriotism, humor, horror, and obscenity in just the proportions his audiences desired."[52] "Filthy Fulton," as he was known in the Catholic press, was also the author of a steady stream of anti-Catholic literature, including one book entitled *Why Priests Should Wed*, which was declared "obscene and indecent" by its publisher, Rand and Avery. When a censored version finally appeared under a different publisher, Benjamin Bradbury (a Tremont Temple deacon) displayed it in his drugstore window, behind iron bars. "A Catholic historian may recall with no great regrets," one such recalled, "that more than one brick was hurled by indignant Catholics through the windows of the drugstore."[53]

Fulton was flanked by a variety of other equally eccentric and controversial figures. The Sunday afternoon meetings featured a regular array of "converts" from Catholicism, including T. E. Leyden, who was pastor of a tiny congregation of "reformed Catholics" in Gordon's Clarendon Street Baptist Church, and the infamous Father Chiniquy, the author of a lurid volume entitled *The Priest, the Woman, and the Confessional.* The most popular lecturer turned out to be Margaret Shepherd, an "escaped nun" with a graphic tale of Catholic intrigue that, to the ultimate dismay of her supporters, did not even begin to surpass the scandalizing truth of her personal life.[54]

British-Americans

Hastings and Davis had plenty of other allies as well. Their most vocal champions turned out to be the city's British-American immigrant community, including many Scotch-Irish Protestant immigrants from the Canadian Maritimes and Great Britain.[55] The alliance is not surprising: Maritime Protestants came from some of the most conservative evangelical stock in Canada, with a British legacy of cultural and religious animosity toward Catholics and the "truculent spirit of the Orange lodges, to which they commonly belonged."[56]

In the post–Civil War era, Boston's leading evangelicals prized their transatlantic connections. Following in the footsteps of Dwight L. Moody, who conducted groundbreaking crusades in the British Isles in the 1870s, A. J. Gordon traveled and spoke there regularly, conducting an extended tour in 1886.[57] Hastings claimed to have crossed the Atlantic six times between 1872 and 1888 for evangelistic campaigns.[58] Boston's transatlantic evangelicals shared beliefs as well as geographic ties. Gordon's close British associate, H. Grattan Guinness, also wrote on anti-Catholic themes, including a series of premillennialist lectures reprinted by a Boston publishing house in 1890, *Romanism and the Reformation from the Standpoint of Prophecy.*[59] The evangelist George C. Needham was another well-known figure on both the anti-Catholic and premillennial circuits. Born an Irish Protestant, he became an associate of Guinness and the famed British preacher Charles Spurgeon in the 1860s; in 1886 Needham and Guinness joined in an evangelistic tour of Northern Ireland. After meeting Moody in London in 1867, Needham came to America and married a woman from Boston, and the couple took up work among Reformed Catholics.[60]

British-Americans also had a specific grievance against Boston's Irish Catholics. On June 21, 1887, expatriate English and Scottish citizens of Boston held a banquet in Faneuil Hall in honor of Queen Victoria's jubilee. But the participants were hardly in a celebratory mood. The night before, John Boyle O'Reilly, editor of the *Pilot,* had held a boisterous counterrally, and passions were running high. The British-American banqueters were beset by an angry

Irish mob, and only the intervention of several hundred police kept a full-scale riot from breaking out. Reverend David Gregg, pastor of the Park Street Church, shouted his after-dinner remarks over the din of a "noisy and dangerous demonstration" outside.[61]

A few months later and still fuming over the episode, the Evangelical Ministers' Association appointed a committee, headed by H. L. Hastings and including A. J. Gordon and Joseph Cook, to encourage more immigration from the British Isles. Since Britain was hopelessly overcrowded, the committee reasoned, and New England's farms were empty and her cities overrun with undesirables, they proposed to invite "industrious Christian people" to restock "the waste places, strengthen the decimated schools and churches, give stability and consistency to society, and serve to counterbalance other less desirable elements, whose presence and whose influence upon our political and educational institutions is a matter of grave concern to intelligent Christians and patriots."[62] Not much came of the effort, which sounded oddly reminiscent of Boston's earlier Emigrant Aid Society, which had sent settlers, as well as "Beecher's Bibles," to Kansas in the 1850s; but the passions behind it were real and permanent, and they soon found other more effective outlets for expression.

Anti-Masonry

During the late 1880s, conspiracy thinking among Boston's evangelicals also drew from a renewed campaign against lodges and secret societies. Its largely church-based constituency included many retired abolitionists and anti-Masonic crusaders of the 1830s and 1840s, a time when anti-Catholicism "Know-Nothingism" also joined forces with anti-Masonry. Like the anti-Catholic movement, post–Civil War anti-Masonry had a national (and strongly midwestern) dimension and a theologically conservative agenda. The campaign against the fraternal lodge, which was centered in the National Christian Association, began in Aurora, Illinois, in 1867 and was led by Jonathan and Charles Blanchard, the father and son presidents of the evangelical Wheaton College.[63]

Historians have found a strong link between post–Civil War anti-Masonry and emergent fundamentalism. The Blanchards, for example, had little truck with liberals and regularly featured premillennial discourses by Dwight Moody in their anti-Masonic periodical the *Christian Cynosure*. In 1871 Blanchard publicly attacked Alonzo Quint, editor of the *Congregational Quarterly* and secretary of the National Council of Congregational Churches, for his role as senior chaplain of the Masonic Grand Lodge of Massachusetts. The common denominator between anti-Masonry and premillennialism, as Blanchard perceived them, was the conviction that "society was in rebellion against God." And nowhere, did it seem, was the battle more stark than in New England, a place Blanchard believed was ruled by "men whose pulpits make no secret of denying the atonement."[64]

Women's groups also held a stake in the success of anti-Masonry. In late nineteenth-century America, the elaborate rituals of the Red Men, Knights of Pythias, Odd Fellows, and Masons were enormously popular among middle-class Protestant men. The historian Mark Carnes has argued that for many of them the lodge operated as a masculine parallel to the female-dominated Protestant churches.[65] There is no doubt that secret societies were popular with men in Boston. Blanchard himself estimated that in 1889 there were twice as many lodges as churches in the city, some 571 compared to 223. Indeed, the 1885 city directory, which listed only a page and a half of churches and ministers, included six pages of listings for Masonic Societies, Odd Fellows, Knights of Pythias, the Benevolent and Protective Order of Elks, and Good Templars.[66]

Many Protestant women viewed these numbers with alarm. Although the national WCTU was more tolerant of male ritual (the WCTU's president, Frances Willard, made common cause with the Knights of Labor, an organization many Protestants viewed as a secret society), New England women fervently disagreed. Women, above all, had the highest stake in shutting down Masonic lodges, for it was in those secret conclaves that all the forms of masculine vice—alcoholic consumption being the chief of all crimes—were allowed to flourish.[67]

In Boston, many evangelical Protestants connected the lodge problem with the rising strength of the Catholic Church. The Blanchards' *Christian Cynosure* received the news of the arrests on Boston Common with great eagerness and alarm, and ran regular updates on events as they unfolded, including eyewitness accounts from Davis himself.[68] To evangelicals, the lodges and the Catholic Church drew from a common set of spiritual ills. "The devil-head of evil in this world," D. P. Mathews wrote in a "Boston Letter" to the *Christian Cynosure*, "consists of the trinity of Rum, Romanism and Lodgery." Taken in sum, Mathews argued, all three amounted to the same thing: rebellion against God.[69]

That conclusion required only a few leaps in logic. True, in 1884 the Third Plenary Council in Baltimore had condemned secret societies, and relatively few Roman Catholic men belonged to them. Moreover, as even the leaders of the National Christian Association admitted, the vast majority of lodge members were upstanding Protestant laymen. But in the eyes of critics, both the Catholic Church and the lodge drew the unwitting into the same web of godless ritual. "The secret lodges," one such critic complained, "with their prayers from which the name of Jesus is excluded, their mutilated extracts of the Scriptures, their solemn hymns, their chaplains, priests, prelates, altars, baptisms, burial services and consecrations are directly leading men to help for salvation without Jesus." A. J. Gordon similarly urged "the duty of

separation—separation from associations that...hold men together by com-
pacts and oaths when they ought to be free to yield with their full force to the
attractions of Christ."[70]

Evangelical Protestants saw the lodge and the Catholic Church as twin
agents of urban vice. "Five hundred and seventy-one lodges in the capital of
New England draw your young men from Christ's prayer meeting, in the
proportion of two-and-a-half to one," the *Christian Cynosure* reported in 1889.

> It swallows their money by thousands, consumes their time till the
> late hours of night, and turns them out on the street between two
> lights, one before the saloon and the other at the door of the brothel!
> And, if they chance to escape one of these roads to hell, it teaches
> them to loathe Christianity in the person of the preachers whom they
> have helped to blindfold.

As the WCTU lecturer Mrs. E. A. Gleason concluded, "you will seldom
find an active member of a secret society earnestly engaged in reform work."[71]

In especially suspicious minds, Masons and Catholics could be imagined
to be working in tandem. In 1889, for example, the *British-American* reported
on a "secret war" waged by Jesuits and Masons. More explicitly, W. H. Davis
imagined a vast conspiracy of irreligion in the city of Boston, linked by
"private winks, and signs, and passwords, and grips, and plots, and secret
meetings." "Whatever names these men may apply to themselves," he concluded sourly, "they are really members of the Catholic Apostate, Canish,
Sodomite, Baalamite, Nicolaitain, Romish, Rumish, Jesuit, Mormon, Masonic, Tobacco, Satanic Church."[72]

Not surprisingly, many of the same evangelical spokesmen appeared on
anti-Masonic and anti-Catholic platforms. The leaders of the New England
branch of the National Christian Association were all at the center of political
conflict in Boston: A. J. Gordon and Maria Gordon, as well as James M. Gray,
Joseph Cook, and L. T. Townsend.[73] A well-publicized Boston conference
against masonry in December 1889 featured all of the city's evangelical leadership. Gordon presided over a stellar list of conservative spokesmen, including Charles A. Blanchard as well as James M. Gray, the Congregationalist
O. P. Gifford, A. A. Miner, the Baptist editor George Merriam, and, of course,
Horace Hastings and W. F. Davis, the latter billed as the "Boston Common
evangelist."[74] T. E. Leyden, the "reformed Catholic evangelist," labored to
draw a direct connection between Rome and the lodge. "Though he had never
been a Mason, he could testify to the great similarity between Masonry and
Catholicism," one observer reported. Adding that he knew many Odd-Fellows
who were also "good Catholics," Leyden predicted that "Masonry will be
wedded to Romanism, as a means to help the latter gain the supreme power
in our country."[75]

Women to the Fore

In August 1887, Mayor O'Brien awarded the famed bare-knuckle boxer John L. Sullivan, the "Boston Strong Boy," a huge, gold-encrusted belt valued at some ten thousand dollars, pronouncing him champion of the world. Four thousand men, including seven members of the city council, thronged the Boston Theater to witness the crowning of Boston's Irish-American champion.[76] Hastings lost no time in denouncing this debauched display of "Rum, Romanism, and Pugilism."[77] The cover page of the *Safeguard* that week was a four-paneled sketch comparing Sullivan's violent career with Davis's unjust jail term (see fig. 4.3). Hastings was also quick to remind his readers of Sullivan's own history as a "notorious drunkard and wife-beater"—in other words, the living antithesis of evangelical morality.[78]

Among Catholics, however, the triumphant Sullivan was an Irish Christian hero. Thanks in part to his personal popularity, prizefighting was losing its violent, disreputable aura and fast becoming a respectable form of middle-class entertainment.[79] And as such, Sullivan's success brought glory to Irish Catholics everywhere. In 1888 John Boyle O'Reilly published *The Ethics of Boxing and Manly Sport*, arguing that a well-rounded Catholic had to be both morally and physically fit. When a delegation from the Gaelic Athletic Association arrived in Boston in the fall of that same year, the *Pilot* praised the "stalwart, bright-eyed, muscular, strapping" young men as true representatives of "Ireland's muscular Christianity."[80]

For their part, evangelicals measured the superiority of their faith against the stereotype of the wild, brawling Irishman. In the nineteenth century the prevailing Protestant ethic of "manliness" emphasized self-mastery, not just over drink and sexual temptation but over destructive emotions as well.[81] Irish Catholic men, in Protestant eyes, failed on all counts. In March 1888 Hastings published a drawing of a brutish Irishman leaning over a broken chair, with wife and children cowering nearby. The accompanying article excoriated Catholic manhood as "ruled by appetite, by passion, by priestcraft, by ignorance, by prejudice, and by secret and irresponsible clans, leagues, and organizations." The list continued:

> They break law, they disturb order, they drink whiskey, they abuse
> their wives, they neglect their children, and then to defend them-
> selves against the poverty, misery, helplessness and stupidity brought
> on by their ignorance and intemperance, they join some secret
> clan . . . go on strikes, hang around saloons, mob peaceable people,
> and commit crimes and depradations, which violate law, disturb
> order, and finally bring trouble and ruin upon them. [82]

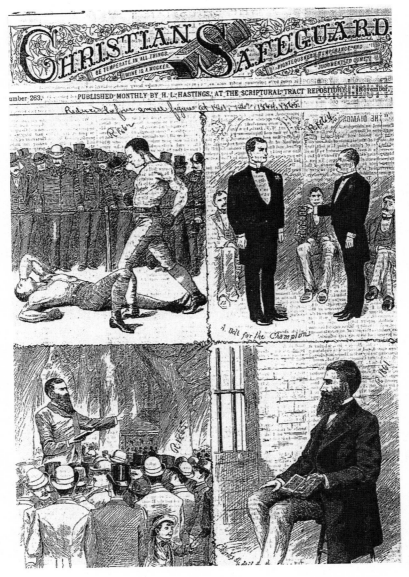

FIGURE 4.3. How Boston Honors Prize-Fighters and Preachers. Cover, *Christian Safeguard* 22 (November 1887).

Opposition to Catholics also drew out a strain of prudery in late nineteenth-century Protestant culture. Anti-Catholic literature made much of the private confessional, a rite that, in Fulton's fervent imagination, "affords the Fathers great freedom to accomplish the purpose they may entertain." Fulton cited "abundant evidence" not only that "confessors have seduced women who have confessed to them" but "that the priest is screened by priest, by bishop and by pope, and that to a certain extent incontinence is counted on, and is treated as a matter of course. It would be indelicate," Fulton added coyly, "to quote at length, or indeed, at all; and yet, could we do so, we could see how the priest is hedged about with protection, and how the widest door to prostituting the virtues of his people is opened before him."[83]

Catholic manhood was deficient on all counts. Fulton even excoriated Catholicism for being overly feminized, through the worship of a "woman-god." "Wherever Mary is worshiped," he charged, "brain power, education and manhood departs, as fashion and triviality bear sway." The true antidote to Romanism, Fulton argued, was a "manly Christianity" with "strength, character, a free foot to walk on and a strong arm to swing the blade." "It claims the right to let God rule with a rod of iron in business, in politics, as in religion."[84]

The problem for evangelical men, of course, was that their own campaign against Catholic priests and politicians was largely run by women. The pragmatic reasons for enlisting women's groups were clear: in the late nineteenth century, Protestant women had the most organizational skill and experience needed to mount a public crusade. The local WCTU, for example, was a well-orchestrated group under highly competent leadership. When Boston women began to come out to vote in 1888, temperance women had already organized themselves by precinct; Maria Gordon appointed workers for each local polling place and even provided them with printed directions and a list of women who had registered.[85] But women's prominent role also placed limits on Protestant success, not least by visibly undercutting the rhetoric of masculine superiority. During the intensely acrimonious days of the late 1880s, the highly moralistic presence of women in the school campaign also placed an unrealistically heavy burden on their supposed natural religiousity. Protestant hopes rose—and eventually fell—around an increasingly uncertain store of feminine virtue.

In the spring of 1888, two events involving school board politics opened a new round of interreligious bickering. First, in May, the state board of education attempted to gain control over Catholic education by passing a Bill for the Inspection of Private Schools. The controversy extended further over the use of an anti-Catholic textbook by a history teacher, Charles B. Travis, at the English High School. The book had enraged Catholics by describing the Reformation-era practice of selling indulgences, famously condemned by Martin Luther, as "permission to sin." The school board began by barring Travis from teaching history (they sent him to the English department, where he would presumably do less harm) and discontinued use of the offending text. These relatively mild acts led, in the description of a Catholic historian, to "an almost unparalleled explosion of rage among the anti-Catholic crusaders." Indeed, the same author described the summer of 1888 as "Pandemonium."

That July, evangelical leaders organized a Committee of One Hundred, which issued a stream of "rabid tracts" and organized the local Tremont Temple oratory into a New England–wide lecture circuit. The Committee of One Hundred also began to recruit new voters for the upcoming school board election that December.[86]

But they were already second in line. A month before, in June 1888, 150 evangelical Protestant women had formed their own anti-Catholic political organization, the Loyal Women of American Liberty, and chosen Margaret Shepherd, the famous "escaped nun" to be their president. A well-known figure in Boston and surrounding New England towns, Shepherd and her specialty talks "for women only" entitled "The Roman Catholic Confessional," were a favorite of Tremont Temple audiences. She had only arrived in Boston in early 1887, but within a few months was wielding a notice of public endorsement signed by all of the city's leading evangelicals, including Joseph Cook, Maria Gordon, M. R. Deming of the YMCA, and L. T. Townsend of Boston University.[87] The Loyal Women immediately set to work registering female voters, monitoring polling places, and holding mass meetings all over Boston. In 1888, they reported registering some 20,252 women, 96 percent of whom voted in the December 1888 election. In the final tally that year, female voters accounted for one-quarter of total ballots cast.[88]

The victory went to the local Republicans, who swept the school board ticket and elected eight aldermen. More significantly, the December 1888 election spelled the end of Hugh O'Brien's mayoral career. The beleaguered O'Brien lost to the Republican Thomas N. Hart by a scant two thousand votes, most of them cast in the heat of the school board fray. Evangelicals recognized the hand of divine providence in his defeat, but Massachusetts Republicans graciously attributed the win to the female voters and the "incendiary preachers" who supported them.[89]

Success, however, created new enemies. The public school inspection bill, which, according to Catholic memory, was supported by a coalition of "Evangelicals and British-Americans," failed in 1888 because of influential opposition by elite Protestants, including the Unitarian pastor Cyrus Bartol, President Charles Eliot of Harvard, Colonel Thomas Wentworth Higginson, and Francis Walker, the president of the Massachusetts Institute of Technology. These men also had influential female allies, a coalition of Republican moderates, Unitarians, and woman suffragists who formed the Public School Union, championing parental rights, religious tolerance, and private enterprise. Though liberals did not defeat the inspection bill outright, they managed to water it down into a harmless version of the original.[90]

Conservative tempers flared. The *British-American Citizen* described the Public School Union as "educated and (mostly) childless people," "eighty per cent. spinsters and fifteen per cent.[sic] 'parents' who consider children neither a necessity nor a pleasure." This timid group of liberals hoped only to promote "a delightful spirit of love for everybody, and a general absence of anything resembling a backbone."[91]

Clearly, anti-Catholicism was widening some old fissures between liberal and conservative Protestants.[92] The class resentments that resonated across this divide dated back at least to the 1830s, when Protestants had burned an Ursuline convent in Charlestown. Patronized by the daughters of upper-class Unitarians and wealthy Catholics, the doomed convent not only represented to evangelical Protestants an "unholy alliance" between infidels but "symbolized the breach between rich and poor." Its palatial rooms and terraces, just a stone's throw from the working-class neighborhoods of Charlestown, spoke eloquently of class privilege as well as the debauched goings-on of nuns and priests.[93]

The alliance between Brahmins and Catholics survived the fire and in succeeding decades found a home of sorts in the popular lore of both Protestant and Catholic novelists. Henry Morgan's breathless bestseller *Boston Inside Out!* was first published in 1880 and promised to expose the "sins of a great city." Indeed, the main character, Augustus Gildersleeve, was a wealthy Brahmin whose daughter Gertrude attended a Catholic finishing school headed by the cynical Father Titus. In tipsy conversation with a liberal clergyman, Titus boasted that his church was "filling even from men of your own creed, Brother Poindexter." "There is a culminating point in faith as well as in physics," the priest continued, "when all beyond is chaos. Liberalism tends to that point. When reached, then the work of the Catholic Church begins."[94] A popular Catholic novel published in 1911 made much the same point. Here the hero was Reverend Josiah Danforth, a Unitarian minister with a crucifix in his study and a close friendship with the local Catholic priest, Father Hanlon. The story's female lead, Dorothy Wakefield, embraced the theology of both men, dreaming of a "great, all-conquering faith" joining the "mystical depth of Catholicism and the rational, modern freedom of Unitarianism."[95]

In early 1890, the rupture between conservative and liberal Protestants became a public matter in Boston, when both the *Congregationalist* and the Unitarian *Christian Register* editorialized against anti-Catholic agitation. The Roman Catholic *Pilot* quoted both approvingly, to the dismay and disgust of the evangelicals, who were described in all accounts as "fanatics" and "so-called Protestants." Barely able to contain his rage, one evangelical (who preferred to remain anonymous) fulminated against the "heretical professors at Andover" and the "cultured readers of the *Christian Register* and *Pilot*" who together opposed the "able, learned, Christian men who, in the performance of pious duty, have ventured to proclaim plain and needed truth, to the people of this city, and the country at large."[96] Accumulated resentments against liberal Protestants, based as much on social class as theology, laced his angry diatribe. He reminded his readers that during the Revolutionary War, the wealthy "elite" had supported the king, and that they in turn had been supported by the press. These "men and women of Anglo-Saxon blood, and Puritan ancestry" who boasted "education, culture, and a so-called respectability" were still arrayed against their poorer but more patriotic countrymen. "We have the same sort of feeling [for them] that inspired our ancestors," the author growled, "when they made Boston too hot for the tories and traitors who were glad to leave for Europe and Nova Scotia."[97]

Margaret's Downfall

As the 1880s drew to a close, attempts at compromise only stirred up more determined opposition. In the fall of 1889, Eliza Trask Hill, president of the Charlestown branch of the Loyal Women of American Liberty, organized a new women's group, the Independent Women Voters. The daughter of a temperance, antislavery, and antitobacco minister, Trask was a leading suffragist and a charter member of the local WCTU.[98] The purpose of her group was to take Margaret Shepherd's Loyal Women of American Liberty one step further. In January 1890, the first issue of her periodical, the *Woman's Voice and Public School Citizen*, announced a new forum for Boston's female voters, one that would have "breadth and scope" to "give to *Boston's women's work* the attention it needs and must have." School committee politics were, of course, central, but the *Woman's Voice* also promised to articulate a new range of women's concerns, from temperance to proper housekeeping. The periodical ran regular reports on organizations like the "King's Daughters," a New York–based Christian women's society bent on widening "the circle of helpfulness."[99] It also carried advertisements for a Protestant Employment Bureau, based at Tremont Temple, which placed young Protestant girls as domestic servants in homes worried about hiring a Catholic. The list of contributors also included names now familiar to Boston's evangelicals as veterans of the Boston Common incident or leaders of anti-Masonic or anti-Catholic meetings. Indeed, the first issue of the *Woman's Voice* included a transcript of an anti-Catholic Music Hall meeting in which the main speaker, J. W. Hamilton, rehearsed the entire story of the arrests on the Common to great dramatic effect.[100]

The editorial policy of the *Woman's Voice* was a potent mixture of women's rights, animosity against Catholics, and orthodox theology. The Independent Women Voters echoed the moral rhetoric of the WCTU, championing women as the active force in religion and dismissing Boston's Protestant men as too "absorbed in business affairs" to be politically useful.[101] Contributors to the *Woman's Voice* took particular umbrage at Irish Catholic manhood, the self-styled "lords of creation" who "talk infidelity while their wives take in washing."[102]

Of course, the invective ran both ways. The popular Catholic writer Shirley Dale attended one of Fulton's Music Hall meetings and reported back with gleeful descriptions of the "furrowed brows" and "pugnacious, bristly faces" of the female audience, gloating over this salacious mix of "pruriency seasoned with piety." "Never anywhere did I ever see such fearfully fascinating ugly faces as those pretended pietists grimacing at each other," he wrote. But, Dale concluded, "it is not the freckled, toad-brown complexion, the wisp of dry hair or the face all knobs and hollows, which makes these women repulsive. It is the ill-disposition which prints itself in the features, and may be read there as plainly as lunacy or disease, an imprint of low spites, jealousies and grudges."[103]

But, for Catholics, the best was yet to come. In mid-May 1891 the *Pilot*, quoting a dispatch to the *Boston Herald* from the Chicago press, announced that Margaret Shepherd was in trouble. Public accusations of deceit and immorality first surfaced at a meeting of the Chicago branch of the Loyal Women, where William Barclay, the editor of the *Western British-American*, who had investigated her past in London, revealed that Shepard was passing off two different men as her husband. One lived in Boston, and another, the Reverend O. E. Murray, a former priest and pastor of the Wabash Avenue Methodist Church, lived in Chicago. Barclay also uncovered evidence of theft and "loose living" during Shepherd's early life in London. Even worse, the Boston papers told of a conversation between Shepherd and the evangelist T. E. Leyden, in which she was reported to have said "'I am in this cause for the money.'"[104]

At first Shepherd denied the charges and sought seclusion. Many of the Chicago women refused to believe the evidence against her, dismissing it as "part of the persecution that Mrs. Sheperd has often had to endure." But Maria Shipley, one of Sheperd's opponents in Chicago, took the charges to the Boston chapter of the Loyal Women, even though they were "so awful that it was almost impossible to read them." Shepherd was forced to resign.[105] The *Woman's Voice*, trying to put a good face on the debacle, admitted the truth of the charges against its former ally and then added weakly that "it is but still one more proof of the kind of people the Roman Catholic Church produces, and proves conclusively that we ought to be all the more on our guard as to how we trust the sacred interests of our beloved country in Romanists' hands."[106]

But Catholics had the final word. Shepherd's immoral past not only discredited her leadership but dramatized the repressed, prurient nature of the anti-Catholic campaign. Her exposure put to rest the easy equation between feminine virtue and public morality that had won so many school committee elections for Protestants. Not surprisingly perhaps, early reports of the incident in the Protestant press contained rumors that the discredited Shepherd had returned to her Catholic faith. But they were hardly so fortunate: Shepherd quickly quashed the gossip, declaring "I am a Protestant, and will remain one."[107]

By the early 1890s, evangelical Protestants were showing signs of unease about aggressive women. In December 1892, the *Woman's Voice* reported angrily about a revival meeting in Philadelphia in which the Tremont Temple pastor George Lorimer had criticized Protestant women for usurping authority in the churches. "He believes that the drift of the times is bringing women so prominently forward in society and religious circle," the *Voice* noted, "that there is danger that the men may be relegated to the rear and obligated to take a back seat."[108] That same year the *Woman's Voice* also raised a complaint about Justin Fulton's conservative attitudes toward women, suggesting that "the good brother asked God to enlarge his heart that he may deal justly by women." Just a moment's contemplation of a church "entirely supported by men" might "help him to appreciate women better."[109]

In the early 1890s, Protestant women also ran into determined political opposition. In 1892, the city abolished the poll tax for men, bringing in some ten thousand more male, Democratic, voters. (Later the same year, the city also abolished the poll tax for women.) The Independent Women Voters won their school committee slate in 1892, but they were not able to push the Republican party to victory in the city at large, nor were they able to carry a vote on alcohol licensing. In 1893, the Republicans finally wearied of their aggressive feminine allies and formed a joint ticket with the Democrats, endorsed by the Public School Union. The Independent Women Voters were not able to elect a single candidate. Suffrage leaders also publicly disavowed the political agenda of "ultra-Protestant women," whose unrestrained militancy was at least partly responsible for the defeat of a statewide suffrage referendum in 1895. In 1905, Eliza Trask Hill took ill, leaving her movement leaderless. Ten years later, the battle was officially over when the Massachusetts legislature reduced the number of seats on the Boston School Committee from twenty-four to five, all to be elected at large, not by district. A small, determined female minority could no longer avert the will of the city's masculine majority.

By the mid-1890s, Boston was sick of religious bickering. On July 4, 1895, Protestant crusaders attempted to wheel a "little red schoolhouse" in the East Boston Independence Day parade. The area was heavily Catholic, and initially the local carnival committee refused the request. But the crusaders appealed to Governor Frederick Greenhalge, who granted a permit and ordered a 350-man police escort. Despite this show of law and order, a number of spectators and marchers came armed with guns and swords; as the parade was breaking up, a confrontation between "rowdies" on both sides ended in sudden violence. Several men were wounded, and one John Ross, an "Ulsterman and a British subject," shot and killed one John W. Willis, "a Catholic."[110]

By this time, neither the Catholic or Protestant press will willing to defend such "ruffianism." "Each successive outbreak of prejudice in Boston has been milder than its predecessors," a Catholic historian noted optimistically in 1899. "Zealots may bluster and hold aloof, but thousands look daily into each other's eyes and learn that they do not belong to any particular kind of men so much as to humanity. And this is practical Charity, which, let us hope, will grow until it covers our multitude of sins."[111]

Though in succeeding years overt interreligious hostility faded, it had already left a permanent impact on the shape of Protestant resistance in Boston—and on twentieth-century evangelical culture. Conservative evangelicals then, as now, learned to express their anger through patriotic zeal; they protested their powerlessness through ever louder affirmations of American individualism and personal freedom. The irony, of course, is that in the late twentieth century evangelicals would take on much the same stigma that Catholics had decades before; although anti-Catholicism still persists, fundamentalism has become the new symbol of intolerance, a threat to free speech and democratic pluralism.

The decline of religious hostilities in Boston did not signal the end of an aggressive evangelical presence. The same energy that was behind the anti-Catholic bigotry of the 1880s fired a new wave of street evangelism and separatist zeal. Some of New England's most well-known evangelical institutions—Gordon College and Seminary, and the Evangelistic Association of New England—date from the civic turmoil of these years. I turn to that story in the next chapter.

5

Occupying the City

Boston Hymn
For Outdoor Preachers
Sung at Tremont Temple
At the 198th Boston Monday Lecture, February 27, 1888

1. O Thou who in the wilderness
The sheep unshepherded didst bless,
By whom the hungry hosts were fed
With heavenly and with earthly bread,
Help us beside all streams to sow,
And preach Thy word where'er we go.
. . . .

4. Mid earth's confusion, scoffing, doubt,
Still may Thy wisdom cry without,
And, where the chiefest concourse rolls,
Renew her call to dying souls;
Nor fear the prison, nor the chain,
While sounding loud the Saviour's name.

5. And now behold the threatenings, Lord,
And boldness grant to speak Thy word;
Stretch forth Thy mighty hand divine,
Bid light through all the nations shine;
Grant us Thy power, for help we call;
May Thy great grace be on us all!

On the Sunday following his arrest in 1885, A. J. Gordon addressed his astonished congregation. With news of the odd incident splashed across the secular press, the newly famous Baptist pastor returned to his church pulpit determined to mount an aggressive defense of his actions. He appealed first to history, reminding his congregation of their city's long tradition of outdoor Protestant preaching, a story stretching back to the eighteenth-century evangelist George Whitefield's fiery orations on the Common's pasturelands. Then Gordon denounced his arrest as outrage against "more than a hundred years of unchallenged custom." "No place within our borders," he declared defiantly, "has been more intimately and constantly associated with the preaching of the gospel than Boston Common."[1] And then he reminded the congregation of his own commitment to open-air preaching, practiced regularly over his past fifteen years at Clarendon Baptist. Distancing himself from the conspiratorial antics of Davis and Hastings, Gordon affirmed that he had willingly accepted the YMCA and Evangelical Alliance's invitation to conduct outdoor services that Sunday—despite the risks involved.

But the central point of Gordon's sermon was a call for more open-air evangelism aimed at the city's "unchurched masses." "There are 380,000 people in Boston of whom not more than 50,000 attend church on the Lord's day," he pleaded. The city's unchurched were not just atheists and scoffers but the respectable—and potentially redeemable—working poor. "Many of the remaining 300,000 are kept from the sanctuary, because they are too poor to dress decently," Gordon declared. "Such a class of people can only be reached by going where they are."[2]

Gordon offered little in the way of strategy, nor did he seem concerned that a large majority of the "unchurched" multitude would have been Roman Catholic. The largest hurdle for Clarendon Baptist's people was psychological: like too many of Boston's evangelicals, they were afraid to venture out into their own city. Confronted with the "oncoming tide of poverty and illiteracy," most Protestant churches had, in Gordon's view, covered their retreat to the suburbs "by throwing out a picket-line of mission stations." Resigned timidity, not entrepreneurial vision, explained why "most of the churches that were born at the north end of the city are now huddled together at the south end and on the Back Bay—the newest portions of the town—so close that they can almost catch each other's eavesdroppings." Gordon wanted his people to open their doors and breach the walls that separated Boston's middle-class Protestants from their poor and working-class neighbors. "If the great mass of Christians would come into heart-to-heart relation with the so-called dangerous class," he declared, "much might be done to change its character. But here is where we fail. We have too many family churches and too few missionary churches."[3]

The people at Clarendon Baptist Church supported Gordon enthusiastically. More than a decade later, a study of the South End reported them still busily engaged in "systematic house to house visitation," holding meetings in "wharves and cheap lodging houses," and "carrying tracts and flowers to the sick in hospitals."[4] They also found missionary-minded Protestant allies across the city of Boston. In the summer of 1885 a legion of open-air preachers pressed forward into parks, beaches, and urban neighborhoods. Through the religious turmoil of the 1880s and 1890s, they erected "gospel tents," held an evangelists' conference at Crescent Beach, and sent a continual array of preachers to the Common, often in knowing defiance of the city ordinance.

This chapter deals with the institutional legacy of the anti-Catholic crusade, focusing on two organizations that formed in the mid-1880s, the Evangelistic Association of New England (EANE) and the Gordon School of Missions. Their strength and permanence—both still exist today—argue against the common assumption that anti-Catholicism was a transient, politically driven passion of a few nineteenth-century Protestants. Rather, the story of these institutions demonstrates that, in late nineteenth-century Boston, opposition to Rome was fundamental to evangelical identity, providing a sense of urgency and injecting a new energy into efforts at outreach.

This chapter also demonstrates the deep ambivalence of Boston's evangelicals toward building up earthly kingdoms. Thoroughly pragmatic and consciously leery of the "Romanist" tendency toward institutional excess, they organized institutes and schools with sometimes visible reluctance. Not surprisingly, perhaps, women were important to this stage of the story, cast in a central role by virtue of their distance from real institutional power in Protestant churches. The spare, demanding tenor of evangelical piety clearly appealed to female leaders like Maria Gordon and the hundreds of others who had taken on Catholic voters in the 1880s. But the evangelical crusade was not exclusively female: in print and devotional resources, Boston's preachers and teachers constantly urged each other to "empty themselves" before God, shunning power and public recognition even as they declared their intention to win their city for God.

As the century drew to a close, however, that goal seemed distant and unwinnable. Gordon's death in 1895 was a severe blow, coming during a time of political as well as theological disarray. The early years of the twentieth century were in fact a difficult decade for Boston's evangelicals, marked by internal dissension and declining membership in the city's largest conservative revivalist churches. Modern times, as subsequent chapters will reveal, would require a far more concerted effort than short-term political campaigns or scattered street preaching could provide.

Street Preachers

Despite the unresolved legal situation in the summer of 1885, the Common remained a popular venue for open-air evangelism. H. L. Hastings continued to preach there regularly, as did a growing number of his emboldened disciples. In late June, Lemuel B. Bates, evangelist at the East Boston Bethel ministry to seamen, preached to a crowd estimated to number around a thousand.[5] Not to be outdone, Hastings claimed to be holding as many as five services on most Sunday afternoons, to crowds sometimes as large as two thousand.[6] The YMCA also continued to sponsor outdoor preachers that summer, including, at least once, Gordon himself.[7] The impetus continued throughout the next decade: in the summer of 1894, Hastings reported some six to eight meetings on the Common every Sunday. Interest in outdoor preaching even crossed denominational lines: in May 1895 a thousand Unitarians met on the Common to hear a rousing sermon by Edward Everett Hale.[8]

Open-air preachers also fanned out across the city, holding forth on local beaches and neighborhood parks. In September 1885, the Massachusetts Home Missionary Society and the YMCA jointly sponsored nightly meetings in the South End. There the evangelist E. W. Bliss led the crowd with music from his cornet, followed up by "pungent, plain and practical" preaching.[9] The YMCA also sponsored a four-day Bible conference at Crescent Beach in Revere, just north of the city. It was "Northfield all over again," the *Congregationalist* exulted, invoking the beloved memory of Dwight L. Moody's summer institutes for young evangelists. The Crescent Beach meeting boasted a lineup of local and national talent, including Leander Munhall from Tremont Temple, George and Elizabeth Needham, and George Pentecost.[10]

Recognizing that many of the outdoor preachers were laypeople, Hastings offered professional tips on everything from drawing a crowd to the mysteries of voice projection. Even people in a hurry will stop to hear "good, hearty singing," he counseled; the real trick was to keep them around for the sermon. He warned against talking or singing into the wind, and advised the would-be evangelist to position himself in front of a building or wall for maximum effect. Hastings also urged his preachers to "avoid lightness, frivolity, controversy, and bitterness" and to "contrive if possible to march your congregation from your outdoor service to the mission hall or meeting place near by." A wise evangelist also kept a few extra tracts on hand, just in case the sermon failed to sustain interest.[11]

Obviously, any serious effort to reach the city's working poor would have had to include Catholics, but Gordon and his fellows rarely urged aggressive proselytizing in hostile territory. In 1887, a group of Boston University students found out why after a visit to the North End to assist the superintendent of the mission there. "We organized something after the model of the Salvation Army," one of them later reported. The adventurous students "formed a line, four abreast, and assisted by a cornet player, thirty of us marched through some of the wickedest streets of Boston." Not surprisingly, one of them related, they quickly found themselves "surrounded by the wildest crowd I ever saw; clubs, dirt, sticks and stones were thrown at us, but strange to say no one was seriously injured." The crowd pressed in on the would-be evangelists, "kicking, striking, tripping, pushing," and knocking their hats off with sticks. The young men "were obliged to walk backwards a good part of the way in order to keep them from trampling upon us." Needless to say, the gospel meeting that followed was marred with "much disturbance" and produced little in the way of spiritual results. The next morning, the young men arranged a visit with the two parish priests to complain about their treatment but received little satisfaction. One begged off the matter entirely with claims of busyness, and the other "reminded them that [the] North End was a Catholic community" and "they had no right down there." The determined evangelists did return on succeeding nights, but with a small police escort, and presumably without the cornet.[12]

By 1887, open-air preaching had become so popular that a group of local pastors, led by Gordon, formed the EANE. The original purpose of the organization was simple: to promote open-air preaching by any means possible, and to reinforce efforts already in place on the Common and in Boston's city parks. The EANE persisted, however, and eventually established itself at the center of the region's conservative Protestant outreach. When it was renamed "Vision New England" in 2001, the EANE presided over a network of some five thousand churches in eighty denominations, all from suburban headquarters in Burlington, Massachusetts.[13]

The EANE's founders worked with a minimum of institutional structure. In the summer of 1888, after they had failed to receive a preaching permit from the mayor (despite repeated requests), they decided upon a tactic of "mobile evangelism," employing a roving "Gospel Carriage" with a preaching platform.[14] Finding new recruits was not a problem. By 1889 the EANE was supporting twenty-three professional evangelists and had begun ordaining willing laypeople as "out-door" preachers. The organization also reported, in the course of one year, between June 1888 and 1889, sixteen meetings on the Common, thirteen at Crescent Beach, thirteen in the North End, and seven in suburban locations.[15]

When Gordon finally obtained a park permit in 1891, the EANE had become a more formal enterprise, operating in some ways as a denominational substitute. From its offices in Tremont Temple, the organization served as a reliable clearinghouse for orthodox men hoping to fill church pulpits. The Examining Committee, representing six denominations, interviewed seminarians desiring permanent posts, as well as evangelists looking for steady employment. In 1891 a Ministerial Department took over this work more formally. But the EANE also worked with laypeople, sponsoring a conference for "Pastors, Evangelists, and Businessmen" in 1890. And in the following years, the EANE never gave up on public evangelism, organizing regular noon services in downtown churches for "business and working men" out on lunch breaks.[16] Probably more entertaining than theological, popular speakers included Ferdinand Schiverea, a former vaudeville comedian, and Charles H. Potter, better known as the "Banker Evangelist."[17]

Increasingly, the inherent social risks of outdoor preaching drew a dividing line between evangelicals and other Protestants. In November 1885, the Suffolk South conference of Congregational clergy discussed Gordon's claims about the unchurched masses and came to a sharply different conclusion. They argued that Boston's unchurched were not necessarily the poor and outcast but might be anyone—in theory, they were "all who disregard or oppose the gospel." That meant that Congregationalists need not haunt the Boston park system but could seek conversions among their neighbors and friends. Eschewing the highways and byways, the ministers urged "every Christian [to] try to win the next and nearest unbeliever," a task that would require "a vigorous toning up of our own personal piety."[18] Austin Phelps, the editor of the *Congregationalist*, tended to agree that confrontational outdoor preaching was a method of last resort. "The latitude of Boston is too high to test the value of preaching in the open air," he wrote in June 1885, adding that "even Whitefield seldom preached on the Common when a church was open to him."[19] Although for political reasons Phelps supported Gordon against city hall, he had no truck with the "boisterous" and "shallow" techniques of open-air revivalists.[20]

In the 1890s few Protestants could have told the difference, at least in theological terms, between a Social Gospel church like Berkeley Temple and Gordon's staunchly evangelical Clarendon Street Baptist congregation. Concern for the poor and unemployed did not necessarily rule out street evangelism, nor did conservative churches uniformly shun the humanitarian emphasis associated with "institutional churches."[21] As the next chapter will show in more detail, Tremont Temple enjoyed a well-deserved reputation as a full-service congregation, and even the conservative Ruggles Baptist Church advertised itself, with justification, as a Social Gospel outpost in the South End.[22]

The difference was in the way they occupied urban space. Gordon envisioned a church militant, its doors open wide and its members streaming outward onto the streets of Boston in search of lost souls. Social Gospel churches attempted to reverse the direction of the flow, inviting the masses to find salvation within the walls of large, well-equipped buildings. Neither, of course, seems at first glance intrinsically "conservative" or "liberal." If anything, Clarendon's street evangelists seemed the least afraid of witnessing urban poverty and confronting the ethnic clannishness of their city. Arguing with run-of-the-mill people on a street corner had to be far riskier for middle-class Protestants than ministering to their wants in a well-lit church building.

But the internal logic of street preaching was still deeply separatist. Evangelism did not draw world and church together but constantly dramatized the gulf between the two. "'How to reach the masses' is an oft considered question," Gordon's associate F. L. Chappell wrote in 1891. In his estimation, the only "proper and pertinent" answer was "sound[ing] the Gospel invitation in every ear"; other efforts aimed simply at bringing the masses to Sunday service were to Chappell "a flat rejection of God's idea of the church." The true Christian observed, without reservation, God's call to " 'Come ye out and be ye separate.' "[23] Evangelical street preachers lived with the paradoxical awareness that, in the end, sidewalk confrontations and temperance parades were not meant to win over the city of Boston to Christianity but to build a core of believers who knew firsthand the hostility of the world around them. Doubtless not a few street preachers internalized the truth of this dictum as they were fleeing the police on the Common or dodging missiles from Catholic rowdies in the North End.

Feminine Piety

Women's involvement in public preaching also reinforced its separatist tendencies. Though women drove the political agenda of Protestant protest, their involvement did not signal long-term commitment to such measures. To many of their allies, women's presence was a sign that God was about to wrap up the history of the world, and end it all with a flourish. "We count it among the most significant signs of the times," the *Watchword* announced gleefully in 1891, "that so many women are moved by the Spirit of God to tell out the story of redemption, and to lend their help in the work of gathering in the harvest of souls." These were no ordinary times. Citing the example of an Austrian "Hebrew Prophetess" who had held a two-week revival at the Clarendon Baptist Church, the editor rejoiced "that in these days of lax theology and feeble preaching of the doctrines of grace such a witness has been raised up—so sound, so clear, so fearless."[24]

Within the larger fundamentalist movement, especially in strict dispensationalist circles, enthusiasm for female preachers hardly ran this strong. Conservatives like James Brookes, the editor of *The Truth*, insisted that the prominence of women was a sign of decadence and a signal that God was moving world events toward a disastrous close. Worried about the increasing "infidelity among women" in the latter days, Brookes insisted that godly women recognized the necessity of submission to God's "divine order." Others, like Arno Gaebelein, frankly admitted their dislike of loud, hysterical females, which they associated with the ecstatic disorder of the pentecostal movement.[25]

In Boston, the rising popularity of female evangelists owed much to the emerging holiness movement. Though often associated with the rural south, the movement was also strong in New England. Just north of Boston, at a popular campground in Old Orchard Beach, Maine, A. B. Simpson's Christian and Missionary Alliance sponsored training institutes aimed at promoting the "higher Christian life" of spiritual consecration. Elizabeth Tobey, who was president of the Massachusetts WCTU and deeply involved in the public school crusade, was one of six women named to Simpson's forty-member General Committee in 1887. In its early days, the Christian Alliance movement openly championed women's leadership, listing "the ministry of women" as one of its five fundamental pillars and a sign of divine grace being poured out in the "last days."[26] Tobey herself was a great advocate of women in the pulpit. In her presidential address to the Boston WCTU in 1887, she urged temperance women to cultivate a "more courageous faith" and to lose their "timidity in praying or speaking in the presence of others." "Dear sisters," Tobey pleaded,

> I am sure many of you feel this bondage which trammels you in the service and retards the gospel. . . . Will you not consider a plan for having an evangelist course in your town or city and hold special services both for fuller consecration of Christians and for bringing sinners to Christ?[27]

Female evangelists also found an ally in A. J. Gordon.[28] Though not institutionally allied with the holiness movement, the Baptist pastor shared the conviction that the increasing incidence of preaching gifts among women was a sign of Christ's imminent return. Though, like Brookes, a dispensationalist, Gordon did not believe that women's subordination was a permanent condition of Adam and Eve's sin. Like many holiness preachers, he chose to emphasize the prediction from the Hebrew prophet Joel that both "sons and daughters" would prophesy during the Spirit's final outpouring. "It seems as if the Churches of God in this century need to have the scales taken from their eyes," Gordon wrote in 1887, "that they may see God wants women to prophesy in the power of the Holy Ghost. Shall we not break down the barriers that God has never set up, but that Satan has put in the way[?]"[29] These endorsements did not, of course, occur in a political vacuum: Gordon's support for women's activism coincided with the voter registration campaign and school committee elections in the late 1880s. But once committed, he did not change his views. Gordon's best-known statement on the subject was an article, "The Ministry of Women," published in 1894. Writing to a missionary audience, Gordon took a firm pragmatic line, warning against wasting women's gifts when the great need of the world was an army of dedicated preachers undifferentiated by sex.[30]

His wife Maria perhaps served as his inspiration. "In these last days," she told a meeting of young women that same year, in 1894, "it would seem as if the Master were saying to every woman, 'Behold, I have set before *you* an open door.' Doors which have long been shut through a misapprehension of Scripture truth are now flung wide open . . . and the majority of Christian churches will bid them 'God speed.' "[31] Maria Gordon was an accomplished, dynamic woman who often protested that she rarely enjoyed public speaking. During a trip to Great Britain in 1888, she preached to great effect under the Midland Arches in East London; however, she consistently spoke of her evangelistic work as an onerous duty. When Dwight L. Moody pressed her into service at the 1893 World's Fair in Chicago, Maria confided to her children: "I am enjoying it each time *after it is over.*... I am always so distressed because I haven't anything to say."[32] On the platform, Mrs. Gordon simply told her own life story, describing the moment when, after one particularly moving Northfield Conference, she "place[d] herself entirely in the Lord's hands for service, willing even to be a fool for Christ's sake." In her view, it took "about as much humility to take a place on the platform as to sit on a back seat."[33] Of course, Maria Gordon was hardly this self-effacing in every circumstance, and after her husband passed away in 1895 she actively pursued her own agenda for evangelistic work in Boston.[34] On her daughter Haley's thirty-eighth birthday, she wrote to her "as a woman of gifts and position," reminding her that "I covet for you leadership in every line of Christian service which opens before you," urging her to become a "spiritual mother of many souls."[35]

Like her husband, Maria Gordon led Boston's Protestants onto the Common. As president of the local WCTU, she organized day-long temperance rallies there every Fourth of July. These featured a large tent with a platform and seating for musical performances, big banners ("The True Declaration of Independence—The Total Abstinence Pledge"), and of course, large tubs of ice water. "Here is the place to 'reach the masses,'" she reminded her fellow temperance enthusiasts in 1891. With crowds of the "foreign-born" congregating in a spot "brimful of patriotism," wise Protestants recognized that it was not just their patriotic duty but a fact of "self-preservation" to "win them to right views" on subjects "which so vitally affect our national welfare."[36]

The Short-Cut School

The new militancy among Boston's evangelicals found institutional form in a Missionary Training School, which opened for classes in October 1889.[37] The initial inspiration came during the Moody revival in 1877, especially among members of Gordon's Clarendon Street congregation. But they did little for the next twelve years, until Gordon's missionary colleague H. Grattan Guinness came to Boston for a visit during the height of the anti-Catholic campaign. The Irish-born Guinness was a renowned evangelist, teacher of dispensational theology, and head of the Missionary Institute of London; he also shared Gordon's belief that "Romanism" was a portent of the End Times. In 1889 Guiness was touring the United States in search of more missionaries to send to the Livingston Inland Mission to the Congo, and he urged Gordon to open his own "recruiting station" in Boston.[38]

The early leaders of the Missionary Training School came from the heart of Boston's conservative evangelical leadership. The school's first location was the old West End, in property owned by M. R. Deming's Bowdoin Square Tabernacle, "the only gospel lighthouse in a stormy human sea."[39] The two buildings on Chardon Street that initially housed the school had previously been houses of prostitution, purchased by Gordon and Deming with the idea of setting up a "Young Men's Institute." Gordon himself was the first president, and Maria was secretary, later treasurer as well; after her husband's death she became a Bible instructor. F. L. Chappell, a Baptist pastor and leading member of the Christian and Missionary Alliance, was the first resident instructor and later dean of the school.

James M. Gray, soon to become president of Moody Bible Institute, taught Bible study methods.[40] In 1901, the list of teachers also included Alice Coleman, a member of the Clarendon Church, Blanche Tilton, who specialized in vocal and instrumental training for evangelistic singing, and Julia Morton Plummer, "widely known in Boston for many years for her remarkable humanitarian work," teaching practical physiology and hygiene.[41] With a minimum of institutional structure, the school saw modest but steady growth. In 1891 the catalog reported a total of fifty students in the day and evening classes, hailing from everywhere from New York to Kansas.[42]

That same year, to accommodate the growing number of women students, the Missionary Training School moved to quarters on Clarendon Street. The young women lived in a house around the corner on Brookline Street, "under Mrs. Gordon's next-door supervision."[43] Registration figures, though sketchy for the early period, show that in the early 1900s the school was graduating twice as many women as men. In the early days, women from Clarendon Street and neighboring churches constituted "a considerable part of the enrolment [sic]," many of them joining the "forenoon classes to enrich their non-professional life and work." According to Chappell, "it was even suggested once that it should be a ladies' School entirely."[44]

The students' daily work was infused with an urgent awareness of Christ's Second Coming, a fact that earned Gordon public criticism for running a "short cut school."[45] Many of these complaints came from the Baptist press, quite reasonably worried about the erosion of educational standards under the premillennial slant of the school's curriculum. The training school did not require tuition, impose a set curriculum, or maintain a list of students. The school song, "We're Going to Take the Congo for Jesus," kept students' eyes focused on a spiritual ideal. "There was to be no text-book except the Bible," Nathan Wood later wrote;

no curriculum of study except what the teachers might be led to adopt; no corporation or incorporation except the bond of the Spirit; no endowment or pledged support except what funds the Lord might send; no buildings, except such rooms as might be tendered; no age limit or mental qualification in the students except such general ones as prudence and spiritual discernment could dictate.

At the heart of the curriculum was the "unpopular truth" that the world might end at any time, in a cataclysmic Second Advent.[46]

The Missionary Training School reflected Gordon's measured dislike of human contrivances. As pastor at Clarendon he doggedly pared down the worship service, ejecting paid soloists and the expensive accoutrements characteristic of Victorian churches. "If the Church had faith to lean less on human wisdom, to trust less in prudential methods, to administer less by mechanical rules," and to look to the "supernatural power" at its disposal, Gordon wrote in 1894, "who can doubt that the . . . demonstration of the Spirit [would] be far more apparent?"[47] In a similar vein, Chappell declared that "missions and holiness, rather than ecclesiastical organization and moral reform, are the spheres in which we must chiefly exert ourselves. Perfected Christian character is what God now wants, more than any external arrangement of church, or state, or social order."[48]

Increasingly, evangelicals differentiated themselves from other Protestants by their disdain for organizational structure. This much is suggested in a letter written by his eldest son, Ernest, to Maria in 1891 on the subject of "religious dissolution." The aptly named Ernest considered Boston's Unitarians and Congregationalists prime examples of this sad outcome but observed "the first symptoms of the same tendency" in the "hyper-respectability" and "magnificence" of a few local Baptists. "Dr. Moxom's gown," Ernest noted in wry reference to the stuffy pastor over at the wealthy First Baptist Church, "might be mentioned along with the Andover theology." In the younger Gordon's view, the popular Episcopalian cleric Phillips Brooks was equally culpable of "gorgeous worldliness," "purseproud magnificence" and "toleration of everything and everybody no matter how absurd the claim on our charity." "I doubt not," he concluded, with more than a hint of youthful righteousness, "that within a century and a half the Salvation Army will be struggling with questions of church aesthetics and ecclesiastical architecture."[49]

For many of Boston's conservative evangelicals in those heady days, God seemed to be unusually present, and prone to timely, dramatic appearances. Nathan E. Wood, who headed the Training School when it was briefly merged with the Newton Theological Institute, decided to take a position at the First Baptist Church after experiencing a supernatural vision. While guest preacher at First Baptist, he saw a "cloud of light" shining before him during his entire time in the pulpit. "No lights caused it. No others saw it," Wood said, but he was convinced that the luminous display was a divine command to stay on and revive the First Baptist Church—which he did quite successfully.[50] Gordon spoke often about a divine visitation he had received in a dream. Having fallen asleep under the stress of Saturday night sermon preparation, he dreamed himself standing in his pulpit and watching a stranger enter the church from the back, proceed up the aisle, and slide into a pew. The stranger's dress was "exceedingly humble" and his expression one of "great sorrow," and as he preached Gordon kept wondering who he was. Alas, the mysterious visitor slipped out of church as soon as the benediction was pronounced, but his seatmate told Gordon quite confidently that this was none other than "Jesus of Nazareth." In the dream, Gordon was bitterly disappointed to have missed a direct encounter with the second person of the Trinity, but the parishioner assured him that Christ would undoubtedly return. " 'He has been here to-day, and no doubt he will come again.' " Then followed a torrent of emotion: awe, fear, and anxiety that Christ had been offended by mundane and superficial worship. Gordon, by his own account, would never again "have the smallest curiosity as to what men might say of preaching, worship, or church if I could only know that he had not been displeased, that he would not withhold his feet from coming again because he had been grieved at what he might have seen or heard."[51]

Gordon put little faith in human striving. "The surrendered will, the yielded body, the emptied heart," Gordon wrote, "are the great requisites to [God's] incoming. And when he has come and filled the believer, the result is a kind of passive activity as one wrought upon and controlled rather than of one directing his own efforts."[52] In one of Gordon's last communications to his parishioners, he reminded them that "the wind always blows toward a vacuum. Let your heart be empty of self-confidence, and of self-will, and the Spirit can come in and bear you whither God would have you to go."[53]

Gordon made a permanent impact on Boston church life, but this was never his intent. As he reminded his congregation in a pastoral letter shortly before his death, "your first and principle business as a disciple of Christ is to give the Gospel to those who have it not. . . . Ask yourself daily what the Lord would have you do in connection with the work of carrying the news of salvation to the perishing millions." Nothing less than absolute consecration would do. "I warn you," Gordon wrote, in tones that a Social Gospel prophet would have appreciated, "that it will go hard with you when the Lord comes to reckon with you if he finds your wealth invested in superfluous luxuries or hoarded up in needless accumulations instead of being sacredly devoted to giving the Gospel to the lost."[54]

Hard Times

Gordon's death in February 1895 was a deep blow to Boston's evangelicals. His end came suddenly: within a few days a nagging cold turned into bronchitis, and from there escalated into a mortal bout with pneumonia. Surrounded by family and distraught church members, the city's leading Protestant died at the comparatively young age of fifty-eight. At the huge memorial service that followed his funeral, emotional tributes, especially from women, flowed without restraint. One after the other, women from the congregation and wives of prominent Boston evangelicals rose to speak from Gordon's pulpit. Mrs. James M. Gray offered a devotional, and Mrs. Joseph Cook spoke about Gordon's philanthropic work. Emily McLaughlin, president of the Boston WCTU, lauded his support for temperance, and several women from Clarendon Baptist praised him as a kind and willing pastor. "Rarely is such a tribute given to any man, however beloved," the *Watchman* reported, "as was paid to Dr. Gordon by the different speakers. All through the service, at the least mention of his kind words and deeds, the feelings of the congregation could not be restrained, and the air was filled with sounds of grief."[55]

Clarendon Street Baptist Church never recovered from its loss. In years following, the congregation struggled and failed to accept a new pastor in Gordon's place, and could not stem the tide of middle-class retreat to Boston's suburbs. In the early twentieth century, Clarendon faded as Tremont Temple and then the Park Street Church assumed ascendancy. In 1912, Baptist leaders opted to unite Clarendon with another struggling city church, the Bowdoin Square Tabernacle, recognizing that neither was likely to survive on its own in an area now heavily Catholic and increasingly African American.[56]

After Gordon's death, ardor for Christ's Second Coming began to dim. In 1901, the Clarendon church hosted a Prophetic Conference, which was attended by all of the leading lights of the premillennial movement but virtually ignored by the religious and secular press.[57] Some of the speakers were local figures: A. C. Dixon, just arriving at Ruggles Street Baptist, James M. Gray, and Robert Cameron, editor the *Watchword and Truth*. Others were regulars on the prophecy conference circuit: the theologians William G. Moorehead and William J. Erdman, the missionary spokesman Arthur T. Pierson, the evangelists Henry Varley and Leander Munhall, and Len Broughton of the Atlanta Baptist Tabernacle.

But most Bostonians, religious and otherwise, perceived the conference as a quaint religious curiosity, hardly a threat to the standing order. The *Congregationalist and Christian World* briefly covered the proceedings and backhandedly urged its readers to be tolerant, for "prominent at this meeting were men who cannot be dismissed as cranks or enthusiasts," including a large proportion of Baptists.[58] Another Congregationalist, Allen Chesterfield, endorsed the Prophetic Conference as yet another example of Boston's famed religious "diversity." On the same day in Boston, he recounted, the Civil Service League met in Cambridge to discuss the needs of workingmen, the Social Gospellers were at the South End House "discussing ways and means," a group of "red-hot gospellers" were "turning handsprings" in the Mechanics Hall, and the International Prophetic Conference was in "full swing at Clarendon Street." "Who says that Boston is slow and provincial?" Chesterfield exulted. "Here were children of the same Father, possessing the same rational faculties, inhabitants of the same world, and yet what was meat and drink to one set of persons was pure drivel to the other, or a riddle past understanding."[59]

For its part, however, the local Baptist press distanced itself from the Prophetic Conference, declaring that "those who attend it represent no one but themselves." Fretting over the literalistic tendency of the premillennialists to "abridge Christianity into one or two doctrines," the *Watchman* billed the meeting as simply an opportunity for "those who hold to the pre-millennial doctrine to get together and compare notes."[60] Doctrinaire fundamentalist belief, including premillennialism or biblical inerrancy, made relatively few inroads into Boston at the turn of the century. Conservative Protestant identity, at least as it was developing to this point, did not revolve around adherence to a particular set of ideas but engaged a complex cross-section of institutional alliances, cultural loyalties, and moralistic political programs.

After Gordon's death, the Missionary Training School took his name but proceeded down a different path from what he would have charted. In 1907, sagging attendance figures prompted a brief and unhappy merger with the Newton Theological Institute, a Baptist seminary headed by the staunchly evangelical Nathan E. Wood. But by 1917, buoyed by a large financial bequest, the newly renamed Gordon Bible School had become an independent institution, no longer housed in the heterogeneous—and increasingly African American—districts of the South End but settled into more comfortable quarters in the Fenway district of the Back Bay. Though still heavily Baptist, the school's official stance was interdenominational and its theological leanings defined as more broadly "christocentric" rather than narrowly dispensational.[61]

The school attracted the avid support of leading evangelical businessmen, including the Rhodes brothers from Tremont Temple, Franklin McElwain, who owned a shoe company (later Thom McAn), and Frank Wyman, a member of the Park Street Church and owner of a Boston department store. By 1925, the renamed Gordon College of Theology and Missions offered a regular undergraduate curriculum and a separate ministerial course, and a few years later divided into two separate institutions, Gordon College and Gordon Divinity School. Isabel Wood, a college English teacher with an advanced degree in education, played a central role, introducing departmental organization, a system of marks and scholastic records, and requirements for promotion and graduation. "These innovations, which seem so natural now," her husband wrote, "met some earnest objection, on the ground that they were contrary to the policies of the School, and far worse, were departures from the leadership of the Spirit!"[62]

In subsequent years, the Training School became the hub of a network of conservative evangelical churches, summer camps, and religious education programs across New England. By the 1930s, Gordon alumni dominated Baptist pulpits in Boston and the surrounding region. "In the four Boston Baptist Associations," Nathan Wood wrote, "of 98 pastors, 48 were Gordon Alumni or students." In 1933, Gordon alums held positions as moderators of all of the local Boston Associations. Half of New Hampshire's ninety-six Baptist pastors were "Gordon men" and twenty-five more "close friends of the School." The Rhode Island Chapter of Gordon Alumni numbered some twenty-two pastors, and Maine was reportedly "full of Gordon men and women and Gordon influence." During the 1930s, as many as eight evangelistic teams went out from Gordon every week, a "network of evangelism" that staffed city missions, foreign-language Sunday Schools, and radio broadcast booths.[63]

In the Bible Institute's early days, this expanding network depended heavily on female recruits, many of them ordained ministers and evangelists. In 1925, for example, the Gordon News-Letter reported the death of Reverend Christina MacKenzie, an ordained pastor in southern New Hampshire for many years. "Word has often come to us," the account ran, "of her notable work and of the esteem in which she was held." The author concluded by emphasizing that "an influence like hers is a great example to all of our Gordon girls."[64] In 1929, the News-Letter reported the ordination of Norma M. Farnham (class of 1928), the "first Baptist woman pastor in Rhode Island," to a congregational call instead of the mission field. President Nathan Wood preached the ordination sermon.[65] That same year, Caroline Ferguson took a post as full-time pastor in Epping, New Hampshire, "probably the first Congregational woman to be ordained" in that state.[66] In 1934, Nathan Wood reported several women in rural pastorates who had opened closed churches, including at least one, Clarice Stilphen, who was an ordained assistant pastor.[67]

But by the 1930s, women preachers were fast going the way of dispensationalism; as the Bible Institute achieved greater educational respectability, its female students began to disappear. In 1930, Gordon's trustees implemented a quota on incoming students, limiting women to one-third of each new class. In the following years, as the school turned away numbers of disappointed women, their proportion fell steadily. Between 1932 and 1937, the percentage of female students in the divinity school dropped from 50 percent to 17.5 percent, and even during World War II, when male seminary students were at a premium, continued to descend into the single digits.[68]

In the end, the Bible Institute left Boston entirely. In 1947, Gordon's trustees set out to purchase a landed estate some twenty-five miles northeast of the city center. During the mid–twentieth century, the school eventually settled into its elegant semirural surroundings, maintaining its urban connection largely through the construction of Highway 128, which ran just beyond the campus. By the 1960s, when the divinity school had merged with another seminary originally from Philadelphia, Gordon College and Gordon-Conwell Theological School became separate institutions, on separate estates in a wealthy district of Boston's North Shore. The new setting was a considerable distance, both physically and theologically, from the renovated brothels on Chardon Street. It suggested that Boston's evangelicals felt themselves increasingly at home in the world—or, at least, in a world defined not by the streets of Boston but by the borders of New England and the world beyond.

6

The Stranger's Sabbath Home

Tremont Temple Baptist Church

> If a man is pastor of a large church he can part his hair where he pleases. But if he is pastor of a small church he must part his hair in the middle or he will upset the boat.
>
> —Lemuel Haynes, Pastor, Tremont Temple

Though only a block or so apart in the heart of downtown, Tremont Temple and Park Street Church were very different places. Tremont, with its marquee exterior and theater-style sanctuary, never aspired to the Puritan elegance of Park Street's famous spire and plain white sanctuary. Squeezed awkwardly between "marts of trade" and eighteenth-century monuments, in the post–Civil War years Tremont Temple defined popular revivalism for the people of Boston. By the turn of the century, many more across New England and the United States knew Tremont Temple as "the stranger's sabbath home."[1]

Tremont Temple was unique, but by the early twentieth century it was one of the nation's leading "people's churches" and a model for other urban fundamentalist pastors. In Minneapolis, William Bell Riley remodeled First Baptist into a "metropolitan center of soul-winning" after a visit to Boston in 1889 left him "enamored and en-thralled" with Tremont's success.[2] Scores of other nationally known congregations followed a similar pattern: the Moody Church in Chicago, the First Baptist Church in Minneapolis, New York's Calvary Baptist, Seattle's First Presbyterian, and Temple Baptist in Detroit all headlined a controversial pulpiteer adept at bringing in the masses with vivid sermon titles. Most of the great fundamentalist leaders of the day—Riley, Mark Matthews, J. Frank Norris, John Roach Straton, A. C. Dixon—honed their oratorical skills every Sunday before vast audiences.[3] Membership in these churches regularly numbered in the thousands, and attendance figures ran even higher. During its peak years in the 1920s, Tremont Temple topped four thousand and regularly turned away thousands from its doors; Mark Matthews's First Presbyterian in Seattle, with over eight thousand by 1935, was the largest Presbyterian church in the country. Although these congregations boasted huge yearly budgets, most of them attracted a generally "blue-collar" audience. As a member of J. Frank Norris's congregation in Detroit put it, "that particular type of ministry did not appeal to upper level people."[4]

In many ways, these early twentieth-century preaching centers anticipated the modern-day "megachurch." Their primary purpose was evangelizing the lost and sinful, not changing society, and they catered to a predominantly young, transient urban population. Although some pastors, like Seattle's Mark Matthews, used their churches as "bully pulpits" to press for social reforms, most of the daily activity in urban fundamentalist churches centered around soul-winning, religious education, and opportunities for harmless fun. Churches like Tremont Temple also filled an important social role in big-city culture. Much like the baseball parks, city newspapers, department stores, and vaudeville houses chronicled in Gunther Barth's study of "city people," urban fundamentalist churches helped ease the transition into the anonymity of modern urban life.[5] No less than a championship baseball game, a revival

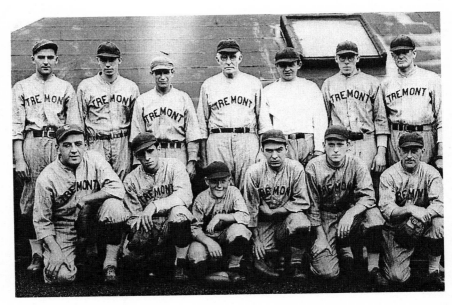

FIGURE 6.1. Tremont Temple Baseball Team. From *Tremont Temple Baptist Church: A Light in the City for 150 Years* (Boston: Tremont Temple Baptist Church, 1989).

service at Tremont Temple drew strangers together into a powerful temporary community, unified by hope, fear, and fervent conviction (see fig. 6.1).

A People's Church

Tremont Temple was a product of nineteenth-century Protestant idealism. In 1838, the antislavery activist Timothy Gilbert left the wealthy Charles Street Baptist Church in protest, after deacons refused to allow an African American friend to enter his rented pew. He immediately organized a new congregation with a simple name—the Free Church—that proclaimed its egalitarian mission.[6] In keeping with the social ethics of antebellum Protestant reform, Gilbert's church refused membership to slaveowners, rumsellers, and drunkards; however, everyone else in Boston was welcome at the "people's church." With pew rents no longer a requirement for membership, the new congregation attracted a varied group: black and white, rich and poor. Despite the predictable number of "erratic and aggressive souls" in Gilbert's initial exodus, the Free Church grew quickly. By 1841, the congregation had grown to 325 members, and in the following year, under the throes of a revival, 138 more were baptized. By then the congregation had moved to Tremont Street, just a block or so from its eventual home.[7]

In its early years, the Free Church was regularly fired by religious passions. At the center of abolitionist sentiment, the congregation hosted a wrenching visit by the evangelist Jacob Knapp in 1842. "He was a man after their own heart," the pastor George Lorimer wrote, several decades later: "sharp, decisive, aggressive, uncompromising, and at times vituperatively denunciatory."[8] Under Knapp's direction, the young congregation quickly identified its true rival in the city of Boston. Situated just a few blocks away from the theater district and spurred by revival enthusiasm, these Yankee Baptists eagerly locked in battle with Boston's theatrical establishment. Knapp's fiery preaching brought some businesses to the brink of bankruptcy; years afterward, the memory of his denunciations remained so strong that some theater owners simply called their establishments "Museums" to avoid negative attention. In 1843, adding insult to injury, the Free Baptists purchased the defunct Tremont Theater and invited the legendary the opponent of vice Lyman Beecher to preach one of the first sermons in their new quarters.

But difficult times lay ahead. In 1852, one day after the resignation of their first pastor, Nathaniel Colver, the church burned to the ground. Rebuilding proved expensive and dangerously drained limited financial resources. Over the next few years, several ministers came and went, all unable to reduce the congregation's indebtedness. Finally in 1857, local Baptists banded together on behalf of the independent Free Church. They formed a new body, the Evangelical Baptist Benevolent and Missionary Society, as a city-wide group authorized to supervise the rental of building facilities for religious as well as secular purposes.[9] Even so, resources remained at a "low ebb," and in 1863 fifty volunteers from the Tremont Street church and the neighboring Union Baptist Church joined together to form the Union Temple Baptist Church on the Tremont Street site. They called Justin Dewey Fulton as their pastor, and under his charismatic leadership their fortunes began to turn. Fulton led with a stern hand, insisting on stricter adherence to baptism as a condition of church membership and restricting participation in the Eucharist to members only. Instead of relying solely on rental income, he instituted a pledge system of monthly payments, and eventually regular congregational giving accounted for two-thirds of the yearly budget. Fulton also attempted to introduce congregational singing, though apparently with less success.[10]

From its inception, Tremont Temple took on a dual role in the city, as both a church and a public building. This intersection of sacred and secular was, of course, hardly unprecedented in Boston; by the early nineteenth century, the heirs of New England's Puritans had assumed a leading role in political affairs for some three hundred years. When Timothy Gilbert left Charles Street Baptist in 1838, the full disestablishment of Massachusetts churches was only five years along. And even though Baptist principles insisted on a strict separation of church and state, they did not chart an other-worldly course. But the new intersection of secular and sacred was economic, not political, reflecting the rising power of market forces in the shaping of American society.

Deprived of income from pew rents, in its early years Tremont Temple rented space to anyone who was able to pay. For many years, before the construction of the Music Hall, Tremont Temple's was the largest auditorium in the city, and, for largely this pragmatic reason, the auditorium became the epicenter of Boston's political debate, intellectual culture, and social reform. As George Lorimer explained, "the public did not think of it as a church, or associate with it pre-eminently the religious idea." Tremont Temple was simply "a great hall, where during the week, entertainments were given, debates were held, where truth and error with singular impartiality were allowed to propound their theories." On Sunday, the building was turned over to the "unchurched multitudes" in need of salvation.[11]

The arrangement was not without problems. Throughout the late nineteenth century, an odd assortment of popular entertainers and famous lecturers occupied its stage, sometimes in vivid juxtaposition with the Sunday work of saving souls. During the Civil War, a full riot broke on in the Temple during a confrontation between white and African American abolitionists and their opponents, a raucous combination of "Cotton Whigs," "broadcloth rowdies," and Irish laborers.[12]

Indeed, a thin line often separated Tremont Temple from its secular surroundings, especially the nearby theater district. Justin Fulton was only one of a long line of dynamic pulpiteers who filled the auditorium to capacity. Perhaps more than any of his peers, the indefatigable anti-Catholic crusader knew that controversy brought attention, and ultimately more members, to the church. After provoking a public confrontation with the Unitarian patriarch Theodore Parker (reviewing his theology and pronouncing him "damned"), the volatile pastor found the results "surprising" but gratifying: "No more compliments were received by me from wicked men," he observed with evident satisfaction, "but God blessed us in the Church and gave us power in the city." Fulton saw himself as a something of a populist, remarking that "The people flock to hear me. . . . I am willing to make a fool of myself for Christ's sake." He was, without doubt, a guaranteed showman, all the more exciting for his unpredictability. "There is something queer about me," he once explained. "Drifts and gusts of feeling sweep through me and may cause me to say things that I never thought of before. I say what comes into my mind, and sometimes make desperate mistakes. Indeed, I cannot account for it."[13]

The pursuit of "legitimate sensationalism," as the pastor Cortland Myers termed it, sometimes meant that sheer volume substituted for the finer points of orthodoxy. Years after his death, the Tremont Temple pastor Poindexter S. Henson's friends recalled that, after being complimented on his sermon, he "confessed to having had to spend ten minutes in the midst of the discourse 'just hollering' until he could remember a point he had planned to make but had forgotten in the midst of the discourse." But as Henson's friends remembered later, "that was the best part of his sermon."[14]

One of the Tremont Temple's most beloved ministers was George Lorimer, who served twice, from 1873 to 1879, and from 1891 to 1903 (see fig. 6.2). Lorimer came to Tremont after many years on the professional stage. Born in Scotland, he grew up in a theatrical family (his stepfather was manager of the Theater Royale) and made a living as an actor before he experienced conversion. His "tall, erect form," "smooth face," and "piercing eye" suggested the measure of his gift, but as one admirer related, "this canny, level-headed Scotchman chose early in life to put his talents at his Master's disposal and to use them in the pulpit for the illumination, and the enforcement of the Christian gospel." On a typical Sunday, Lorimer came to the pulpit with a small army of assistant pastors and laymen to lead the preliminaries, saving himself for the full dramatic impact of his sermon, which he preached without notes for forty-five minutes at a time.[15] Though obviously more refined than Fulton, the dignified Lorimer kept carefully abreast of local issues and "did not hesitate to announce topics which may seem at first to have a secular ring," though all were "invariably treated from the standpoint of evangelical Christianity."[16]

FIGURE 6.2. George Lorimer. From *Tremont Temple Baptist Church: A Light in the City for 150 Years* (Boston: Tremont Temple Baptist Church, 1989).

Under Cortland Myers, pastor from 1909 to 1921, social controversy became almost routine. Though claiming to preach only the gospel, the fiery pastor regularly weighed in on local and national political issues. Moreover, unlike some of his more staid predecessors, Myers was not afraid to pick a fight. When he angered a local Irish politician with some intemperate public remarks, the irascible preacher published his office hours in the local press and promised to "wipe up the floor" with the offending politico if he had the courage to confront him in public.[17] A Tremont Temple deacon recalled of Myers that he would take "the outstanding event of the day which held the public interest and discussion, whether catastrophe, politics, a sporting event, or what not" and draw "from it a striking title for his discourse," suitable for a headline in the local papers or a splashy advertising marquee. "The public, curious to hear his view, came in such numbers that 500 to 1,000 were turned away almost every Sunday night." Though the church ended up issuing tickets to guarantee seats in the auditorium, "when the doors opened to the public, people literally ran down the aisles. Every available seat would be filled in about four minutes, and the side aisles packed with standees, who also formed a crowd at every door."[18]

Literally housed in a theater and led by clergymen with both professional and amateur acting credentials, Tremont Temple emerged in the mid–nineteenth century as a focal point of revivalist Protestantism in Boston. Certainly it did not follow the typical New England way, either socially or architecturally. But Tremont Temple's nonconformity allowed it to carve out a unique role in the city, albeit one that required constant and vigilant redefinition.

An Urban Community

"Ask the average, well-informed man in California if he has ever heard of Tremont Temple," one observer noted in 1901, "and the chances are he will respond, 'Why, yes, that's the big people's affair in Boston.'" At the turn of the century, Tremont Temple was approaching its heyday, its auditorium regularly filled with people eager for a good show and some spiritual inspiration along the way.[19] After a fire destroyed their building in 1893, the congregation rebuilt in splendid style: the new edifice was seven stories tall, and its exterior was made of light sandstone, white terra cotta, and colored marble, modeled after a Venetian palace (see fig. 6.3).

Converse Hall, the main auditorium, provided seating for over twenty-five hundred and featured two tiers of balconies and a spacious main floor, each chair appointed in mahogany, red plush, and the finest quality saddle leather. The ceiling, a mosaic of eight-foot panels richly ornamented in white and gold, rose to a commanding height of fifty-four feet. Over the preaching platform, an enormous mural, headed by winged angels, doves, and haloed figures, framed a huge theater-style organ (see fig. 6.4). The auditorium seats were rarely empty: although the church's numbers fluctuated, by the late nineteenth century growth was steady, and total membership passed two thousand in 1898.

Popularity created both problems and opportunities. To begin with, continuing dependence on rental income instead of pew rents made Tremont Temple increasingly susceptible to the rise and fall of the local economy, and too easily forced into hosting unwanted tenants. In 1893, George Lorimer began a campaign to tighten the church's policy on renting out to the public. Though the congregation earned a tidy sum by allowing a wide variety of lectures, meetings, and rallies in its auditorium, more often than not they had to turn a blind eye to undesirable proceedings. This Lorimer was no longer willing to do once the grand new building was under construction.

FIGURE 6.3. Tremont Temple Exterior. From *Tremont Temple Sketch Book* (Boston: St. Botolph Press, 1896).

Thoroughly annoyed by the "sound of stamping feet, bands of music, and other merriment" constantly echoing through the building, Lorimer threatened to resign unless the church devoted its building to more specifically religious purposes. "I decidedly object to any of the halls in the new building being rented for atheistic or free religious lectures or banquets," he declared in a formal letter to the congregation. "I also object to gatherings for purposes of spiritualism and for the alleged healing of the sick in the main room on week-day mornings by so-called doctors, who use the standing of the building to give them a larger notoriety. And, further, I cannot approve of any entertainments of a semi-theatrical kind," the former actor stormed, "or of negro minstrels, or dancing on the platform by men, women, or even children." Instead, Lorimer urged rentals for lectures, concerts, and celebrations "in which Christianity is not to be ridiculed, Protestantism assailed, and the proprieties which are recognized among ladies and gentlemen ignored." He

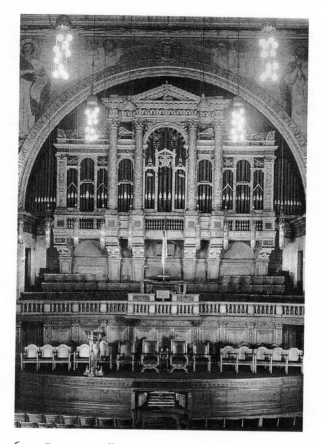

FIGURE 6.4. Converse Hall. From *Tremont Temple Baptist Church: A Light in the City for 150 Years* (Boston: Tremont Temple Baptist Church, 1989).

condoned a variety of meetings for the consideration of Christianity, philanthropy, reforms, patriotism and education—even political rallies— "providing that the gentlemen engaging the rooms...are willing to comply with the ordinary rules of decency, forbidding smoking, chewing, and swearing." The congregation adopted his recommendations in 1895, even though this plunged them into a debt crisis: deprived of rental income, the church struggled to repay the $523,000 owed for their recent rebuilding effort.[20]

The policy also underlined the growing importance of businessmen in the congregation. Edgar Rhodes, who owned a grocery business with his brother Leonard, played a major role in balancing Tremont's budget in 1903. Born in Camden, Maine, in 1863, he came to Boston at seventeen, "spurred on by a dominating purpose to succeed," as one admiring tribute put it. The young man was "faithful and zealous in the performance of his duties" and "frugal in his habits," and did not have to wait long for success. In 1883 he was baptized and became a member of Tremont Temple, and the next year began the Rhodes Brothers business. Appointed deacon in 1902 and "life deacon" twenty years later, Rhodes was a leading figure at Tremont Temple and in Boston's business community. A trustee of Gordon College for twenty-three years, he was also a member of the Boston Chamber of Commerce, the Woodland Golf Club, and the Masons.[21]

Other laypeople also played an influential role in helping Tremont Temple maintain its reputation as "the stranger's sabbath home." At the turn of the century, a small army of young men and women worked as pastor's assistants, busily keeping tabs on the church's geographically scattered membership. One of the best known of Tremont Temple's lay evangelists was Amanda Ricker, widow of a Baptist pastor who worked alongside George Lorimer. Hardworking and determined, she led a round of Sunday school and service classes for young women, visited the sick and evangelized with vigor. "If ever a woman had a 'passion for souls,'" a friend recalled her at her death in 1905, "Mrs. Ricker had that passion. There was always a burden on her heart for somebody." In fact, "if a new member came Mrs. Ricker would soon find out whether she were a Christian or not, and if not, she would not rest until she had persuaded her to become one."[22] Pastor's assistants at Tremont Temple also made regular visits to the church's members in their homes across the greater Boston area, despite the increasing amounts of labor involved. In 1888, the church missionary Sylvester King, for example, logged 4,779 family calls and forty-five visits to "criminals" and distributed an untold number of tracts and religious leaflets.[23] As the congregation became more geographically dispersed, the number of pastoral visits declined, though they continued to be a regular practice. In 1904, W. W. Everts, who met with every member at least once a year, reported a total of 1,544 visits on his afternoon rounds, accomplished almost entirely on public transportation.[24] In 1908, the pastor's assistant Charles Jeffrey clocked similar numbers. "In former years," he observed,

> a large per cent of our congregation inhabited the section of the city known as the West and South Ends, which are located within a very few minute's walk of the Temple, but owing to an increased foreign population in these sections during the past few years the greater portion of our members have gradually relocated to the numerous suburban cities and towns.

But, at least in part because of his efforts and because of Tremont Temple's reliance on the new system of subways and trolleys, suburban members still made the trek into town for regular services. "Owing to the excellent railroad facilities," he commented, "a few minutes ride from any direction within a circuit of many miles will bring our attendants to the Park Street terminus or to Scollay Square."[25]

Laypeople also took up the task. Under Lorimer's leadership, two young people's groups, the Minute Men and the Daughters of the Temple, pledged themselves to "at a minute's notice, God helping them, [to] do whatever the pastor and officers of the church may require." They also fanned out across the city, investigating boarding houses, looking after the sick, finding work for the unemployed, and cultivating "the spirit of comradeship."[26] Tremont Temple's energies did not even stop at the city line. In 1892, the church founded a Lay Preacher's Association, aimed at supplying pulpits and convening revivals around New England.[27] By the 1920s, with membership passing three thousand and spread across fifty-seven different towns and cities, the church organized a visiting system of lay "templars," twenty-four groups of ten, headed by a deacon or church leader. Each individual member pledged to stay in touch with the other ten, visiting them regularly and greeting them on Sundays, trying "in every possible way to create friendship and Love [sic] for the Temple and all of its activities."[28]

By the early twentieth century, Tremont Temple prided itself on being highly accessible to the public, though not in the typical Social Gospel mold. In 1889, the pastor's assistant Charles Roundy described Tremont as "a religious center, a kind of world's parsonage, widely known as a place in which to find most every sort of aid of a proper kind needed by stranger living or dying." Open to every kind of appeal from the citizens of Boston, the Tremont Street building would be, in Roundy's enthusiastic words, "a *city* church, yea, a *people's* church, yea, a *missionary* church!" "We are willing to be at the beck and call of the community," he promised, "if we can only recommend the blessed religion of Christ and be of Christian service to even a few."[29] Unlike the dedicated Social Gospel tabernacles in the South End, however, Tremont Temple's aid to the poor was generally in the form of old-fashioned charity, and directed primarily to its own members. The "aged and poor" within the congregation received regular help with money, employment, coal, and clothing, nearly all of it dispensed by the church's busy pastoral assistants.

By the turn of the century, Tremont Temple was clearly not an "institutional church." "The main thing is the able and earnest proclamation of the gospel," a Baptist admirer declared, and clearly the interior architecture of the building supported this goal. Besides the main auditorium, Tremont could accommodate preaching in two smaller settings, Chipman and Lorimer Halls. The church had little in the way of recreational or educational facilities; most of the upper floors were composed of rented office space. Nearly alone among Boston's Baptist churches, Tremont Temple championed a "virile, as well as persuasive and tender" presentation of the gospel, aimed at the individual. "Tempting baits and wasteful bribes are not the sinews that give these churches their sturdy grip on down-town fields," the admirer continued. "They tell of a grace that gives a man a grip of his own."[30]

But the growing reliance on vivid, topical preaching made Tremont Temple increasingly detached from social conditions in the city of Boston. Though the Temple was at the center of political fervor in the 1880s and 1890s, the church's pastors and people were far less engaged with local issues by the early twentieth century. Though other sources suggest that dispensational premillennialism, a vivid theology of the impending End Times, was popular at Tremont Temple, theology alone did not impel retreat from social involvement. The following two sections discuss two other factors—one dealing with the pews and the other with the pulpit—that softened the hard edges of fundamentalist opposition.

People

At the turn of the century, Tremont Temple's enormous popular appeal was painfully clear to its less fortunate neighbors on a Sunday morning. Large crowds exited the subway only a few yards from the front door of the struggling Park Street Church but walked right past it another two blocks down Tremont Street. As the *Watchman* observed in 1901, Tremont Temple was thriving because it attracted a wide variety of people from all over the city. The congregation was "not an assembly of 'bums' and bedraggled women," the author noted (perhaps a bit defensively), but

> the best of the hotel people, both of the guests and of the help. They get many respectable families held down-town by their occupations— superintendents, janitors, engineers, elevator-men in great buildings. Then there is the boarding-house population—married couples, and the great army of young men and women that vast industries and professional schools call from rural districts and from adjacent states.[31]

"The Tremont Temple audience is recruited from the homes of the city itself," another observer confirmed, "and of fifty suburban cities and towns. Young people abound—clerks, stenographers, dress-makers, milliners, carpenters, plumbers, railroad men, the young from the country or the provinces, [and] plain old women in neat but rather well-worn garments."[32] George Lorimer described his congregation in similar terms: students, strangers, and "young business people," as well as "the usual proportion of 'dead-heads' and religious tramps." ("It would not be Boston," he added ruefully, "if we did not have a fair-sized contingent of cranks.") The congregation was also, according to Lorimer, composed of both rich and poor, though "the poor are stupendously in the majority."[33] By the early twentieth century, Tremont Temple was growing because of the uprootedness and transience of Boston's city life, not in spite of it.

Tremont's church records allow an unusually human glimpse into this side of American fundamentalism. Membership cards provide a revealing view of its people—their names and neighborhoods, the places where they were born, their ages and occupations. Annual reports document the daily routines of church life: the irritations that beset a busy pastor and the many miles clocked by Tremont's indefatigable pastoral assistants as they visited thousands of church members across the city and in its growing suburban neighborhoods.

As these records reveal, Tremont Temple's membership grew steadily from the late nineteenth century into the early twentieth, though with regular fluctuations (see fig. 6.5).

Beginning with 327 members in 1864, the church passed fifteen hundred in the wake of the Moody revival in 1877. By 1878, its Sunday school alone had grown to over eight hundred; one class, taught by Russell Conwell, reached 620 members. As enthusiasm waned in the following years, numbers dipped somewhat predictably; however, during the 1880s and 1890s, a time when Tremont Temple was at the center of anti-Catholic and temperance controversy, Boston's people steadily flocked to its doors. Membership passed two thousand in 1898, propelled by the completion of a new building and Lorimer's successful second pastorate. Yet the early years of the twentieth century brought new difficulties: for two years the church was without a pastor, and numbers dropped precipitously. "It is impossible to fish for pearls in a troubled sea," the church clerk noted sadly in 1903, when membership had dropped to 1,628, "and our Church has been agitated all through the year

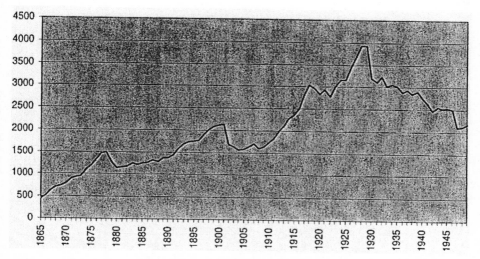

FIGURE 6.5. Tremont Temple total membership by year. From Tremont Temple membership records, Boston, Mass.

by the important question, 'Who shall be pastor?' "[34] Tremont Temple's fortunes soon changed for the better, however. Cortland Myers's arrival in 1909 coincided with a major city-wide revival, described in the next chapter; in 1912 membership passed two thousand once again and continued to grow spectacularly, approaching four thousand by the end of Jasper C. Massee's successful pastorate in 1929. But the gains were not permanent. The following decades saw consistent decline, and by 1949, Tremont Temple's membership had fallen back to the two thousand mark.[35]

Who were Tremont Temple's people? The annual reports offer only names and numbers; the church's membership files, however, offer more detailed information on more than five thousand of the Tremont Temple faithful.[36] Though only about half of the church's members went through the process of filling out cards, which were used sporadically to track attendance, those who did listed their local address, date and place of birth, and occupation. It's likely, of course, that this is a fairly select sample of more dedicated members; however, in a few important respects—gender for example—the information from the cards affirms the picture presented in the annual reports.

Both sources clearly affirm that the majority of Tremont Temple's members were women (see fig. 6.6). Throughout the late nineteenth century, the proportion of female members was high, ranging from about two-thirds to as much as 83 percent during Lorimer's second stint as pastor. New male members rarely accounted for more than about 40 percent of the total, even during a revival year, in which men were specifically targeted for conversion. This disproportion was, of course, normal for Protestant churches, where

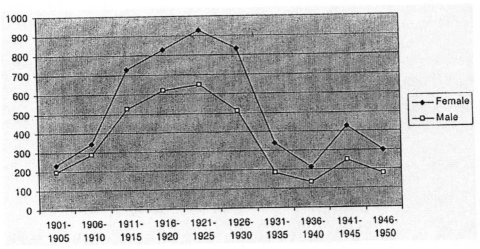

FIGURE 6.6. Tremont Temple new members, male and female. From Tremont Temple membership records, Boston, Mass.

women formed the consistent two-thirds majority. But in the early twentieth century, Tremont Temple took special pains to attract and hold men. A Men's League was formed in 1905 with 125 members and by 1907 had nearly doubled that figure. In 1911 the church hired David Lockrow to lead a Tremont Temple Brotherhood, which by 1912 listed over five hundred active members, with an average of 325 attending a weekly Sunday school class. It was said to be the largest Bible class in North America.[37] Buoyed by the Billy Sunday revivals in 1916–17, the Brotherhood enjoyed its best year ever, sending out evangelistic teams to the Common on Sunday afternoons, and fielding a baseball team and a bowling league. By then more than thirteen hundred men had joined the organization, which offered them Bible classes and lectures, as well as piano lessons, gymnastics, a bowling league, and an employment bureau.[38] The emphasis on activity and outreach drew from the current understanding of the kind of religion that attracted men. In his book *Why Men Do Not Go to Church*, Cortland Myers urged strong leadership and well-organized programs to draw in reluctant laymen. "The church should be a magnet," he wrote, "to disturb the sleeping particles of manhood on Sunday, and draw them to a place of worship."[39]

The racial and ethnic composition of Tremont Temple's membership is more difficult to determine. Established on abolitionist principles, the church certainly posed few institutional barriers to an interracial membership. Scattered indications in membership and photographic records point to a consistent, but small, minority of African Americans. Since Tremont Street bordered on Boston's Chinatown, the congregation also included a similarly small but regular influx of American- and foreign-born Chinese. In the 1890s, 19 percent of new members had been born outside the United States and Canada, most of them in Europe; in following decades the proportion stayed high, around 10 percent, before declining as a result of the anti-immigration ethos of the 1920s.

Rarely, from the 1890s through the Depression years, did the proportion of native Bostonians make up more than a third of the new members listed. Over the early twentieth century, the majority of incoming members (tracked by membership cards) were natives of rural New England—specifically, the five New England states, excluding Boston and its near suburbs—or the Canadian Maritimes (see fig. 6.7).

The largest single group came from eastern Canada, a region long characterized by strict Baptist faith.[40] At the turn of the century, fully a quarter of new members named Nova Scotia, New Brunswick, or Prince Edward Island as their place of birth. The proportion did not fall below 20 percent until the 1930s, when immigration laws and declining economic opportunity cut off the flow of Canadians into New England.[41] By that time, Tremont Temple was known in many quarters as "the Canadian church." "It seemed nearly every

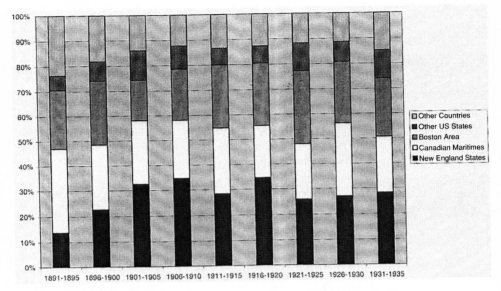

FIGURE 6.7. Tremont Temple new members, place of birth. From Tremont Temple membership records, Boston, Mass.

one you spoke to there was a Canadian," recalled a New Brunswick emigrant who arrived around 1913. "They'd have a Canadian night there once a year...[and] ask the Canadians to stand, all those that were born of Canadian parents. And really, there wouldn't seem to be anybody sitting down. It seemed that the whole church would get up."[42]

It is not surprising that immigrants from the Maritimes found a stranger's sabbath home at Tremont Temple. Atlantic Canadians had long perceived New England as one part of a single region, drawn together by a common maritime economy and English-speaking culture. Separated from the rest of Canada by Roman Catholic French Quebec, Protestants from the Maritime provinces easily identified "the Boston state" as a cultural partner and as an economic destination. Indeed, by 1913, when railroad and steamship lines provided direct and easy transportation, Boston had more Canadian-born inhabitants than Winnipeg (two hundred thousand).[43]

Canadian immigration to the United States followed different patterns from the usual European type. Like the majority of Tremont Temple members, Maritime immigrants also tended to be young, unmarried, and female.[44] Most left rural homes to take up city work as domestics, clerical workers, waitress, and, by the 1920s, student nurses. To a degree, moving to Boston was a response to economic distress, caused by the decline of coastal trade and the shipbuilding industry; but increasingly it was simply "the thing to do," a "rite of passage into adulthood" for adventurous young women and men.

Unlike European immigrants, who came as extended families and segregated themselves in ethnic neighborhoods, Canadians in Boston had a "sense of familiarity" with the region and many friends and relatives to provide companionship and economic support.[45] Even Tremont Temple's anti-Catholic reputation would have given many Maritimers a familiar link with the past; their own region's history was rife with similar tensions between English Protestants and Irish Catholics.[46]

The presence of large numbers of Canadian immigrants strengthens the impression that Tremont Temple was a church for the hardworking and comfortably ambitious, not the alienated. The common picture of Protestant fundamentalists as angry, dispossessed people simply does not wash with the congregational history of Tremont Temple. This is not to say that militant rhetoric was unimportant—certainly during the 1880s it provided an important stimulus for growth and visibility. But long-term success as a city church required something more.

Fundamentalism

By the 1920s, Tremont Temple had become an important site for fundamentalism in New England. As a regular stop on the revival and Bible conference circuit, the church hosted a constant flow of luminaries from the national movement. Two of its pastors, J. C. Massee and J. Whitcomb Brougher, brought solid credentials as leaders of conservative orthodoxy within the northern Baptist church.[47]

But Tremont Temple was not always fundamentalist in the expected ways, suggesting the occasional gulf between the standards of a national movement and the pragmatic compromises necessary to the life of a local congregation. Though, for example, opposition to Masonry was a staple of Protestant protest in the 1880s, George Lorimer preached from a lectern presented to him by the DeMolay Commandery and the Knights Templars. Seven of the first eight of Tremont Temple's pastors were Masons or Knights Templar, and Lorimer himself was a thirty-third-degree Mason, the highest ever connected with the church.[48] Tremont Temple was also not averse to forms of popular entertainment usually considered anathema to doctrinaire fundamentalists. Beginning in Myer's pastorate, Tremont Temple began to meet its expenses by showing feature films, thanks in part to the assistance of Lyman Howe, a member who owned a movie business. In 1912 a six-months run of the coronation of George V—shown in color—brought in some ten thousand dollars toward church expenses. Between 1908 and 1926, the congregation averaged more than twenty-five thousand dollars a year from film revenue. Though the practice was controversial, all of the movies were said to be "clean": The Count of Monte Cristo, Pollyanna, Daddy Longlegs, and The Hunchback of Notre Dame. And because it was lucrative, it was hard to argue against. Proceeds from movie nights eventually liquidated half a million dollars' worth of church debt and financed a new organ.[49]

Tremont Temple reached its peak in terms of membership and national influence during the pastorate of J. C. Massee (1922–29), traversing the most contentious decade of fundamentalist debate.[50] Massee was a formidable pulpit presence, tall and eloquent, with a dignified mane of flowing white hair (see fig. 6.8).

A leader in the national fundamentalist movement among Baptists, he was born in rural Georgia in 1871, the youngest of thirteen children. Massee rose to national prominence through his speaking gifts and solid reputation for orthodoxy. After graduating from Mercer University in 1892, he spent a year at the Southern Baptist Seminary in Louisville, and then served a series

FIGURE 6.8. J. C. Massee, From *Tremont Temple Baptist Church: A Light in the City for 150 Years* (Boston: Tremont Temple Baptist Church, 1989).

of relatively short pastorates in Florida, Kentucky, Ohio, North Carolina, and Tennessee, before arriving at the Baptist Temple in Brooklyn in 1920.

There he entered a hotbed of Baptist fundamentalism. At his installation service, John Roach Straton, the pastor of New York's Calvary Baptist Church and a leader in the national movement, was on hand to issue the welcome. At that time, Straton was approaching the height of his somewhat dubious popularity. He was by all accounts an experienced controversialist, known for leading graphic tours of New York's vice district, issuing lurid denunciations of Hollywood sin, and headlining a series of raucous public debates with the Unitarian Charles Potter in 1923 and 1924. The cranky Baptist minister seemed to flourish in the glare of public limelight; according to some sources, he served as Sinclair Lewis's model for the venial evangelist Elmer Gantry.[51]

The year that Massee came to Brooklyn was a troubled one for northern Baptists. Just before the denomination convened its national convention in Buffalo, a small group of clergy and laymen met to organize a protest, pledging to defend "the Fundamentals of our Baptist faith" against the inroads of modernism in Baptist schools and among Baptist missionaries. Massee played a leading role in stirring up controversy; he presided over the protest meeting and subsequently became president of the newly formed Fundamentalist Federation in the Northern Baptist Convention. Along with Straton and William Bell Riley, pastor of the First Baptist Church in Minneapolis, Massee emerged at the center of a rapidly growing tumult in the denomination, focused on the orthodoxy of Baptist schools and seminaries.[52] Massee clearly embraced the cause, and was in fact so zealous early on that he sent out his own separate questionnaire to Baptist alumni. When the survey brought back troubling results—only 40 percent reported that their faculty were faithful to the Scriptures—he led the fundamentalist effort to push through a written standard of Baptist orthodoxy at the Des Moines convention in 1921. Ever alert to the dangers of an all-out controversy, however, Baptist leaders consistently headed off fundamentalist efforts; as a result, angry conservatives began to take steps toward separating from the denomination, organizing a militant Baptist Bible Union in 1923.

But this time Massee did not go along. Because he became increasingly uncomfortable with divisive tactics of the fundamentalist minority, his stay among the militants was relatively brief. In 1925 Massee resigned as president of the Fundamentalist Federation and withdrew from active participation in Baptist polemics, pausing only to address the national convention in 1926. At that point, in an address entitled "The Laodicean Lament," he called for a six-month truce and urged all Baptists to renew their efforts toward a common goal of evangelistic outreach. But the attempt at conciliation did little to heal the wounds of theological controversy and earned him permanent scorn from Riley and Straton—both denounced him as an apostate. Still, Massee felt he had no other choice. "I left the fundamentalists to save my own spirit," he wrote to James M. Gray in 1926; "they became so self-righteous, so critical, so unchristian, so destructive, so incapable of being fair that I had to go elsewhere for spiritual nourishment."[53]

During his years at Tremont Temple, Massee's public reputation was generally positive; even those outside the movement could see that he was a conservative but not a hardline fundamentalist. Comparing Massee to the pugnacious William Bell Riley in 1926, one journalist reached the somewhat backhanded conclusion that "if either lives at all in the thought realm of the twentieth century, it is Dr. Massie [sic]. Dr. Riley sees only absolutes, that is, only absolute rights and wrongs, truths and lies, blacks and whites. One suspects that Dr. Massie can distinguish grays at least and maybe reds."[54]

Even so, Massee knew the value of a good public uproar. Early in his career, during his pastorate in Raleigh, North Carolina, he found himself in the thick of one, when some incidental remarks from a midweek service ended up in the local newspaper headlines. Massee had been discussing a passage from the Book of Job in which the suffering Job denied ever having oppressed a wage earner. No social radical, Massee used the occasion to decry the oppressively low wages given to blacks, declaring that "in the sight of God one stands condemns who does it." That was enough to bring enemies out of the woodwork. For the next several weeks, Josephus Daniels, the editor of the local paper (and later secretary of the Navy), mercilessly lambasted the young pastor in front-page editorials, denouncing his politics and calling for his resignation. The tactic was brutally effective in silencing social critique: Massee would never preach the "social gospel" from his pulpit again. But this harrowing experience also brought another important lesson, evident the Sunday morning after the first editorial appeared: when Massee ascended his pulpit, the church was overflowing with curious listeners. The crowd spilled out of the building and onto the street, and at the close of the service, hundreds came forward vowing their personal loyalty. The application was not lost on Massee. "Early in my ministry," he later confided to a Boston journalist, "I learned that the very best way to gather support is to have the good fortune to be unjustly assailed."[55]

Massee's rough introduction to Boston in the spring of 1922 must have reminded him of Raleigh in 1903. Since late February, the Unitarian *Christian Register* had been running editorials denouncing the "horrendous creed" of premillennialism, as well as the benighted insistence that "God alone wrote the Bible, set the type, made the paper, bound the pages, dedicated the societies, and appointed the colporteurs to distribute the infallible work."[56] Some writers went so far as to directly implicate Gordon Bible College, the EANE, and Park Street Church in fomenting the "freak" theology of the Second Coming. Tremont Temple, however, was the center of the problem, for there premillennialism had "reached the hot fanatical stage."[57]

Public trouble began in April at the Ford Hall Forum, a prestigious lecture program endowed, ironically enough, by a venerable local organization, the Boston Baptist Social Union.[58] There, Albert Dieffenbach, pastor of the Arlington Street Unitarian Church, launched a public attack on fundamentalism and on Massee himself, urging the "decent people of Boston" to prevent him from coming to Tremont Temple.[59] As proof, Dieffenbach cited a lurid passage from the dispensationalist writer Isaac M. Haldeman and warned the audience that this violent, blood-drenched theology proclaiming a "Kaiser Jesus" was being disseminated in the heart of Boston. He named the Gordon Bible College, Park Street Church, and Tremont Temple as the primary source of what appeared to be a Bolshevik-style conspiracy, and ended with the baleful pronouncement that "they are getting ready." Indeed, "if tomorrow one of their recognized spokesmen should say the end has come, we should witness a spectacle the most awful in the world's record of wars and massacres."[60] Perhaps also recognizing the value of a religious controversy, the Boston Herald took Dieffenbach's side, editorializing against Massee as a representative of the "Religious Ku-Klux" and offering the self-fulfilling prophecy that "Tremont Temple will shortly be the storm center of a religious controversy."[61]

But Massee said little in return. Undoubtedly, in the spring of 1922 he had little stomach for theological arguments; his arrival at Tremont Temple coincided with his disillusionment over the militant spirit of the Baptist Bible Union, and as a Boston pastor, he never joined in public doctrinal controversy. Instead, Massee sat down for a long personal interview with the Herald, a feat described somewhat enviously by his Unitarian opponents as a "magnificent use of the public press."[62] And he let the Baptist press do the primary work of defending him. The conservative Watchman-Examiner proved a staunch ally, attacking the "angry, bitter-spirited, irresponsible Unitarian minister" who elected to "pour out the phials of his wrath on able, representative and consecrated men serving in prominent pulpits of the Baptist denomination."[63]

Despite the dire predictions, Massee brought to Tremont Temple a relatively generous form of Protestant orthodoxy. As he told an interviewer in 1926, "I am not a debater. I am not a controversialist." Though there were certainly many with whom he differed, Massee vowed not to "engage in battle with them. . . . My attitude, I hope, is one of charity."[64] More than once, he made good on this promise in the pulpit. In a 1925 sermon on religious doubt, Massee described himself as only "somewhat" of a fundamentalist and took the occasion to warn his congregation against the "dry rot of orthodox thinking" as a substitute for Christian love.[65]

Many of Massee's sermons during his Brooklyn and Boston years were, perhaps not surprisingly given the makeup of his congregation, about family issues. "I don't know, but I suspect," he told a Tremont Temple audience in 1924, "that the vast majority of you who are here tonight were born somewhere else than in Boston and you are thinking of an old home about which your heart entwines its tendrils." God, Massee said, could be that one "whose voice is familiar, whose presence is constant, whose friendship does not change, who has courage in the midst of disasters, who enthuses, comforts, strengthens our hearts and encourages our souls."[66] According to his personal records, between January 1920 and June 1927, Massee preached on women's roles eighteen times, on the home eight times, on men's conduct six times, on marriage and divorce seven times, and on sex five times. Most of these sermons were devotional rather than legalistic, emphasizing personal purity rather than adherence to a set of rules. And they were often sentimental. "I feel quite sure," he told his congregation in 1924, "that if I should ask every man here to night to tell me the honest truth about the things that have gone into his life to make up what he is, without a single exception, you would all stand up to say that the most telling and lasting influence, and the influence to which you were most willing to pay tribute, was the influence of some woman, a maid or a mistress, a wife or a daughter." Massee's tribute to his mother, "My Mother's Legacy," followed this pattern, recounting her constant presence in his life, as a voice of reproof and encouragement.[67] The tone of these sermons was generally conservative. Massee did not object to woman suffrage, but he insisted that women's role in the home was primary, and that men should take leadership there. "I have no limitations, no criticisms for women," he declared in a 1924 sermon, "The Man in the Home." "But there is one thing that God almighty never contemplated, and that is that man should lose his place as the head of the family."[68]

Massee's religion was thoroughly evangelistic. Throughout his pastorate he held regular revival meetings, often in January or February, hosting an array of colorful, attention-grabbing musicians and evangelists. In 1925 the Aida Brass Quartet of Brooklyn performed in Egyptian costumes. In 1928, Tremont Temple hosted John Brown, the "Moody of the South," or, as he was popularly known, the "laughing evangelist." Brown's description captured two of the dominant cultural motifs of popular culture in the 1920s. He was first of all a "rapid-fire salesman who feels it is his business to tell the world the one thing he feels it needs—Jesus Christ."[69] And he was an athlete: "God's full back, and he's carrying the ball!"[70] Though undoubtedly entertaining, Massee's revivals were not all fun. He also used the revival platform to call out the opposition. Modernist theology, he told one reporter, "tends to unbridle lust, looses lawlessness, sets free the dogs of war, breaks down the moral fibre, pulls down governments and destroys the human race. The gauntlet has been thrown down at our feet," he declared. "We will meet the issue by hurling the lies back whence they have come."[71]

Nor did Massee avoid confrontation with the people of Boston. In 1925 he created a minor sensation by declaring the city "Satan's Branch Office." New York, as always, took first billing as a center of wickedness, but, to the delight of Boston journalists, Massee allowed that the prince of darkness had set up a "secondary throne" in the Hub, under which "godless business, godless pleasure and a bloodless religion thrive."[72] During his pastorate, Tremont Temple began to broadcast revival sermons on a local radio station, sending them out across the Common from a loudspeaker on the nearby Stearns Department Store.[73] The move prompted a round of liberal Protestant protest, with Dieffenbach the first to denounce the "wretched business." "Into thousands of homes the evil things about a fiendish, murderous God are poured in the name of the religion of Christ," he thundered. "It is terrible."[74] Nevertheless, in January 1924, Tremont Temple announced plans to run its own radio station, WBDR, "to meet the challenge of the religious modernists and spread the fundamentalist gospel as never before." Not just Boston but the entire New England area could now hear messages from Tremont Temple. "We will make it a part of not only the religious community for which it was, of course, primarily established," Massee told the press, "but for the whole social community as well."[75]

But in the end, Boston journalists stopped taking Massee seriously. In March 1925 he gave a memorable sermon against women smoking, decrying it as an affectation of the rich and intellectual, enjoyed by "women of personality and influence who think they can set aside [social] conventions." Massee, now arguing for social convention as "the standards of the living God," excoriated "men and women everywhere" who failed to see the "deep religious conviction" behind the assumption that women should not smoke cigarettes. And, of course, cigarettes were a health hazard, primarily through the arsenic used to bleach the rolling paper. Inhaling this chemical, Massee explained, thickens the mucous membranes in the lungs and creates "impure blood," which is then carried into the heart and brain, where it "debates the judgment, inflames the imagination, arouses unholy desires, and accomplishes a deadly reaction on the physical health." In a quick aside, he also suggested that, if a woman had to smoke, a pipe was probably a better choice, since "there is not enough nicotene in the tobacco of a cigarette to kill a flea."[76]

The local papers loved the story, running photos of young women who had given up cigarettes and taken to smoking pipes instead. "If you must flirt with Lady Nicotene, girls," one caption read, "by all means hit the pipe." Massee's endorsement of female pipe-smoking garnered attention even beyond the confines of New England. The *Pittsburgh Daily Pictoral* ran pictures of a young actress smoking a pipe and declaring that "her decision came about by The Rev. Dr. J. C. Masse [sic] of Boston, who said that a pipe was by far the more sanitary and advisable."[77]

Courting public attention was risky business. For all of the public attention that Massee's sensational statements gave Tremont Temple, they probably did not win many converts to evangelical Christianity. If anything, Massee's case suggests that during the 1920s, conservative Protestant belief was not so much falling victim to liberal attack as becoming the punch line to a secular joke. By the late 1920s, religion was an object of fun. This much is clear in Paul Kemeny's insightful analysis of the demise of Boston's Watch and Ward Society, a process that chronologically paralleled Massee's departure. For many decades, the society effectively policed the borders of public decency in the city, bringing the powerful cultural prestige of its liberal Protestant membership to bear against "obscene" literature and unwise booksellers. In the late 1920s, free speech advocates, led by H. L. Mencken, exposed the Society's weakness through ridicule. Once the public learned to laugh at earnest Victorian moralisms, targeting "Puritanism" as an object of modern derision, the battle against censorship was effectively over.[78]

By the 1930s, popular revivalism had lost whatever political edge it had once sought to gain. Part of this was no doubt due to Prohibition: with the Eighteenth Amendment safely in hand, Massee and his successors had no need to press a public agenda. But, as the following two chapters demonstrate, this slippage was already well underway by the 1920s. The Chapman revival campaign in 1909 and Billy Sunday's crusade in the winter of 1916–17 illustrate a process of conservative Protestant disengagement from secular citizenship in the city of Boston. Ironically, during the 1920s, a decade that historians have assumed was the climax of theological confrontation between liberal and orthodox, religion itself was becoming a joke. More a form of entertainment than a political threat, it was in many ways no longer genuinely divisive.

With Massee's departure in 1929, Tremont Temple faced difficult times. Economic depression, coupled with the fairly swift decline of immigration from Canada, cut into membership. In 1930, a purging of membership rolls resulted in a net loss of 740 people, 646 of whom were untraceable; similar investigations in 1933 and 1936 brought a net loss of 350 more. Though new members continued to join Tremont Temple, total membership slid steadily downward, dropping toward two thousand by the late 1940s.[79] Half a century later, the church had weathered more demographic transitions, doggedly refashioning itself into a doctrinally conservative, multiethnic congregation in the heart of the city. By the 1980s and 1990s, the new members came from Cambodia, Brazil, and the Philippines; the new tenants are Hispanic evangelicals, Korean Presbyterians, and Ethiopian Baptists. But on any given weekday, the hallways of the old building are far quieter than in the past; Tremont Temple's persistent presence in downtown Boston has not come easily.

These losses coincided with the rising fortunes of Park Street Church in the late 1930s and 1940s. Under Harold John Ockenga, who arrived there in 1935, conservative Protestant faith took on a more polished and newly aggressive public face. If the decline of Tremont Temple marked the decreasing appeal of popular revivalism, the success of Park Street indicated a new form of conservative evangelical faith in both Boston and New England.

PART II

Separating

7

Civic Revivalism

J. Wilbur Chapman's Boston Crusade, 1909

"Yes, sir," said Lapham, in a strain which Bartley was careful not to interrupt again, "a man never sees all that his mother has been to him till it's too late to let her know that he sees it. Why *my* mother—" he stopped. "It gives me a lump in the throat," he said apologetically, with an attempt at a laugh. Then he went on: "... She got time to go to church, and to teach us to read the Bible, and to misunderstand it in the old way. She was *good*. But it ain't her on her knees in church that comes back to me so much like the sight of an angel as her on her knees before me at night, washing my poor, dirty feet, that I'd run bare in all day, and making me decent for bed."
—William Dean Howells, *The Rise of Silas Lapham*

It was shortly before noon in the heart of Boston's business district, and thousands of men gathered in front of Tremont Temple, spilling out onto the street and temporarily blocking the busy thoroughfare. They stood in packed, restless rows, a sea of black bowler hats, shuffling against the biting cold of late January. Most of them clutched small paper tickets in their hands, advertising the midday revival service for "men only," but most of them knew that these would not guarantee a spot inside. Once the great doors of Tremont Temple swung open and the three thousand seats in Lorimer Hall were filled, hundreds of men would be left on the sidewalk, waiting another day to hear the great evangelist J. Wilbur Chapman and his legendary song leader Charles M. Alexander.[1]

Though less renowned than Dwight Moody and less notorious than Billy Sunday, Chapman was one of the leading evangelists of his day. His Boston campaign, conducted from January 26 to

February 21, 1909, was one of his most successful ever, dramatically show-casing his broad-based appeal in one of the nation's largest cities. Every weekday at noon, Chapman filled Tremont Temple's auditorium with thou-sands of businessmen from nearby shops and offices, and every evening he addressed an equally enthusiastic cross-section of men and women from around the city. Not surprisingly, perhaps, by the end of the campaign, Boston seemed to many observers a city transformed. "If this is what is meant by a revival of religion," the New Bedford *Standard* concluded, somewhat envi-ously, then it "would be a mighty good thing for more cities than Boston."[2]

The revival was as much an organizational feat as a spiritual one. Chap-man's meetings in Tremont Temple were actually the centerpiece of a vast, coordinated effort involving 166 area churches, billed as a "simultaneous" crusade for Boston's soul. Every weekday beginning January 26, while Chap-man held noon and evening services at Tremont Temple, his entourage of twenty-five trained evangelists fanned out across the city and its surrounding suburbs. Reinforced by an army of trained laypeople, the Chapman campaign held daily revivals in packed suburban churches, "quiet hour" meetings in wealthy Back Bay salons, and boisterous songfests at East Boston rescue missions.

Chapman sought to alienate no one. His campaign incorporated every religious denomination willing to grant him a hearing, from Universalists and Episcopalians to Swedish Baptists and Adventists. Herbert Johnson, the local chair of the publicity committee, even preached in Temple Israel, encouraging Jews and Catholics to support the revival.[3] On the eve of his first public meeting, Chapman issued an address to the people of Boston, printed on the front page of the *Boston Globe*, urging them to forego their differences and unite behind a common cause. "It is not my disposition in any city to oppose men who ... do not agree with my theology," he said. "I am too busy to fight anything but sin, too much concerned for men who are in need to waste my energy in opposing other Christian workers who may not believe just as I do."[4]

Boston quickly succumbed to the evangelistic onslaught. Beginning with a city-wide audience of twenty-five thousand on January 26, attendance reports were reaching sixty thousand a night five days later. A week later the number of simultaneous meetings had more than doubled, from 25 to 56.[5] Some two weeks into the campaign, on Sunday, February 7, over three hundred area churches held revival services in conjunction with the Chapman crusade, in-cluding fourteen for "men only," four just for women, and seven geared to-ward children.[6] By February 19, Chapman's crowds were so large that they regularly impeded traffic on Tremont Street, and the evangelist was forced to move his meetings to Mechanics Hall, which had a seating capacity of eight thousand. The massive response, evident from the very first week of the campaign, moved one reporter to concede that "Boston has been completely captured by the army of evangelists that have invaded the city under the leadership of the Rev. J. Wilbur Chapman."[7]

Had he been alive, A. J. Gordon might have blinked in wonderment. Barely twenty years earlier, evangelical Protestants had been an angry, beleaguered group, united by a common distrust of the Catholic Church and their city government. Their impulse toward separatism was moderated only by their determination to challenge Catholic encroachment on Protestant control of public schools and city park space. But in the winter of 1909, the enemy was nowhere in sight. Again and again, evangelical Protestants proclaimed an optimistic commitment to civic uplift, basking in the rapt attention of the secular press and the broad support of area churches.

A major religious event in the heart of the Progressive Era, the Chapman revival was an important marker in the history of Boston's evangelical Protestants. Though the revival itself was—like all such—ephemeral in its spiritual effects, its rhetoric and organizational structure speak volumes about the way that conservative Protestants had come to envision their public role. Once fervently bound to local city politics, twentieth-century evangelicals viewed their urban setting in increasingly generic terms, as a broadly moral but not specifically political problem. Part of the reason for this was the steady exodus of Protestants into Boston's streetcar suburbs. But beneath that trend were other, more subtle social mechanisms facilitating evangelicals' gradual disengagement from the city over the course of the early twentieth century.

The change in evangelical Protestant presence mirrored a transformation of the city's political culture, a process that also reached a significant turning point in 1909. A recent study of Progressive-era Boston by the historian James Connolly tracks changes in the city's political structures that make sense in light of the religious events of the late nineteenth and early twentieth centuries; in both cases, small, local battles were giving way to broader cultural conflicts based on symbolic loyalties and managed by charismatic leadership. Connolly's story begins with the tumultuous turf battles over public schools in the 1880s and attributes the decline of these hostilities to concerted efforts by city leaders to forge new, less volatile ties between politicians and voters. The new city charter, signed in 1909, hastened the demise of old-style ward politics by awarding citizens' interest groups, particularly reform-minded civic and business organizations, primary access to city hall. As a result, Connolly argues, politicians came to rely less on ward-based party loyalties to mobilize their constituencies and more on "broadly gauged policies designed to ignite collective action." What this meant in Boston's context was that populist figures like James Michael Curley and John F. "Honey Fitz" Fitzgerald energized their Irish Catholic constituency by employing the language of Progressive reform—a discourse that historians normally associate with middle-class and elite Yankee Republicans. Echoing Protestant reformers' condemnations of urban vice and corruption, Curley and his lieutenants rallied their constituents by pinning the problem on Yankee greed and selfishness. Connolly traces Boston's fabled ethnic clashes, which rose to a height in the busing crisis of the 1970s, to these broadly polarizing tactics, fully evident by the 1920s. As Yankee Protestants increasingly left the city for the suburbs, he explains, Irish voters were free to believe the worst about people who were no longer around to argue back.[8]

Connolly's argument that "politics shaped society as much as society shaped politics" is broadly useful for understanding early twentieth-century religious change, particularly the structural changes to American religion brought on by fundamentalism.[9] The previous chapters have demonstrated some of the reasons why religious realignment proceeded relatively slowly in Boston: during the late nineteenth century, evangelical Protestant identity revolved around smaller loyalties to centuries-old churches, denominations, and geographical turf. But during the Progressive Era, Protestants across the country, and even in Boston, began to call themselves "fundamentalists." Although American Protestantism was no stranger to factions or schisms, up to this point most of these had occurred within denominational structures, pitting revivalists against antirevivalists or proslavery forces against abolitionists. Fundamentalism, however, recast Protestant identities around a common set of ideas and on a national scale, in many ways paralleling the way Boston's political alignments became less local and more symbolic in the early twentieth century. The apparent urgency of the theological issues at stake prompted like-minded conservatives to cross denominational boundaries and act as interest groups within American religious culture. By the end of the twentieth century, when denominational labels had come to mean relatively little to many rank-and-file believers, and conservative Protestant subcultures seemed almost completely dominated by high-profile national leaders, parachurch organizations, and political interest groups, a transformation rooted in the Progressive era had reached its logical conclusion.[10]

The emergence of fundamentalism as a movement also involved gender. Though women had played a central role in the local battles of the late nineteenth century, men would dominate the rhetoric of Progressive-era Protestantism in Boston. Chapman and Sunday both aimed their message at religiously inert male church members, recognizing their potentially powerful political and civic role. In a broad sense, the masculine rhetoric of both these campaigns signaled a reaction against overly "feminized" Victorian Protestantism; but the focus on male converts also meant that Protestant concern was moving beyond the divisive battles over urban turf that women had once led. The shift toward a more masculine Protestantism meant a shift away from particular loyalties; rather than fight for Boston by preaching street by street, Protestants could join in a broader effort to simply claim the entire city for God.[11]

In many ways, Boston's two city-wide revivals recast Protestant identity. Certainly many Protestants continued to perceive Chapman through a denominational frame of reference: Congregationalists and even many Unitarians applauded the high ethical tone of his preaching,[12] Methodists marveled at his adeptness in the "science" of revivals,[13] and conservative Baptists applauded him for preaching the "old fashioned gospel" without apology.[14] But Chapman's language of civic reform also helped evangelical Protestants envision themselves not just as members of competing denominations but as part of a broader coalition of resistance to various aspects of modernity.

Iniquity Galore

The language of civic reform pervaded the revival. "It is in the interest of cleaner politics and better surroundings that this campaign is to be held here," the Congregational pastor Herbert S. Johnson told the press the week before Chapman arrived. Highlighting low wages as a source of moral peril, especially to young women, Johnson announced that the campaign would "stir up the ideals of city life" and strengthen especially the business community "against all forms of civic corruption we hope."[15] "It is foolish to close our eyes and say Boston has no plague spots," A. Z. Conrad concurred. "There is iniquity galore. . . . The whole social and civic life needs toning up."[16]

Most Bostonians would have agreed. The city was notoriously unreceptive to moralistic politics, but in the shadow of the Progressive movement it fielded sporadic bursts of moral outrage. In 1907 a Finance Commission, appointed by Mayor John Fitzgerald, began an investigation of illegal ties between business and city government. No earth-shaking scandals emerged, mostly petty larcenies and tawdry betrayals of the public trust. By Chicago or New York standards it wasn't much; but it was sufficient to alert the citizens of Boston. Propelled by a wave of public cynicism and disgust, the Finance Commission successfully pushed through a new reform-oriented city charter in 1909.[17]

Chapman came to Boston that same year with a message of civic righteousness, framed in the language of efficiency and order. "The King's business" was his catchphrase, printed on thousands of lapel pins and tickets, conveying in simple terms his conviction that "a man can succeed in business and be a Christian."[18] Chapman demonstrated the truth of his own dictum in the deft, businesslike way he ran the revival. From his very first day in Boston he avidly courted the secular press, who sat together on a long table to one side on the platform at every public meeting. In return, all of the local newspapers gave the campaign regular front-page coverage, and at the end of the campaign Chapman rewarded them with a banquet, at which a group of reporters (which even included a few Roman Catholics) gave him a commemorative pocket Bible as a parting gift.[19]

Visibly, Chapman exemplified managerial values. A graduate of Oberlin College and Lane Seminary, he determined to become a minister after his conversion at a Moody revival in Chicago in 1877. Although rumors circulated that he was demanding ten thousand dollars up front before he would come to Boston, in reality he lived a fairly frugal life and never directly profited from his revival work.[20] Nonetheless, Chapman looked solid and successful; he was a "suave and urbane" man who "dressed like a banker," with gold-rimmed glasses, neatly combed hair parted on the left, and silk ties held in place by a pearl tie pin.[21] Before Chapman arrived, A. Z. Conrad replied to an anti-revivalist editorial in the *Boston Transcript* by endorsing him as a "discriminating scholar, a refined, cultivated gentleman ... [and] a tactful sympathetic teacher." "Just as there are newspapers and *newspapers*," Conrad chided the *Transcript's* largely Brahmin readership, "so there are evangelists and *evangelists*," noting that Chapman had been endorsed by "literally thousands of the brainiest and must successful business and professional men" in cities across the country.[22]

Chapman was a classic go-getter. He transformed his first pastorate, the Reformed Church in Albany, New York, from a sleepy conservative showpiece to an "aggressive evangelistic organization" overflowing with new members. In his first three years as successor to A. T. Pierson at Philadelphia's Bethany Church, Chapman brought in eleven hundred new members. In 1889 he became pastor of New York's prestigious Fourth Presbyterian Church and enjoyed the same "glorious success" he had found elsewhere. As a full-time evangelist, Chapman pioneered new methods, in particular the simultaneous city-wide campaign that was so effective in Boston and other cities around the country.[23]

The simultaneous crusade, a method that Chapman perfected, was itself a feat of organizational skill, requiring immense preparation and commitment on the part of local churches. Two years before Chapman's arrival, Boston's Evangelical Alliance began to plan the city-wide event, and in the preceding seven months began scheduling meetings and incorporating financial support from churches around the entire Boston area.[24] After each service, scores of "personal workers" filled out cards for each new convert and sent them on to a central committee, where they were tabulated and sent on to a pastor if a church preference was indicated. "It was all done," A. Z. Conrad explained, "in a methodical, business-like way."[25]

Not surprisingly, Chapman's gift for organization elicited continual admiration from middle-class Bostonians. The Methodist *Zion's Herald* described him as a "marvelous manager" who "has reduced the matter of evangelistic services to a sane, scientific, and persuasively victorious system. He is a man to study," the editor concluded, for "in perfect self-control, knowing men and how to use them ... he preaches ... with an intelligence, discrimination, and convincing power that very few men possess."[26] Another columnist praised Chapman's "genius for combination and management," which "would have entitled him to the baton of a major-general in a military campaign."[27] Thomas Lawson, a local drama critic, concluded that Chapman was "the most finished artist I have ever listened to," unequalled as a "delicious mind, brain and heart stirrer."[28]

The sins of the business world were central to Chapman's message. Boston, like many large urban centers of its time, was undergoing a painful economic transition, as the small shops and offices of the post–Civil War era were being absorbed into large companies. Many of the clerks who attended Chapman's rallies were also encountering an increasingly feminine work-force, as office work became increasingly the province of young unmarried women. Few would have had opportunity to own their own business; most clerks were employed by large firms with elaborate hierarchies, and they rarely encountered any bosses beyond their immediate superiors.[29] In such an impersonal setting, small moral infractions and petty cheating might seem fairly harmless.

Though Chapman insisted that capitalism and Christianity need not clash, he was careful to warn his audiences of a conflict of interest. "There is danger," he declared in the public press, "that business men in their pursuit of wealth may forget the needs of their souls" and that "the old ideals, which were the inspiration of our parents, may be lowered in this commercial age." To lower ideals, Chapman warned, "is to prophesy ultimate failure."[30]

A Message for Men

Though he held special services for shop girls and, according to press ac-counts, women predominated at most of the evening meetings, Chapman recognized that men were key to the city's moral and spiritual renewal. Within the context of the revival, the "remasculinization" of early twentieth-century Protestantism was not just a way of redressing the female imbalance in churches and religious organizations but a means of articulating a new civic agenda.

Gender politics were common in Progressive-era Boston. The election of John F. Fitzgerald as mayor in 1910 marked the beginning of a new style of populist leadership; "Honey Fitz" became the first Irish Democrat to hold a four-year term as mayor of Boston, defeating the Yankee candidate, James Jackson Storrow, in a campaign of "Manhood Against Money."[31] His successor, James Michael Curley, came into office in 1914 and raised personality politics to an entirely new level. The gregarious Irishman openly baited Boston's old blue-blood leadership, declaring that Boston needed " 'men and mothers of men, not gabbling spinsters and dog-raising matrons in federation assembled.' " The "Rascal King," who held his swearing-in ceremony in Tremont Temple, simi-larly taunted the Democratic City Committee as a "collection of chowderheads" and the Brahmin aristocracy as "clubs of female faddists" and "old gentlemen with disordered livers."[32]

Curley's counterpart in the Catholic Church was Cardinal William O'Connell. Bishop and then archbishop of Boston between 1907 and 1944, O'Connell dominated ecclesiastical politics as a shrewd administrator, centralizing diocesan control over Boston's scattered parish churches, while Curley solidified his personal rule in city hall. O'Connell was also a powerful spokesman for Catholic antimodernism, following the Vatican's policy of caution against rapid embrace of American culture.[33]

But Chapman's audiences soon discovered, to their delight, that he was easily these men's match. "The broad, heavy jaw, blue-tinged by the closely shaven beard, the straight chin and large, firm, thin-lipped mouth," an admiring reporter wrote, "give his face a look of force and determination almost brutal."[34] On the platform, Chapman preached with power and drama. "Not the typical shouting, singing, pleading, sensational revivalist," the *Globe* reporter continued, "this man depends upon simple statements straight from the shoulder [and is] as ready to laugh and joke as he is to preach and pray."[35]

Certainly the city's lackadaisical Protestant men seemed ripe for spiritual prodding. According to the 1906 federal census, male membership in each of the city's major Protestant denominations hovered around one-third, with the lowest proportion among Boston Baptists.[36] Not surprisingly, perhaps, the local Baptist paper observed in 1901 that "no fact in the life of Christian churches excites more attention or is the subject of more anxious thought than the disparity in the membership between men and women."[37]

In this regard, Chapman's efforts seemed to have paid off solidly, if not spectacularly: by the end of the crusade he tallied more male converts than female.[38] Each weekday Tremont Temple's Lorimer Hall was packed to its capacity of three thousand; its ground-level seats and balcony were filled with men taking time from their worldly affairs to attend to higher things. Although some accounts emphasized the economic and social diversity of the crowd,[39] most reports characterized the men in attendance as a solid audience of middle-class businessmen, the "substantial laymen of the greater city" and "the mainstay of Boston church life."[40]

To his noontime audiences, Chapman urged self-mastery over the stereotypically masculine sins of intemperance and adultery. "You never meant to do any wrong when you broke your marriage vows," he chided; "it was one thread around you; when you changed the figures in the books, that was a thread around you, and when you took your first social glass it was a great chord around you. You didn't mean to do wrong, but now you cannot stop yourself." Chapman was sympathetic to masculine temptation but firm in his judgment of spiritual weakness. "I am not talking to you as a preacher," he urged the men in his audience, "but as a man, and any man that dares to look me in the eye and say that he can go on and sin and stop it when he likes is saying what is wrong. He can't; the habit has gripped him."[41]

Often at this point, Chapman had the men stand to take a simple pledge. "First, with God's help I'll try to make my life better," the men promised; "second, with God's help I'll make my influence count in the church." The new convert also vowed to "keep my ears open to the cry of the needy" and to work toward civic uplift: "with God's help I'll put myself in line with every decent man in the city who is trying to make Boston better."[42]

Godliness provided the basis for a broader civic unity. "There is no difference between the man at your side who is clad in rags and yourself," Chapman told his audiences. "Don't measure yourselves by your own standard, or any one else's standard," he challenged, "but by God's standard." Even the society women on Beacon Hill heard the same message. "I preached to them as I do to you," Chapman said, "because with God there is no distinction as to sex or social position."[43]

Even the traditional divide between labor and management dissolved in Chapman's wake. On February 8, the labor activist Morrison Swift confronted Chapman in an elevator with a set of demands for workingmen. The evangelist responded the next day by asking the businessmen in the audience to provide jobs for the unemployed; ten days later, he devoted the noon meeting to "practical Christianity," focusing on the problems of many jobless men in attendance (according to one source, a third of the audience). In a meeting that featured a liberal Congregationalist and a Unitarian, no discordant notes were allowed. When a "dark-complexioned man," who, according to the *Globe* reporter, "looked like one of Swift's lieutenants," stood up to read a petition on behalf of the unemployed, Chapman told him to sit down; when the man refused, he was quickly escorted out by the police.[44]

The Mother's Prayer

In the end, however, the revival's overwhelming bond was sentimental emotion. Many observers remarked on the "great calm" of a Chapman meeting, some (but not all of them) thankful that the revivalist did not shout or scream. At the opening of the campaign, the *Globe* reported with a hint of disappointment that the "speakers were calm and conservative" and the opening addresses "dignified." "In none of the meetings," the front-page article concluded, "was anything sensational reported." Yet most descriptions of the Chapman meetings described deep pathos, which began building on Tremont Street's sidewalks before the meetings began. "It was most pathetic to hear people plead with tears for admission," a Baptist editor related, "some having come twenty, thirty, forty, fifty, or a hundred or more miles to catch the spirit, and take in the blessing." And the tears came not just from women but from grown men, and sometimes even the evangelist himself.[45]

Music played an important role in generating a common emotional experience. Early in the campaign, Chapman's sprightly colleague Charles Alexander announced to the press his aim "to get everybody in Boston singing gospel hymns."[46] He succeeded in "Alexanderizing" them, to use the popular phrase, almost immediately.[47] By the third day of the campaign, as one reporter observed, "the hymns that are sung during the meetings are being whistled on the street, and the sight of many people carrying hymn books in the street cars on their way to the service is a common one."[48] The songs were often boisterous and fun. Alexander's song-leading technique pitted groups against each other, each directed to try and outsing each other. Sometimes the competition was between different sections of the auditorium, sorted by age or by gender. "Gray-headed men vied with beardless youths," the *Globe* reported of one meeting, "in sending out a volume of tone, and the great masculine tone completely drowned out the voices of the chorus and the women."[49] But more often the songs were deeply sentimental, swelling to a high pitch during the verses and ending in a quiet hush. Chapman's crowds loved to hear familiar hymns—"Love That Will Not Let Me Go" or "Safe in the Arms of Jesus"—from male and female soloists.

But the true emotional centerpiece of Chapman's revivals was the love of a mother for her children, a quality that spoke to men but in a larger sense transcended differences of gender. Chapman did not just preach about maternal love—sometimes he exemplified it. Offering a tribute to motherhood before an audience of "aged hearers," Chapman declared, "let me mother Boston, and I will revolutionize it."[50] But most often the evangelist used maternal images to open his listeners' hearts to his message. Chapman often began his meetings with the public reading of letters received from mothers, imploring prayer for their wayward children. Then Alexander would lead a series of crusade favorites: "Where Is My Wandering Boy Tonight?" and "Tell My Mother I'll Be There." One of the favorite hymns of the campaign was "Memories of Mother," with a chorus that pleaded "O, Mother, when I think of Thee / 'Tis but a step to Calvary, Thy gentle hand upon my brow / Is leading me to Jesus now."[51] At that point Chapman would take the stage. "Was it your mother who wrote ... about her boy?" he would gently but directly demand. By now, many in the audience were all but overcome with emotion. During one service, in which Chapman preached on "the old-fashioned home," he had to stop and attend to two young men whose loud weeping was drowning out the sermon. "Come, give me your hand," Chapman beckoned. "I have seen you crying and it has made it hard for me to speak." He asked them both to commit their lives to God, "for the sake of your mothers, boys." Then Chapman turned to the crowd, urging them to "picture your sweet-faced mother, with her hair combed back and smiling tenderly upon you. Can you see her looking upon you, the child she loved? Don't sin against her, don't hurt her then."[52]

This formula was so effective, especially, but not exclusively, with male audiences, that Chapman rarely altered its content, no matter what the occasion. The climax of his midnight meetings in Boston's rowdy Scollay Square—the "psychological moment," as A. Z. Conrad phrased it—was the soloist Virginia Asher's rendition of "The Mother's Prayer." As she sang in a slow, lilting soprano, Chapman called to the down-and-outers in the crowd, "How many of you are aching to hear a woman pray?" As hands slowly raised, Mrs. Asher would offer a simple invocation, "the phrases inspired by her woman's intuition of the circumstances of those among whom she was kneeling."[53]

Clearly sentiment did not mean weakness, as was aptly demonstrated by Virginia Asher's powerfully coercive presence. If by chance a young man managed to steel himself against Chapman's entreaties in Lorimer Hall, he still had to face Mrs. Asher before he was safely outside on Tremont Street. A statuesque woman with a powerful soprano voice and a mound of snowy white hair, she was also a skilled evangelist who often canvassed Boston's red-light districts alongside her husband. In her capacity as the leader of Chapman's "personal workers," Asher stationed herself in a hallway or side room, offering help to souls in conflict as they exited from the auditorium. As one reporter noted, "almost every day she may be found in some corridor or corner of Tremont Temple talking or praying with a sobbing girl or boy, man or woman."[54] Though Asher had no children of her own, she exerted a powerful motherly presence. "If a man approaches her in a spirit of bravado or thinking to get some fun out of it," the reporter continued,

> he soon finds that he has met a real woman, absolutely sincere, entirely convinced of the truth of her message and of the need for her hearer to receive and accept the Christ she follows. She is not to be turned away by any sophistries or argument, but keeps right at her hearer until he drops his eyes, usually tear-filled, and then she has him.[55]

In turn-of-the-century American culture, motherhood came with a variety of emotional hooks for men and women alike. Two of Chapman's campaign workers, Asher and Edith Fox Norton, had lost young children. Asher and Norton both credited their decision to undertake an evangelistic career to the death of their young children. Norton, who, with her husband, supervised the campaign's "personal workers," told the press about the loss of her one-year-old daughter, Margaret. "When she went away," Norton said, "it just seemed to me as though God had called me to mother other girls, and now I feel that I want to work for two, little Margaret and myself.... My love for my baby girl has given me a love for young girls I could not [have] had without her. It has made me have a motherly feeling which I shall always have. Once a mother, always a mother."[56]

Aftermath

On the final day of the campaign, a near riot took at the Mechanics Hall as the crowd rushed inside for seats. All of the injured were women. "Women were crushed, suffocated and carried, limply unconscious or crying hysterically, from the multitude that hurled itself through the doors of the Mechanics Building," the Baptist *Watchman* reported. "Hats, furs, gloves, hymn books, purses were dropped and trampled over heedlessly. Men dragged their wives and daughters along by the arms."[57] Inside, fifty women fainted from the heat and stress of the crowd. "Others, who did not faint, but were weak from the struggle," the *Watchman* noted, "walked limply to some corner of refuge."[58]

Clearly Boston was still a long way from civic righteousness, or from genuine spiritual transformation. The revival caught a few hardened sinners—the press delighted in the testimony of a tearful carnival clown and the public conversion of the mayor of Cambridge—but for the most part, Chapman's audience was composed of at least nominal churchgoers. According to some accounts, many of the same men, including a goodly proportion of clergymen, attended Chapman's noon meetings day after day. "In the front rows on the floor," the *Boston Globe* reporter observed, "there were many familiar faces, for there are scores of men who attend these noon-day meetings regularly and usually succeed in getting desirable seats." The religious press tended to be less charitable toward these men, whom a Baptist paper dismissed as "that stall-fed type of religionist which especially abounds in Boston, who, having little to do, go anywhere and listen to anything in a perpetual abnormal craving for religious excitement." Most of the men and women who stood up to accept salvation did so repeatedly, "a regular stock company of candidates for conversion, who delight in rising at every initiation, and responding to every call, to get themselves into notoriety."[59]

In the weeks following the revival, a chorus of critics argued that any change in behavior—for the worse or the better—was only temporary. First out of the gate was the Unitarian leader Samuel Eliot, who decried the "irrational" element of mass revivalism. This charge was familiar to evangelicals, and they deflected the criticism with familiar ease.[60] But that was hardly the worst of it. In early April 1909, the Congregationalist Samuel Dike published a scathing article in the *Springfield Republican* showing that church records of Boston's past revivals—particularly the Moody one in 1877—indicated very little permanent church growth; indeed, the denominational group with the steadiest increases, the Episcopalians, were notorious nonparticipators.[61] To make matters worse, Dike repeated his charges in a meeting of the Twentieth Century Club, a gathering of men of "advanced views." In the formal study published later that year, Dike declared that the Chapman crusade had little impact on the city as a whole. "The deeper ethical concerns were not touched.

It is doubtful if the municipal reforms of our great cities are coming out of the revivals they have had."[62]

Others echoed similar doubts more quietly. Neither Park Street nor Tremont Temple saw a huge jump in new members, at least partly because of the method used to tabulate conversions. Each convert filled out a card that listed a denominational preference and a local address, and on that basis names were assigned to the closest church. But despite Tremont Temple's highly visible role in the campaign, the congregation netted only 90 names, of which only 64 became new members that year. "As there are few residences in the vicinity of the Temple," assistant pastor Charles Jeffrey reported in 1909, "we received only such cards as were specifically signed 'Tremont Temple' and for various reasons the greater number of these cards were valueless. However," he concluded magnanimously, "we heartily rejoice with some of our sister churches in the suburbs of Boston which happily received four to five hundred cards each; a large portion naturally being of promising material."[63]

Tremont Temple's experience was only the tip of the proverbial iceberg. By the time of the Chapman crusade, few knowledgeable Protestants could have denied that they were fast losing hold of Boston proper. Baptist numbers, according to an in-house study, peaked in 1898, with a total membership of 5,650. But by 1903, urban membership dropped below five thousand and by 1908 to 4,300. Even a revival campaign in 1905 was not sufficient to offset these losses.[64] According to a Congregational survey, between 1886 and 1905, membership in the five leading Congregational churches in Boston fell from 3,408 to 2,902, a loss that also reflected an average 20 percent drop in membership and 45 percent decline in benevolence contributions. By 1902, several Congregational churches, including Park Street, were close to folding.[65] Though Park Street had turned the corner by 1909, A. Z. Conrad admitted in an article first published in the *Boston Transcript* that the church, with its members scattered across twenty-two towns and cities, was "dependent largely upon local transportation facilities" for its survival; contributions from members living in Boston proper "would scarcely suffice to pay the sexton." Tremont Temple, which "owed even more to the transportation systems," was even less a local institution than Park Street. All across Boston, churches stood empty on Sunday morning. According to a survey by D. W. Waldron, " 'If three-fifths of the people of Boston [excluding infants and invalids], who are neither Jews nor Roman Catholics, should desire to attend church at the same hour on Sunday ... there would be room for them all, and 21,625 empty seats besides.' "[66]

Boston itself was undeniably Catholic. Everywhere were signs that bore out the truth of Cardinal O'Connell's famous dictum that "the Puritan has passed, the Catholic remains."[67] According to census returns, in 1890 over three-quarters of Boston's church members were Roman Catholic; by 1906, neighboring towns and suburban communities like Cambridge, Somerville, Lowell, and Lynn posted similar numbers, a sure sign of permanent economic success.[68] In contrast, two of Boston's largest Protestant denominations, Congregationalists and Baptists, each accounted for only 3.2 percent of the population.[69] Indeed, in preparing for the revival, Boston's Protestant leadership estimated the metropolitan area population at around one million, and its combined evangelical forces at a mere 120,000.[70]

The Chapman crusade was not, however, the last word. Seven years later Boston would undergo a new gospel offensive, this time from the redoubtable Billy Sunday. The Sunday campaign engaged the rhetoric of masculine citizenship, sentimental emotion, and the fight for urban righteousness at a much higher level of intensity than Chapman ever had, consciously placing the evangelist's colorful personality front and center. In the end, of course, Sunday was not any more successful than Chapman in saving Boston's soul, and his campaign only served to reinforce the unavoidable fact of Protestant exodus from the city. But in the winter of 1916–17, that hard truth was not yet inescapable.

8

Vaudeville Revivalism

Billy Sunday, 1916–1917

> Came a man to Bean Town—Billy Sunday his name,
> He sure is a corker—he merits his fame;
> He lambastes the Devil with uppercut blows,
> Slams boozers and sinners, too—high brows and lows;
> Middlesex does not care—we are here for our share—
> Good luck, Billy, God is with you.
> —Christian Endeavor Society,
> Middlesex, Massachusetts

During the seven years that elapsed between the 1909 Chapman campaign and Billy Sunday's arrival in Boston in the winter of 1916–17, American fundamentalism transformed from a mood into a movement. With the publication of the twelve-volume series *The Fundamentals* between 1910 and 1915, disgruntled conservatives assembled a full theological agenda of opposition to higher criticism, Darwinism, and liberal theology. In 1910, Presbyterian conservatives drew up a list of five essential doctrines—the inerrancy of the Bible, the virgin birth of Christ, the substitutionary atonement, the bodily resurrection, and the historicity of miracles—to rally their denomination against the inroads of modernist theology.

World War I also pushed fundamentalists into a more militant posture. Since many premillennialists believed that Christ's return was imminent, they initially opposed Woodrow Wilson's call to make the world safe for democracy; in return, liberals easily took them to task for insufficient patriotism. The modernist charges stung badly—so badly that by the end of the war, fundamentalists were rallying loudly behind the American cause and accusing their opponents, known devotees of German biblical scholarship, of open sympathy for the kaiser.[1]

The Sunday campaign was Boston's first public taste of fundamentalist-style rhetoric, served up in a very large dose. Many lesser revivalists had come and gone in the years between 1909 and 1916, but none had anything like Sunday's reputation for liberal-baiting. In contrast to the gentlemanly J. Wilbur Chapman, Sunday was crude, confrontational, and prone to overheated theatrics in the pulpit. A former member of the Chicago White Stockings who had turned to an evangelistic career after his conversion, Sunday was famous for smashing chairs and wrestling with the devil on stage. Not surprisingly, many Protestants worried that his visit to Boston would upset the carefully maintained civility that bound the city's Protestant minority together. As one Congregationalist critic complained, "the man appears like a great big water shed, simply compelling every one to take sides."[2]

The unfolding of the Sunday crusade shows that many of these fears were well grounded. As expected, Sunday offered up a regular course of polarizing rhetoric, attracting huge crowds and media attention. But as his three-week campaign drew to a close, the end results were not what most Protestants had expected. Sunday's campaign injected new energy into religious division, helping Protestants imagine themselves more and more into two warring theological camps. But he also demonstrated to evangelical Protestants their political weakness, especially around issues of moral reform in Boston. A vote on local option, which Sunday championed from his tabernacle pulpit, ended in a humiliating public defeat for temperance forces. But liberals emerged from the revival months almost reborn. In its wake, the Sunday campaign left Boston's Unitarians feeling at least, if not more, as invigorated as their conservative cousins, thoroughly glad to be unrepentent liberals.

The Power of Personality

Even before he set foot in Boston, Sunday opened divisions between liberal and conservative Protestants. More than a few received the news of Sunday's impending campaign with "ill-concealed uneasiness, if not with openly expressed distrust and distress."[3] Even some who had supported J. Wilbur Chapman in 1909 were worried about Sunday. The editor of the Methodist *Zion's Herald* pronounced the upcoming revival a "calamity," prompting a prim rejoinder from the Baptist *Watchman-Examiner* that even if the Methodists were not going to support Sunday, the Baptists and Presbyterians would, and enthusiastically.[4] "The point is not that everybody is glad of his coming," the *Watchman-Examiner* editorialized in late September—"far from that!"

It is time that the theological atmosphere up in this section of the world was cleared of some of its fogs and mists, and that men saw more plainly than many of them now do the difference between things that really differ. It would not be surprising if one of the greatest and most lasting services that Billy Sunday renders New England will prove to be the clearer and more exact delineation of doctrinal thinking and teaching.[5]

No one dreaded Sunday's arrival more than Boston's Unitarians. Many had heard press reports of an earlier revival in Colorado that had ended with an attempt to drive all the Unitarians out of town.[6] Local Unitarians also knew, thanks to a warning from the *Congregationalist*, that A. Z. Conrad had urged Sunday to "come to Boston and give some of the opposition, as you say, the devil." Some even considered mounting a counterevent of their own. In the end wiser heads prevailed; in September the *Christian Register* urged its readers to accept Sunday as a "mixed blessing." "Apart from the slight tendency to nausea which his coming may arouse in us," the article ran, "we should rejoice in the good he will do our cause . . . This vaudeville revivalist . . . will give us what we gladly welcome,—publicity."[7] Unitarian leaders, led by Samuel Eliot, president of the American Unitarian Association, announced that "they will not oppose or antagonize Sunday in any way unless he provokes them to it; that they will let him alone 'if' he will let them alone!" And this was not likely, the *Watchman-Examiner* noted with suppressed excitement, for "our friends on the other side of the doctrinal fence are doubtless in for the fight of their lives and equally doubtless they know it and are preparing for it."[8]

Many liberal and moderate Methodists and Congregationalists were equally dubious, though by the end most of them fell grudgingly into line behind the Sunday forces. The Methodist bishop Edwin H. Hughes, speaking before the Methodist Social Union in early October, reluctantly urged the liberals in his audience to "put aside all our natural mood of criticism and give Mr. Sunday a chance at Boston."[9] The Worcester Congregationalist Frederick Rouse, who had been through the rigors of a Sunday campaign at a previous church in Omaha, warned his brethren that "there is no question that the fulminations of Mr. Sunday do confirm the more conservative brethren in their narrower views; and also tend to unsettle the larger faith of some and weaken the confidence of such in the ministrations of their modern-minded pastor." Still, he advised, it is better to support Sunday than oppose him, for his ability to win souls was beyond question, and, he added, "the anxious mother of a wayward son in Boston [will not] worry much about the date of the dogma of the man whose outstretched hand wins him back to God and home and purity."[10] In the same spirit of guarded welcome, the *Congregationalist* printed an open letter to Sunday, urging him not to bait Protestant liberals and exhorting prospective "non-participants in the Sunday campaign" to sign on, even if just for the excitement the revival promised.[11]

Billy Sunday was going to be hard to avoid. By October, New Englanders in thousands of "cottage prayer" meetings were pressing God on his behalf, and men's Bible study clubs and women's service organizations were gearing up for an enthusiastic reception. In the weeks before his arrival, some twelve to fifteen hundred evangelical women fanned out across the city, visiting "stores, restaurants, hotels, laundries and factories" and inviting working women to special noon luncheon meetings at the Park Street church.[12] On October 30, the exclusive Boston City Club hosted a dinner for four hundred representatives of "big business" on behalf of the Sunday campaign; the invitation committee was headed by the governor of Massachusetts and Mayor Curley of Boston, as well as twelve other mayors representing towns around the city. A stellar array of national business and professional leaders also attended: George M. Studebaker, a pious Indiana Presbyterian and car manufacturer; Howard A. Kelly, a surgeon from Johns Hopkins University; Hugh Birkhead, an Episcopalian rector from Baltimore; Charles R. Erdman of Princeton Theological Seminary; and Hugh M. Tilroe of Syracuse University. Although no grace was said over dinner, the event came off as a ringing success. Even the Roman Catholic Mayor Curley endorsed Sunday, on the grounds that "any force that can make men better citizens and lead them to think more of the hereafter deserves the approval of right-thinking people, irrespective of race or creed."[13] "The attention of those who are inclined to belittle Mr. Sunday and his work is called to this strange phenomenon," the Baptist papers chortled, "and they are respectfully invited to explain it."[14]

Unlike Chapman, who spread his revival across the city in a simultaneous mass effort, Sunday was the central attraction of his crusade. His advance men recruited local leadership, but primarily as assistants under an experienced professional staff, not as speakers or organizers. Beginning in February 1915, Sunday's advance men held a series of publicity meetings for local business leaders and clergy, tantalizing them with stories of enormous success in other cities. But in order to reap the benefits, they would have to get to work immediately. To host a Sunday revival, Bostonians were responsible for raising some twenty thousand volunteers, including two thousand ushers, seven thousand prayer-meeting leaders, and five thousand "personal workers."[15] In addition, organizers asked contributing churches to close through the month of December, and even to cancel Sunday services the first week of the campaign.[16] All of this was designed to enhance the effectiveness of one person, Billy Sunday himself. As the Watchman-Examiner concluded in mid-January, "Billy is himself the principal and all-dominating figure, the 'head-liner,' the directing energy, the manifest power." The tabernacle was "the apex toward which all paths climb, or the reservoir into which all streams flow."[17]

Bostonians had a large physical reminder of Sunday's dominating presence. Since the city had no local auditorium big enough to hold a Sunday audience, the campaign built its own tabernacle on a site bordering the South End and the Back Bay, on Huntington Avenue. The huge structure, made of terra cotta and steel, had a seating capacity of fifteen to eighteen thousand and an acre and a half of floor space for five thousand more. Fire code regulations boosted the cost to forty-five thousand dollars, more than twice the initial estimate for the cost of the campaign. Anticipating the huge crowds, the city constructed an extra street railway track down Huntington Avenue and put up special signs directing passengers toward the Sunday Tabernacle in every subway station.[18]

At the dedication service on November 5, organized by the local chairman Allan C. Emery, a Congregationalist wholesale wool merchant, Boston's religious leaders made a brave show of unity. One by one, an Episcopalian, a Methodist, a Presbyterian, and a Congregationalist conducted brief devotional exercises; a Quaker pronounced the final benediction. But the rest of the service left no doubt about who was really in charge. The main addresses were by James E. Walker, Sunday's personal assistant, and the two local leaders of the Sunday forces, A. Z. Conrad and Cortland Myers. The congregation also participated in a litany, dedicating the tabernacle as "an inspiration to make our virile city a veritable city of God" and an instrument in "the destruction of evil in places high and low."[19]

Expectations stayed at a fever pitch throughout the next week. Sunday's supporters fasted on Thursday and continued to hold cottage prayer meetings on Monday and Wednesday. Two huge revival choruses, composed of a total of forty-five hundred representatives for all of the participating churches, practiced in the tabernacle. Five hundred secretaries and fifteen hundred ushers prepared to greet the crowds and keep a running tally of converts. "Everything is now ready for the campaign," the Methodist *Zion's Herald* reported on November 8. "The churches are thoroughly organized; personal workers have been faithfully trained; the prayers of the Christian communities have been fervent and earnest. And Boston and New England are waiting for a spiritual awakening during the next ten weeks under the leadership of Mr. Sunday."[20]

Bostonians were, of course, prepared for Sunday's arrival in other ways as well: on any given Sunday, they could have witnessed pulpit antics similar to Sunday's by the city's leading conservative pastors. When Cortland Myers arrived at Tremont Temple in 1909, his skill in "the art of legitimate sensationalism" and strident, topical Sunday evening sermons attracted huge crowds. During his tenure, some five hundred to one thousand people were regularly turned away from the evening meetings in Lorimer Hall.[21] Over at the Park Street Church, Arcturus Zodiac Conrad held forth in a similar manner in his Sunday evening question-and-answer session. At his death, the local press remembered Conrad—somewhat fondly—as "a man of few doubts" whose "natural inclinations were to attack" if controversy promised a larger audience.[22]

It's not surprising, then, that many Bostonians eagerly awaited Sunday's arrival. When the evangelist disembarked from the Twentieth Century Limited at Boston's South Station on Saturday, November 11, the waiting crowd quickly turned into a parade and escorted him all the way to his temporary home on Commonwealth Avenue.[23] For the next three weeks, Sunday and his entourage would stay in the family home of ex-governor John Davis Long, a few blocks' walk from the tabernacle. Sunday was accompanied by his wife, casually known to thousands of Americans as "Ma Sunday," his son George acting as business manager, James Walker, his advance man, and his popular song leader Homer Rodeheaver. The Baptist papers enthusiastically described "Sunday's people" as "wide awake, well fed, good dressers, jolly"; they were "just a lot of good-looking people such as one would be likely to meet on the golf links, or driving an automobile, or in the draw-room, but whose high spirits and 'pep' have been consecrated to kingdom purposes and work."[24]

The rest of Sunday's assistants were women, all of them thoroughly experienced organizers. Virginia Asher, who had assisted Chapman in 1909, was back to lead in "extension work." Grace Saxe led a three o'clock Bible study every afternoon in the tabernacle, Alice Gamlin directed work with young children, and Florence Kinney organized meetings for local college students. Frances Miller, known as the "female Billy Sunday," held lunch meetings at the Park Street Church three times a week for five hundred to one thousand shop girls and secretaries working in the downtown area. A team of local women, led by Grace Coleman Lathrop, organized two thousand volunteers to supply the five-cent lunches. "No organization connected with the Sunday campaign," the *Globe* announced in early January, "is doing finer work with less confusion" than those connected with the businesswomen's work. Miller's team also assembled two hundred volunteers and sent them out in pairs to canvass all of the offices and stores in the vicinity of Park Street, inviting the female clerks and stenographers to attend the luncheons.[25]

Unitarians

Sunday's Boston campaign began on Sunday, November 12; his three meetings were attended by a total of some forty-eight thousand people, with another twelve thousand turned away. To the disappointment of some, and the relief of others, he started slowly, preaching in a powerful but controlled manner and ending each service without the customary altar call. "He laid aside his athletic gyrations and his slang," the *Boston Herald* reported, "and he talked to them as minister to minister. He led them through the tortuous paths of theology. He got acquainted with them, and they with him; and when he had finished they applauded."[26] Herbert Atchison Jump, writing to his fellow Congregationalists, reported that "Boston now has had her first amazing taste of Billy Sunday, and she is not at all disliking the taste. She is for the moment smiling good-naturedly," though "shuddering a bit now and then up over old Beacon Hill and out Brookline way." Sunday himself was pleased with his initial reception, declaring, "You can't beat Boston for open-mindedness, enthusiasm, and appreciativeness. The audiences today didn't miss a Biblical or historical reference. Nothing got by them, in-curve, out-shoot, or spit-ball."[27]

Then Sunday moved on to the Unitarians. On Monday afternoon, he addressed a meeting at the Second Unitarian Church on Beacon Street, convened by the Boston Association of pastors. The evangelist was there in response to an olive branch tendered the previous October, but all bets were off on his behavior. Scores of Boston's leading liberals and a full contingent of the local press were on hand, hoping for a story to take back home. But Sunday disappointed them all, sticking close to his printed manuscripts and punctuating the address with his trademark charismatic smile. "Straight-out theology it was," Herbert Jump reported, "Hodge, Shedd and the Westminster Confession accepted in their entirety," but also some conciliatory words on the Social Gospel and a few self-deprecating jokes about evolution.[28] The meeting concluded with thunderous applause, after a brief word from Ma Sunday, and a solo by Homer Rodeheaver. The presiding pastor offered a motion of thanks to Billy, and those present carried it by unanimous vote.[29]

Initially, at least, some Unitarians were cautiously sympathetic toward the revival campaign, if not to Sunday himself. "As far as I could judge," moderator James Huxtable concluded, "the ministers present were glad to hear Mr. Sunday,—glad to shake hands with him, and glad of the opportunity to study him at close range."[30] Some were even openly curious about his proven success. "We have the best set of brains I know of," the Brookline pastor Thomas Van Ness commented afterward, "and can say things in the best way.... What is the matter, then, when we come to act? We spend too much time in general criticism. We should get more cooperation."[31] Samuel Eliot similarly concluded that "our churches should take advantage of the tides of religious interest which are sweeping through New England to proclaim ... a pure, rational and spiritual Christianity; but we do not think that this work should be undertaken in any spirit of antagonism or of controversy."[32]

Still, throughout the winter of 1916–17, Boston lived under the constant threat of religious strife. Newspaper editors, from both the secular and Protestant press, watched anxiously for signs of division and cheered on all signs of good behavior. Editorials probed the roots of Sunday's appeal, analyzed his methods, and kept tabs on the mounting numbers of converts. No one, except for Cardinal O'Connell, who forbade Catholics to attend, ventured an outright condemnation.

Both the secular and religious press devoted columns of print to explaining Sunday's appeal. Class-conscious Boston wondered whether the evangelist was simply pandering to uneducated working people, manipulating them into conversion with lurid oratory. One account in the *Boston Evening Transcript* painted a particularly distressing scene in which "young men, pale as death, or green with horror," fainted under the ghastly spell of Sunday's sermon on "booze." "What sort of man would hit the trail at the end of such an outpour of awfulness was a most interesting question," the correspondent wrote. "Sunday's Sunday night audience was of a pretty good class, as far as the eye could estimate," including delegations from the Shawmut Bank and American Express and workingmen from other businesses—"of an unusually intelligent type for the Tabernacle." But few of these people came forward for the altar call. "It was the bottom crust of the audience, if not from underneath it," that streamed forward to shake Sunday's hand. "There were queer strange-looking waifs and swarthy human curiosities. Some of the faces wore a sly smile, as if their owners were coming forward from mere curiosity, for the joke of it."[33]

Still, in the early weeks of Sunday's campaign, most of Boston was a bit baffled, if not reluctantly charmed, by the evangelist's prowess. Sunday's press accounts, though not as glowing as Chapman's, mixed enthusiasm with caution; with the Unitarians temporarily at bay, Sunday's next move was a mystery.

The Battle against Booze

Bostonians would not have to wait long for an answer. In late November, Sunday took the lead in a political fight over the prohibition of alcohol, in a highly contested vote for local option. Since 1906, a licensing board had full control over the expansion of the city's saloon trade. By law, the board could grant one license for every five hundred inhabitants of the city, though never more than a thousand licenses in all. As the city's population began drifting outward into the suburbs, the board stopped granting licenses altogether, and as a result liquor licenses within Boston's city limits were hard to come by and increasingly valuable; in 1915 a dealer could surrender his license to a new-comer for as much as nineteen thousand dollars. Bankruptcy courts and creditors reckoned a liquor license a financial asset.[34]

Every December, the city held a vote on license; in 1916 Boston's businessmen were well aware that Sunday was going to be trouble. Warnings began to circulate the first week of the campaign, and on December 11, the president of the Real Estate Exchange sent a letter to all of its members, alerting them to impending catastrophe.[35] A front-page advertisement in the local papers argued that the city stood to lose over $1.4 million in yearly license fees if no-license passed. Prohibition would put ten thousand people out of work and affect one hundred million dollars' worth of real estate properties where liquor was sold.[36] In response, former governor Eugene S. Foss took out a front-page advertisement in the *Boston Evening Transcript* offering a $1 million bond to offset any such losses, and jobs for all unemployed saloon-workers.[37]

In the early going, Boston's temperance forces had reason to be optimistic. Just a few weeks before he came to Boston, Billy Sunday had held a crusade in Fall River, the third largest city in Massachusetts. Shortly afterward the city voted no-license in an election campaign incorporating many new voters, presumably recent converts from Sunday's crusade.[38] Evangelical leaders expected similar results in Boston. At their urging, Sunday started a regular round of meetings for "men only" several days ahead of his customary campaign schedule, on November 30. At this service, as everyone knew in advance, Sunday would offer his very first "trailhitting" invitation to converts, the surefire dramatic peak of every campaign. Despite a driving rain, every seat in the "Gospel Shed" was filled that night, including vast tracts reserved for church brotherhoods and men's Bible classes. "And all men!" the *Watchman-Examiner* exulted. "Not a woman in the lot! Not a touch of feminine finery or a touch of the bright colors of feminine dress to break the monotony and liven up the dull black and white and gray of men's attire! It was certainly a great sight to see an acre and a half of unbroken masculinity stretching away from the platform in every direction."[39]

Sunday did not disappoint. After the men had sung, clapped, waved flags, and announced the various delegations present, the evangelist set to work. "It was plainly evident," the *Watchman-Examiner* reported, "that this was not mere effervescence of high animal spirits or thoughtless horseplay, but the deep enthusiasm of earnest men pervaded by a serious purpose." Indeed, "everybody felt that the invitation to 'hit the trail' would be given before the evening was over, and everybody was getting ready for it." At the crest of his oratory, sweat streaming off his face, Sunday stood on a chair, with one foot on his pulpit. In ringing tones, he imagined himself as the Scottish warrior Douglas casting the heart of Robert the Bruce into the midst of the Saracens, urging his forces into battle. "Men," he thundered, "I seize the cross of the Son of God, and I wave it over this audience! I hurl the heart of the Saviour out into the ranks of the manhood of Boston, and as I do I cry, 'Lead on, O Christ, and we will follow!' Will you do it? Will you follow? Will you follow? Stand up if you will!"[40]

The scene that followed, according to the *Watchman-Examiner*, was "indescribable." Cheers and applause filled the tabernacle, as thousands of men, tears streaming down their faces, rose to their feet and shouted as one, "We will! We will!" Sunday silenced the tumult with an uplifted hand. "How many of you will say 'Yes,' I will go with you, Bill'?" he demanded. "How many of you will come up here and give me your hand and say, 'I will live for Christ from this time on'? Come on men! Come on!" As Homer Rodeheaver played "Stand Up for Jesus," the men surged forward to shake Sunday's hand and sign the convert's pledge. The final count, some 1,440 trailhitters, was a record for a first-time invitation.[41]

On December 10, Sunday gave his famous "booze sermon," a campaign staple billed "for men only." "Get on the Water Wagon" was a graphic, heart-wringing portrayal of the liquor trade, an hour and forty minutes long. In print it is a fairly ordinary litany of facts and figures, human-interest stories, humorous anecdotes and weepy, pathetic tales of drunken fathers and their powerless victims. But when Sunday delivered it from the stage, the effect was irresistible. "Again and again," one witness recalled,

> his audience broke out in applause and cheers, and as he hurled his defiance at the whole liquor crowd who, he said, had threatened his life and the lives of his family from the Atlantic to the Pacific, those thousands of men rose in a body with their hats waving over their heads and cheered him to the echo.

At the climax of his address, Sunday called nine boys onto the platform, and as he waved an American flag over their heads, he cried: "'There is the raw material of the saloon. It has to have two million recruits a year to keep its infernal business running. Are we going to pay our taxes in *boys*?' And the crowd thundered, '*No, no!*'"[42]

As Election Day approached, Sunday continued to hammer away at the liquor trade. Local clergy distributed special admission tickets to "doubtful" voters in East Boston, South Boston, and Dorchester, all districts they needed to carry to win.[43] On December 18, Sunday preached a sermon entitled "The Trail of the Serpent" to twenty-five thousand men, working so hard that his clothing dripped with perspiration. "In figure," the *Boston Evening Transcript* reported, "he grabbed the saloon, threw it in the air, turned it inside out, 'walloped' it, stood it on its head, threw it down and trampled it into a shapeless mass."[44] That night, ex-governor Eugene Foss stood among the trailhitters at the close of the sermon. "Swinging his stick and carrying his hat with one hand," Foss was hardly a picture of abject repentance. When he reached the front of the line, Sunday "ruffled the ex-Governor's hair as he patted his apprecation."[45]

As moral fervor continued to mount, evangelicals grew hopeful about the prospects for the election, which looked to remain close. "We shall win," the Baptist papers predicted,

> if that part of Boston which considers itself most respectable, and insists that saloons be kept out of its territory, does as well as what are commonly called the cheaper sections.... If Dorchester and the Back Bay do as well as Charlestown and South Boston, there is no doubt of the truth. And Mr. Sunday is undoubtedly lining up these people.[46]

But, in fact, the opposite was true. The election was a huge victory for the "wet" forces, by a margin of 53,431 to 30,380. Only three districts of the city—Hyde Park, Brighton, and Jamaica Plain—voted dry; all the rest stood against prohibition. Even more humiliating, the wet vote was some seven thousand votes larger than in the previous year's election. "It is hardly apparent," the *Transcript* concluded, "how the no-license forces can extract even a grain of comfort from the decisive showdown on the liquor question which the Boston polls have flashed over the country." The embarrassing defeat was news everywhere.[47]

"Looks bad, does it not?" the *Watchman-Examiner* admitted in a sober postmortem editorial. "Well, it is bad!"[48] And the worst part of the defeat—even worse than Sunday's being labeled a "good loser" by the secular press—was the obvious irrelevance of the Sunday campaign to the election's outcome.[49] Weeks of strenuous preaching had finally come to nothing.

In the wake of their disappointment, some evangelical leaders resorted to anti-Catholic rhetoric. Cortland Myers got into a platform wrangle with A. Z. Conrad, charging that Catholic priests had urged their people to vote no-license out of jealousy for the Sunday campaign's success. The two had to be forcibly broken up by Ma Sunday. But in fact, Catholic leaders generally stayed away from the election, sensing little to be gained from bringing victory to the Sunday forces.[50]

But the election did make it clear that, politically, evangelical Protestants had almost no power in the city of Boston. "The churches are in large degree supported and manned by suburbanites," the *Watchman-Examiner* concluded, and a "considerable number of the ministers live outside the city." Indeed, "of the fifty-seven members of the Boston Sunday campaign committee, thirty-seven . . . hold their legal and voting residence in other towns or cities than Boston." Most of those weeping trailhitters at the Sunday meetings, as it turned out, were ineligible to vote in the election in the first place. Since most of Boston's surrounding towns had been dry since the 1880s, it also seemed likely that most of those ostensible converts were only there for the show, not for any real moral improvement.[51]

The Sunday campaign recovered from this humiliating loss with considerable difficulty. A series of heavy snowstorms and the pressures of the Christmas holiday kept the crowds small during the following week. By December 22, when numbers had dropped as low as five hundred, an eavesdropping *Globe* reporter came across an impromptu meeting of frantic local clergy, gathered below the platform and urging each other in panicked whispers not to "say anything" about the vote and to "hush that up" if questions arose.[52]

The limits of Sunday's appeal, even among surburbanites, were also becoming more evident, according to a December 29 eyewitness account in the *Transcript*. The tabernacle services usually included a time for church and business delegations to announce themselves. "Men and women from Newton Centre, from Marlboro, men from Boston & Albany Railroad, men and women from other places and organizations, came forward at Mr. Sunday's call from the top of his pulpit," the correspondent related. "Then he swung his arms and called for the Brookline people, who were in the Tabernacle as an identified body. 'Come on you men of Brookline!' Mr. Sunday shouted, 'Line up for God! Come on Brookline! Are you coming? Last call!' But no one came." Brookline, a prosperous nearby suburb with, as was duly noted, three Unitarian churches, was immune to Sunday's spell. "Everyone knows that Brookline represents the top notch of Massachusetts culture.... Can it be possible," the reporter wondered, "that Mr. Sunday is losing his grip on his audience?"[53]

Still, by the time the campaign wound up on January 22, 1917, few would have denied it was a success. On the closing night, Sunday preached to a crowd of sixty thousand on the "death scene of an unbeliever," and brought a record 5,196 penitents to the stage.[54] All told, Boston remained one of Sunday's best efforts, breaking every previous record for attendance. Tabernacle attendance topped 1.3 million, and tabernacle trailhitters sixty thousand. After a slow start, Bostonians donated over ninety thousand dollars to meet the campaign's expenses, including over fifty thousand dollars in one lump sum.[55] "Boston's batting average for God is 900," Sunday announced in the waning hours of the crusade. "She's not behind in history or culture or hospitality, baseball—or religion. She trails nobody in anything. Goodnight, old Scout."[56]

That Old-Time Arianism

The true results of any revival crusade are always difficult to gauge. None of Sunday's backers expressed open disappointment, even after the failure of the prohibition vote. Indeed, by early January, Roger Babson, a Congregationalist observer, was already noting changes for the better all across the city. "Every one is more serious," he wrote. "Clerks are more interested in their work; factory hands are more desirous to increase production; everyone seems to be more anxious to be of use and to tell the truth than ever before." Customers were more patient in long lines, Babson noted, and commuters less apt to push and shove on the trains.[57] For a time, at least, religion was front-page news in Boston, and the coverage was generally positive.

Certainly, the Sunday crusade was a major victory for Boston's Baptists, who congratulated themselves as the "wheel horse" of the local Sunday team. According to campaign statistics, Baptist trailhitters numbered 11,845; Methodists trailed a distant second at 7,104; and Congregationalists came in third with 6,195.[58] Most of the converts, as everyone knew, were nominal churchgoers seeking an opportunity for reconsecration, but local congregations still stood a chance to benefit richly from the crusade; campaign staffers duly recorded their denominational preferences and forwarded the information to the local church that was geographically closest to the penitent's home. But all told, Sunday did not leave religious harmony in his wake. "Boston has not been shaken to its foundations," the *Congregationalist* concluded on February 8, blaming the presence of "three great indifferent or hostile religious bodies, the Roman Catholic Church, the Christian Science Church and the Unitarian churches."[59]

No doubt, by the time he left Boston, Billy Sunday had stirred up Protestants of all theological stripes. While a few steadfastly attempted to ignore the entire affair, their absence went largely unnoticed. Conservatives cheered his "scathing invective" and "fiery denunciation." "Dogmatism," wrote Joseph Kennard Wilson, the associate editor of the *Watchman-Examiner*, "has had a new and needed vindication." Cortland Myers agreed: "The theological atmosphere has been clarified. Men know what they believe now, and know what other men believe." "One likes Billy Sunday," Nathan Wood declared. "I think, unless one is a saloonkeeper, or a Christian Scientist, or a drifter from the cross and the Word, one cannot help loving him."[60] In keeping with this new spirit of theological clarification, on January 25, the *Watchman-Examiner* announced the beginning of a twelve-part series comparing the "Old and New Theologies" and attempting to answer questions such as "Who are the 'Evangelicals and the Non-Evangelicals'?" and "Who are the 'Conservatives' and the 'Liberals'?"

But Sunday also energized liberals. Throughout the campaign, Unitarian churches across New England featured sermon topics that highlighted their differences with evangelical revivalism. In late January, for example, Unitarian clergy preached on "Salvation and Social Service," setting in "definite contrast the two goals at which orthodox and liberal churches of religion respectively aim." "Boston has heard (and all New England has read) during the past ten weeks a great deal of the appeal to men to save their own individual souls from perdition, and to do this by acceptance of a dogmatic creed," the *Christian Register* noted. "Against the dark background of this reassertion of mediaeval theology and the kind of fear that belongs with the dark ages our ministers have set forth the white figure of truth in the radiating light of hope and unselfishness."[61]

On February 4, Unitarians held what the local Baptist press characterized as a "monster mass rally" at Symphony Hall. The Sunday crusade had given them, they believed, a unique opportunity to step up efforts at "liberal evangelism," highlighting their distinct emphases on "broad-mindedness" and the importance of the "inner spiritual life."[62] In the final weeks of the Sunday campaign, Unitarian clergy distributed five thousand tickets for the meeting, despite the fact that Symphony Hall could only accommodate three thousand. On the night of the rally, overflow crowds filled the Horticultural Hall across the street and Edward Hale's South Congregational Church nearby. They began with a joyous hymn sing and then heard addresses by President-Emeritus Eliot of Harvard, Robert Luce, the ex–lieutenant governor, and Dr. William L. Sullivan of New York.

The platform leadership was careful to set a positive tone. In his opening address, Charles Eliot reminded the enthusiastic crowd:

> We have come hither in mass, first, to rejoice and give thanks for our deliverance from all the creeds, confessions, and dogmas of the older

churches and denominations ... and to congratulate each other that we are able to reverence all saintly lives and to treat with respect all sincere religious beliefs no matter how different the beliefs may be from our own, and no matter how different from our own may be the external manifestations of saintliness.[63]

The *Christian Register* pronounced the meeting, and its enthusiastic aftermath, an "epoch in our Unitarian movement" and its largest single gathering ever. "With its spirit of enthusiasm coupled with reverence, with its broad tolerance coupled with the fearless utterance of truth, its splendid proclamation of service and character as essentials of religion, it was the best possible answer to the recent revival."[64] The accompanying statement denying that the meeting was in any sense "an opposition to the Sunday revival" was met by Baptists with some suspicion. "There are not many people," the *Watchman-Examiner* rejoined a bit sourly, "who will be quite ready to believe that this coming meeting has not been arranged just at this time with the strategic purpose of counteracting whatever effect has been produced in the Unitarian constituency by the tabernacle campaign."[65]

But Unitarians themselves saw the spirit of the post-Sunday meetings as entirely positive. A letter-writer to the *Christian Register* from Sacramento, California, confessed to being "profoundly stirred" by recent events. If Unitarianism were to survive, he said, it needed such a fresh declaration rejecting both "present-day orthodoxy" and the "old-time Arianism." Indeed, by late January the Boston Ministerial Union requested a talk by Frances Greenwood Peabody, Unitarianism's leading advocate of Social Christianity, on "preaching power." Though most Unitarians had experienced the Sunday revival as "a campaign of theological frightfulness," Peabody admitted, few could deny his power—a quality well worth imitating. "Never was it so plain," declared the former Harvard professor, "that a great, unoccupied fertile area of modern life is waiting for a free gospel."[66]

Despite his best efforts, Billy Sunday did not save Boston, either from liquor or from itself. Still, in its galvanizing effect, the Sunday revival was a signal event in the history of fundamentalism in Boston. The crusade cleared the air, like a violent summer thunder-shower, and helped Boston's Protestants visualize both their theological allies and their enemies. But permanent division between fundamentalists and liberals was relatively slow to form within Boston's denominational structure.

The story of Park Street Church, told in the following chapter, demonstrates the expanding geographical range of an emerging conservative Protestant coalition. In the 1930s, Boston-style orthodoxy, originating at Brimstone Corner, would become key not to the city's renewal but to a national movement set to redeem the entire nation.

9

Brimstone Corner

Park Street Church

The Devil and a Gale of Wind
Danced Hand in hand up Winter Street.
The Devil like his demons grinned
To have for comrade so complete
A rascal and a mischief-maker
Who'd drag an oath from any Quaker.

The Wind made sport of hats and hair
That ladies deemed their ornament;
With skirts that frolicked everywhere
Away their prim decorum went;
And worthy citizens lamented
The public spectacles presented.

The Devil beamed with horrid joy,
Til to the Common's rim they came,
Then chuckled, "Wait you here, my boy,
For duties now my presence claim
In yonder church on Brimstone Corner
Where Pleasure's dead and lacks a mourner;

"But play about till I come back."
With that he vanished through the doors,
And since that day the almanac
Has marked the years by tens and scores,

Yet never from those sacred portals
Returns the Enemy of Mortals.

And that is why the faithful Gale
Round Park Street Corner still must blow,
Waiting for him with horns and tail—
At least some people tell me so—
None of your famous antiquarians,
But just some wicked Unitarians.

—Mark Antony DeWolfe Howe,
"A Legend of Brimstone Corner"

Park Street Congregational Church came into being on February 27, 1809, at three o'clock in the afternoon, in a mansion at the top of Beacon Hill. One hundred years later, Deacon Chauncey Brewer reminded a celebratory audience of their distinguished New England bloodlines. Not only was the new congregation's "grandsire" Boston's First Church and "its mother the venerated Old South" but "its birthplace was Boston, the intellectual center of a new republic which was commanding the attention of the world."[1]

Park Street's original members certainly believed their church was born for great things. Convinced of their calling to set a new standard for Protestant orthodoxy, they set out to make the mission known to every passer-by. "'We laid our plan on a very grand scale,'" a charter member recalled. "'Our meeting house must be larger and higher than any other in the city.'" They calibrated their steeple to rise 217 feet, making it just visibly higher than the golden dome of the Massachusetts State House, sitting a block or so away at the top of Beacon Hill.[2]

Despite its auspicious beginnings, however, Park Street took almost a century and a half to fulfill its early promise. Though physically favored with a location on one of Boston's most famous street corners, the young congregation was long overshadowed by the Baptist zeal of its nearby neighbor Tremont Temple, and often hampered by ineffective or erratic clergymen. In fact, as Park Street Church approached its one-hundred-year mark, the congregation seemed near death. But by the 1930s, the relative status of Boston's two largest conservative churches had begun to reverse: Tremont Temple was losing members as its Congregational neighbor's fortunes turned for the better. By the 1940s, Park Street—not Tremont Temple—assumed the defining role in New England's evangelical resurgence, a movement that would have a profound and lasting effect on the direction of conservative Protestant faith across the United States.

Orthodoxy

Orthodoxy was at the core of Park Street's destiny. The church's original members were refugees from William Ellery Channing's First or Federal Street Church—known as a hotbed of Unitarianism—and Congregationalists from Old South. This core group, many of whom had been spiritually prodded by a revival among the Baptists, came from a women's prayer circle yearning for a larger religious awakening in Boston. Despite Deacon Brewer's assertions, the young congregation was more abandoned foundling than cherished offspring: both Old South and Federal Street declined to help with the required procedural steps for constituting a new church body. "There was not a single church in Boston," one supporter later recounted, "that would countenance their purpose."[3]

The early nineteenth century was a difficult time for the heirs of New England's Puritans. Though the revivals of the eighteenth century renewed the experiential faith of many a lagging church member, they forced a theological wedge between orthodox Congregationalists and the Unitarian defenders of "rational religion." Not without cause, many tended to regard as dangerous emotional excess what some saw as authentic spiritual zeal. In 1805, when Harvard College appointed the Unitarian Henry Ware to be the Hollis Professor of Divinity, the orthodox felt beleaguered in their own precincts, and established the alternative Andover Seminary in 1808. But the stakes of the growing divide were not just theological. In Massachusetts, where church parishes traditionally included all of the tax-paying citizens of a town, doctrinal disputes could easily lead to a battle over property rights, one that the orthodox did not always win. In Dedham in 1820, when the surrounding parish voted in a liberal pastor, the regularly attending members refused to accept him. Despite the fact that most of the parish voters rarely darkened the door of the church on Sundays, the Massachusetts court denied the dissenting members ownership of their own church building. In the end, Dedham found itself with two churches, one Unitarian and one Congregationalist, directly across the street from each other, their separate congregations filing defiantly into opposite front doors every Sunday morning. Weary of the confrontation, or perhaps still angry, the Unitarians moved their main entrance around the corner, facing onto a side street.[4]

Park Street's first members were consciously wary of takeover. Guarding against the possibility that their new church might someday fall into Unitarian hands, the men in Park Street's original group designated themselves as trustees with sole ownership of all of the property in question. Then they armed themselves for theological battle. In his dedication sermon, Edward Dorr Griffin, the president of Andover Seminary and Park Street's first pastor, declared: "This house, though not raised for controversial discussions, has been built by those who esteem it far from indifferent what doctrine a man believes."[5]

A. Z. Conrad wrote that the young church "had practically no childhood." Within two years, the new congregation had a fine building, a highly respected pastor, and an indebtedness that was only partially offset by the sale of pews in 1810.[6] Park Street's early years also saw escalating economic tensions with England, turmoil over a federally imposed embargo, and then war. With the Boston Brigade practicing drills just a few yards away over on the Common, the new congregation enthusiastically took on patriotic responsibilities as well. In a move that later become part of the church's local legend, Park Street offered its basement for storage of the brimstone used to manufacture gunpowder.[7]

In the early nineteenth century, the church became a local hub of moderate Protestant social reform. Lyman Beecher's son Edward was pastor from 1826 to 1830 and a leading opponent of slavery, hosting the famous abolitionist William Lloyd Garrison in 1829. Both of these men, however, became much more outspoken in the years after they left Park Street. Garrison announced his conversion to immediate abolition the following year. Beecher left Park Street in 1830 to become president of Jacksonville College in Illinois, where he gradually abandoned the doctrines of total depravity and original sin and became a social radical. As a convinced abolitionist, he stood with the doomed Eliza Lovejoy when a murderous mob destroyed his printing press in 1837.[8]

Park Street also lent its prestige to new religious causes. Its members raised passage money for the first missionaries hired by the American Board of Commissioners for Foreign Missions, and helped organize the first church of converted Hawaiians a few years later. The American Peace Society, formed in 1828, held its annual meetings at Park Street; in 1849 the church's rafters rang to a stirring oration by Massachusetts state senator Charles Sumner. The list of spiritual and cultural accomplishments is long: Park Street hosted the formation of the American Education Society in 1815, the Prison Reform Society in 1824, and in 1826 the American Missionary Association and the American Temperance Society.[9] In 1817 the church opened one of the first Sunday schools in Boston, having already begun a prestigious "singing school" in 1810. A church service on July 4, 1831, saw the first performance of the patriotic hymn "America," composed by Park Street's music director, Samuel Francis Smith.

By midcentury, Park Street's respectability was beyond question. Membership was approaching nine hundred, and the sanctuary was regularly filled with "prominent citizens" from neighboring Beacon Hill, Tremont Street, and the newly built Back Bay.[10] Bostonians knew and admired Park Street's high standards in its impeccable choice of clergymen, its tasteful music program, and its elegant colonial building. While Tremont Temple supplemented its income with storefronts on the first floor, Park Street met its own

FIGURE 9.1. Park Street Interior. From *Twenty Fifth Anniversary, Pastorate of Rev. A. Z. Conrad, Ph.D., D.D.* (Boston, Mass: Park Street Church, 1930).

financial challenges more quietly. Not many knew that a large part of the space in its renovated basement was being sold off to provide space for private burial crypts (see fig. 9.1).

A People's Church?

By the post–Civil War era, Park Street was becoming far more constrained by its social reputation than by evangelistic zeal. The problem became painfully clear in 1868, when the congregation called William Henry Harrison Murray as its pastor. Some fifty years after the fact, Chauncey Brewer described him diplomatically as a man of "eloquent tongue and attractive personality," but Murray's contemporaries might have used different adjectives. Fond of fly fishing and fast horses, Murray cut a dashing, and controversial, figure, coursing through the streets of Boston in his racing trap, an expensive cigar clenched between his teeth. But the handsome young pastor's most troubling aspect was his populist style. Though he "caught the attention of the city and filled the pews to overflowing" with "the curious from near and far," his own congregation did not welcome their spot in the public limelight.[11] Murray was not afraid to insist, even to secular audiences, that Boston's Protestant churches had sunk into a "deplorable state of semi-heathenism." In a lecture series given across the street from Park Street Church at the Music Hall in

1869, Murray urged the well-heeled orthodox to end their "splendid seclusion" and open their doors to all. "Let the wealthiest and the poorest, the strongest and the weakest, the taught and the untaught, worship side by side," he declared. Murray did not lack for suggestions on specifics, urging his fellow clergy to "doff [their] clerical robes and don the blue uniform." A few months walking a police beat in the North End was, in his view, essential training for anyone with an ambition for the ministry. In one unmistakable dig at Park Street's well-funded foreign missionary program, Murray publicly derided churches more interested in the "benighted heathen on some far-distant shore" than in the "men and women living and dying at our very side." "I am not so anxious for the Christianization of Pekin and Calcutta," he declared, "as I am for the Christianization of Boston."[12]

As if that were not enough to rile his congregation, Murray lambasted Park Street's deacons for their dry, loveless orthodoxy and publicly criticized his church for ignoring the needs of Boston's poor. He took particular issue with the pew-rent system. When "a pew in God's house can be speculated in like railroad stock, and change three hundred per cent in market value within five years," and "the poor who live and struggle and die within sight of its steeple have *not* the Gospel preached to them," the spiritual problem was obvious. Murray also demanded in a published open letter that his congregation hire an assistant to help him carry out this task. How could any "but the stupid or thoughtless," Murray queried, "expect any one man to carry the burden alone?"[13]

He did not have to wonder long. Under pressure from his disgruntled deacons, Murray resigned from Park Street in 1874. He did not, however, leave quietly. With nine dissidents—a number that later grew to 145—the charismatic young pastor formed another congregation across Tremont Street in the Music Hall. The New England Church was to be a "metropolitan church," an independent congregation characterized by a "liberal evangelical theology" and "unsectarian policy." Under the spell of Murray's preaching and a vigorous music program that featured congregational singing and an enormous choir, the new church grew so quickly that by 1875 the congregation purchased land and began planning a new building with a seating capacity of four thousand. But then, in 1878, Murray received a year's leave for a fundraising tour and simply disappeared. A few failed business ventures later, and after his wife filed divorce proceedings, the dashing pastor's religious career was effectively over.[14]

But Murray's departure did not mark the end of Park Street's troubles. Determined not to hire another grandstander, the church ended up with a series of capable but relatively lackluster pastors. John Withrow, David Gregg, and Isaac Lansing might have served well in other times, but, especially before the subway system was finished in 1897, they were hard pressed to stem the flow of congregants to Boston's streetcar suburbs. Obscured for several years behind an ugly network of scaffolding as construction crews dug subway tunnels into the Common, Park Street could hardly compete with Lorimer's eloquence at Tremont Temple or Gordon's spiritual appeal at Clarendon Street (see figure 9.2). Even worse, the pew-rent system, which both Lorimer and Gordon's churches had abandoned, eroded the church's financial status; every member who left a Park Street pew for a suburban one took away substantial revenue from the annual budget. In 1894 the congregation was forced to remodel its basement to include retail space (the crypts were quietly removed), and within a few years, Park Street, sporting a florist shop and a fruit vendor, looked at street level much like Tremont Temple. But even with this new source of income, the congregation had to cut Lansing's salary in 1896, and, seeing no real future for the church in the city, he soon left for a more stable pulpit.[15]

The hazards of church rentals, a story already familiar to Tremont Temple's members, soon became clear at Park Street. In 1901, the church opened its sanctuary to a holiness convention, co-led by Seth Rees and the Portsmouth (New Hampshire) Campmeeting Association, and John Pennington and the Salvation Army. The congregation quickly regretted its hospitality. "There was dancing, men embracing on the platform, leaping, enthusiastic hollering, vociferous songs," a *Globe* reporter related, "and a perfect babble of prayer, where a score or more were all at once and nobody first, in all sorts of positions, from the most humble salaam to the erect position, with hands outstretched to heaven to receive the blessing." In the midst of the uproar,

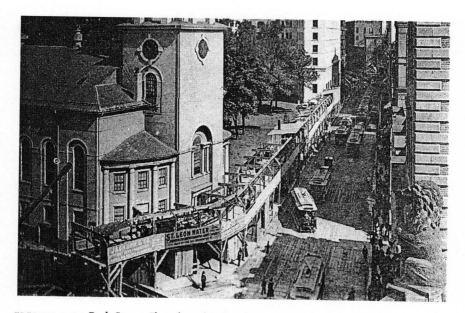

FIGURE 9.2. Park Street Church and Subway Construction. From Park Street Church Records, Congregational Library, Boston, Mass.

Reverend Withrow stormed the stage and rescinded the invitation, though he was already too late to save his church's reputation. The *Globe* reporter noted that Withrow had been forced to respond after receiving complaints from some Unitarians in the neighborhood, put off by the noise and hubbub but no doubt chuckling a bit over the situation. The holiness convention ultimately decamped for the Mechanics Hall, after every other Boston church refused to open its doors. As one of the puzzled enthusiasts told the *Globe*, "It is a very funny thing that we could not secure a hall or suitable place in this city to accommodate a couple of thousand people. It is not as though we did not have the money to pay for the use of the hall, for we have plenty of it."[16] The *Congregationalist* commented in return: "This last remark perhaps indicates their idea of the character of the exhibition they provided, and by no means the idea that the people of the church have of its uses."[17]

Tremont Temple and Park Street faced a common problem, but followed two different paths. The areas of the city immediately surrounding them promised few potential members: the upper-class neighborhoods in the Back Bay and Beacon Hill were predominantly Episcopalian and Unitarian; the working-class neighborhoods were Catholic. Moreover, the exodus of the middle class to the streetcar suburbs meant, at best, widely scattered congregants with varying degrees of loyalty. Tremont Temple met the challenge by deploying its small army of assistant pastors on rigorous rounds of visitation.

For a variety of reasons, Park Street did not follow suit. To begin with, its members were not uniformly wealthy. Situated on the edge of a roominghouse district in the West End, the congregation drew a steady number of working-men, clerks, widows, and housekeepers.[18] At the turn of the century, the pew-rent system exacerbated the problem of middle-class exodus, shrinking the annual budget along with the church rolls. Declining resources, in turn, all but ruled out the possibility of hiring extra staff. But even if they had had the money to do so, Park Street's members would not have adjusted easily to a multiplicity of pastors. Since the church's founding, the ministers' public reputation was a key safeguard of the congregation's moral and theological integrity.

Respectability was in fact central to Park Street's historic role in Boston. In 1890, the men of the church formed the Park Street Club, a debating society under the leadership of the Suffolk University law professor Gleason Archer. The group, which originated as a men's Sunday school class, tended toward the conservative: the first question up for consideration was whether women should vote on the license question, and the negative won by a vote of fourteen to twelve. Men's and women's clubs at Park Street also were more social than their evangelistic counterparts at Tremont Temple; by the 1930s, the women's club usually featured plays and musicales, and, more rarely, low-key discussion of political topics. Park Street's men, who awarded Calvin Coolidge an honorary membership, tended to talk about business.

By 1901 Park Street was barely surviving, its numbers heading for their lowest ebb after a precipitous decline in the late 1890s. From eleven hundred members in 1886, Park Street dropped to 366 in 1901. The remaining male pew-holders—who took a vote and decided to exclude the women from their deliberations—concluded that it was time to relocate outside the city. In a rapid series of events, Boston's fabled Brimstone Corner went up for sale to the highest bidder. Seeing its opportunity, the *Boston Herald* immediately offered one million dollars and announced its plans to tear down the old church and build an eleven-story office building on the site.[19]

In the end, Park Street was saved by its enemies. A Preservation Committee, made up of leading architects and lawyers, vociferously opposed the sale and, with the help of several prominent Unitarians and Episcopalians, raised ten thousand dollars in seed money toward a successful fund drive. More than thirty years later, the *Boston Evening Transcript* was still chuckling over the turn of events: "Unitarians against whom the Park Street pulpit had thundered anathemas for three or four generations" ended up saving the congregation from dissolution.[20] But the Preservation Committee cared relatively little for Park Street's theology; they were much more concerned about the church's role in Boston's civic life. "Churches are quasi-public property," the Committee argued. "The public confers special favors upon church societies; and out of those favors arise corresponding obligations on the part of the church societies to respect the wishes and welfare of the public." Park Street's building was "a beautiful and time-honored feature of Boston, indissolubly bound up with the very thought of Boston in every mind.... Unless something generous and energetic is done, however, the familiar spire will be superseded by a...dry-goods emporium, which will dominate the view of the State House for its principle approach and which at best will be a blot forever on the landscape of the city."[21]

Once revived, however, Park Street exhibited scant gratitude to its benefactors. In 1905 the congregation rallied to a new theological offensive under a new preacher with the unlikely name of Arcturus Zodiac Conrad (see fig. 9.3). A midwestern Presbyterian who had survived an Indian uprising in his boyhood, Conrad was a graduate of Carleton College and Union Theological Seminary. During his lengthy pastorate (he preached regularly until his death in 1937), he financed a new organ, paid off the church's mortgage, and brought in nearly three thousand new members. Conrad even survived a brief scandal when at age seventy-six he married the twenty-seven-year-old church organist, less than a year after the death of his first wife. But first and foremost, Conrad was a man of the pulpit: "I would rather preach than do anything else in the world," he once declared. When the congregation offered to hire an assistant, Conrad adamantly refused—until they mollified him with a raise of two thousand dollars—growling that "a minister does his work a

FIGURE 9.3. A. Z. Conrad. From *Twenty Fifth Anniversary, Pastorate of Rev. A. Z. Conrad, Ph.D., D.D.* (Boston, Mass: Park Street Church, 1930).

good deal more effectually when he does it himself."[22] Under Conrad's aggressive leadership, the congregation began to grow quickly. From 348 members in 1905, it nearly doubled by 1910, and by 1916 had passed one thousand (see fig. 9.4). By the 1930s, Park Street was enjoying some of its biggest numbers, regularly reporting over eighteen hundred members on its rolls.[23]

In the early days of his career in Boston, Conrad was an able partner to Cortland Myers over at Tremont Temple. Besides the Sunday morning sermon, he held regular Sunday evening "question periods" in which he addressed current events of particular concern to his membership. In 1918, for example, Conrad described in vivid detail what he would do "if he were the president," including outlawing beer and calling up another million draftees to

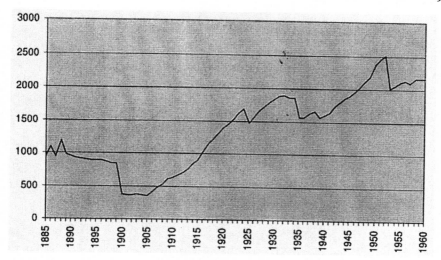

FIGURE 9.4. Park Street Church membership. From Park Street Church Records, Congregational Library, Boston, Mass.

win the war at any cost. "I would immediately intern every avowed pacifist and pro-German," Conrad thundered, "and keep them interned until the victory is won." "I would accept neither explanations nor apologies for failure" from government employees and "immediately and unceremoniously throw out men whose inefficiency and incapacity" kept them from implementing preparedness. And, Conrad concluded a bit superfluously, "I would give unmistakable evidence of vision and supervision backed by blood and iron."[24]

Like his other contemporary at Tremont Temple, J. C. Massee, Conrad also addressed issues surrounding sexuality and family life, but in a far more pugnacious tone. On the "festering iniquities" of the public beach, his criticisms left little to the imagination, evoking a "huge unsanitary wallow" of men and women frolicking in various stages of undress. "The microscopic dots and shreds of color that upon inspection would doubtless prove to be bathing suits," he declared, only served to highlight the "shining nakedness of this herd of human swine." In contrast to the more irenic Massee, Conrad never missed an opportunity to stake out his position. His Mother's Day sermon in 1934 wasted little time on sentiment and ended with denunciations of communism and the worthless habits of "cigaret-smoking [sic], cocktail-drinking women."[25] Still, Conrad, like every other conservative preacher in Boston, attracted consistently more women than men to his congregation throughout his pastorate (see fig. 9.5).

Conrad often insisted that he was not a fundamentalist, but the distinction was probably lost on most of his contemporaries. In 1926 H. L. Mencken's

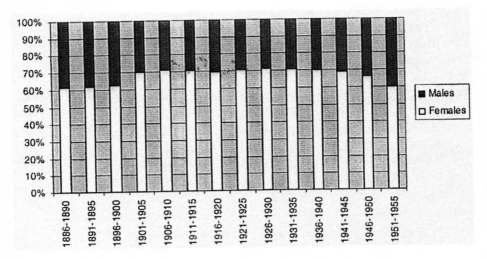

FIGURE 9.5. Park Street Church membership, male and female. From Park Street Church Records, Congregational Library, Boston, Mass.

avidly antifundamentalist *American Mercury* offered up Conrad as a worst-case scenario in bemoaning the "bawling of fundamentalists, theosophists, metaphysical healers, and other such quacks" on the streets of once-literate Boston. "The stimulating clash of metaphysical and theological ideas which so stirred the Boston of the last century is gone," the author lamented, and in its place "the Rev. A. Z. Conrad...speaks in behalf of the virgin birth, the resurrection, and long dresses."[26] And in fact, Conrad's "credo," issued in 1930, did include a list of doctrines associated with the national movement—the unassailable truth of the Bible, the necessity of Christ's virgin birth—all proclaimed without a hint of compromise. "The one thing Jesus Christ despises," Conrad declared, "is *patronage*. He wants no man's applause." Christ demanded full, humble commitment: "Grant him less and he spurns with pity and contempt those who approach him."[27]

But A. Z. Conrad's most enduring legacy to Park Street was his entrepreneurial gift. Within a few years of his arrival in Boston he had become president of the Evangelical Alliance, and thus chiefly responsible for inviting J. Wilbur Chapman to lead his evangelistic campaign in 1909; seven years later, he was one of the primary sponsors of the Billy Sunday revival.[28] Once again in the limelight, Park Street grew steadily. Even the building took on a grander appearance, stripped of several layers of old paint and restored to original brick and white clapboard.[29] But in the years following, Conrad began to look for evidence of revival further afield, beyond the streets of Boston. By the 1930s, he had found it, but this time in New Hampshire.

Reviving New England

One important thread of Boston's modern religious history can be traced to the northern end of the Connecticut River Valley. At the turn of the century, the Vermont–New Hampshire border, a rural, fairly mountainous area, had a scattering of Free Methodist and Freewill Baptist churches, both bodies a legacy of the revival fires that had swept over New England in the late eighteenth and again in the early nineteenth centuries. Whereas in Boston the awakenings brought theological strife and, in Park Street's case, a renewed commitment to orthodoxy, in northern and western New England, the legacy of revival was less divisive. In many parts of rural New England, the revivals lived on in the experiential faith and millennial expectation of Free Will Baptists and Universalists.[30]

Just before the turn of the century, Joel A. Wright, the son of a poor New Hampshire Baptist farmer, felt called by God to leave his Free Methodist church. Convinced that all denominational labels were wrong, Wright began holding tent meetings and advertised them under a label he perhaps felt the local farmers would appreciate, the First Fruit Harvesters' Association. By 1897 Wright had acquired a small, dedicated following and a property in Rumney, New Hampshire, where the group built cottages, an outdoor meeting space, a dining hall, and an orphanage. Soon afterward, a visit to the Christian Missionary and Alliance campground in Old Orchard Beach, Maine, convinced Wright that he could do much the same kind of work in Rumney. Aiming high, the Harvesters dedicated their "World's Missionary Campground" in 1903.[31]

In their early days, Wright's group centered around the pursuit of intense spiritual experience; in 1908, several members received the gift of tongues.[32] In the years following, with "the Holy Ghost in charge," other Harvesters experienced miraculous healing and deliverance from demons after hours of ecstatic prayer at summer campmeetings. They were not always popular with their rural neighbors: in 1908 the Harvesters' chapel in Jefferson, New Hampshire, was razed and then dynamited by a group of townspeople who had tired of the noise and "holy roller" hubbub.[33] But opposition only strengthened their commitment. Convinced that they were living in the End Times before Christ's Second Coming, the Harvesters organized gospel teams and sent them out across northern New England to establish new outposts. By 1924, they had established twenty-four evangelistic centers, mostly in individual homes and staffed by Christian workers or local leaders ordained by the original band in Rumney.[34]

But success brought new problems. To Wright's son Elwin, the Harvesters were starting to look suspiciously like one of the denominations they had rejected a scant three decades earlier. Instead of transcending sectarian divisions, they seemed to be busier than ever perpetuating them. Thus, when the aging Joel Wright stepped down and appointed his son as "lead overseer" in 1924, the younger Wright announced a new direction. The Harvesters' new constitution, issued in 1927, stressed unity around a few "fundamentals" of the faith garnered from the Apostles Creed, and dedication to the common goal of evangelism. "In short," the statement read, "the object of the Association is to cooperate with every Christian in the world in spreading the gospel of Jesus Christ as rapidly as possible and to carry on this work with the minimum amount of 'red tape' and 'machinery.'" Realizing anew the urgency of their task, the Harvesters promised to "ignore denominational and sectarian lines," even if it meant placing less emphasis on pentecostal experience, and to concentrate instead on evangelism."[35] Accordingly, in the summer of 1925 the Harvesters began recruiting support in northern New England's scattered rural churches, hosting inspirational summer conferences for pastors at the Rumney campground. In 1929 Wright renamed the organization the New England Fellowship (NEF), announcing the new goal of revitalizing the entire region.

The early 1920s were an opportune time for this kind of effort. New England had plenty of churches, but never enough pastors. According to one survey, the Northeast was one of the most heavily churched regions in the country, with only 7.5 percent of all communities lacking a church, a proportion far smaller than in mountain states (52 percent) and the Pacific coast (37 percent). But far too many of these churches were empty. During the 1920s, more than 20 percent of New England pulpits were vacant, and consequently the region's rate of church growth was the lowest in the country.[36]

This institutional void provided ample opportunity for the steady supply of pastors, Sunday school teachers, and evangelists from Rumney. Many of them were young women, trained by Wright's assistant, the indefatigable Elizabeth Evans (see fig. 9.6).

Evans arrived in Rumney in 1924, a recent graduate of the Christian and Missionary Alliance training school in Nyack, New York. Though she originally planned to work in the Harvesters' orphanage, she soon became indispensable to Wright's own vision for outreach. Under the rubric of the New England Fellowship, Evans fashioned a multifaceted career as a traveling preacher and evangelist, conference organizer, bookstore manager, and educator. In 1937 Evans began a rural education program that included a full roster of summer Bible schools for children and regular religious instruction during the school year. Encouraged by Wright to "multiply yourself," each year she recruited, trained, and devised curricula (personally mimeographing each workbook) for scores of young women volunteers from local Christian colleges and some twenty-one thousand children in northern New England. The indefatigable Evans also supplied each woman with a car and initiated

FIGURE 9.6. Elizabeth Evans. From Elizabeth Evans, *The Wright Vision: The Story of the New England Fellowship* (Lanham, Md.: University Press of America, 1991).

them into the mysteries of automobile maintenance and winter driving on the often perilous back roads of Vermont and New Hampshire.[37]

Though Rumney's fervent faithful would seem to have had little natural affinity to the genteel orthodox at Park Street, in the 1930s fundamentalism became their common bond. The precipitating event was a conference for pastors held in 1929 that drew in hundreds of men from around the country. The event was so successful that talk began of a New England–wide revival. In 1930, A. Z. Conrad ventured up to Rumney and quickly recognized the potential of the network forming in the New Hampshire woods. Never one to underestimate his own capacities, Conrad quickly embraced Wright's goal of reviving New England, and soon invited him down to Boston to begin work among the city's college students.[38]

In 1932, the New England Fellowship moved its headquarters to 5 Park Street, in an office building adjacent to the church. Before long they had opened a bookstore; the dedication service was preached by A. Z. Conrad. But the Park Street address, soon a "familiar one to thousands," also drew both the NEF and Park Street Church toward the center of a growing conservative Protestant network that spanned Boston as well as much of New England. As the NEF annual report for 1938 enthused, "Here, in the course of the year, come people from all walks of life seeking counsel or spiritual help for themselves or others. Pastors know it as a place where intimate problems may be frankly discussed and definite help received." Five Park Street was fast becoming a reliable "clearing house of information" for evangelicals all around the city.[39]

During the depths of the Depression, and in a city long since acceded to Catholic control, conservative Protestants began to feel optimistic. While many churches struggled to make ends meet, evangelicals were looking for ways to expand. On May 15, 1935, conservative Protestant leaders served notice on the city and its Roman Catholic hierarchy by organizing a huge parade from the Common to a rally at Boston Garden to mark Bible Demonstration Day. Some sixteen thousand of the faithful participated in one admirer dubbed one of the "finest spiritual demonstrations ever attempted in New England"—and a sign that evangelicals were once again ready to take their cause outdoors.[40]

Boston Common, Again

Harold John Ockenga, who became Park Street's pastor in 1936, was by his own account not a fundamentalist. This was not because he lacked orthodox credentials: in 1930, he graduated from Westminister Seminary, the school founded by the Presbyterian controversialist J. Gresham Machen after he was ousted from Princeton Theological Seminary in 1929. Ockenga went on to become a protégé of Clarence Macartney, one of the northern Presbyterian Church's leading conservatives, and with his help acquired an influential pastorate at the Point Breeze Presbyterian Church in Pittsburgh. A leading light in a denomination thoroughly shaken by theological controversy, Ockenga was poised for an influential career as a Presbyterian. But during his thirty-three years at Park Street Church, from 1936 to 1969, Ockenga forged a new identity, not as a fundamentalist but as a self-proclaimed "new evangelical," preaching from one of New England's most famous Congregational pulpits (see fig. 9.7).[41]

New evangelicals emphasized outreach. Though many of them differed little from their fundamentalist cousins on matters of doctrine, they rejected the cultural separatism that had become a hallmark of the movement during the 1930s and 1940s. Ockenga and his peers—men like Carl F. H. Henry,

FIGURE 9.7. Harold John Ockenga. From Harold Lindsell, *Park Street Prophet: A Life of Harold John Ockenga* (Wheaton, Ill.: Van Kampen Press, 1951; reprint, New York: Garland, 1988).

Charles Fuller, and Billy Graham—insisted that conservative Protestants had a responsibility to address the social and intellectual issues of their day. In the late 1940s and 1950s new evangelicals began to filter into secular graduate schools; they began to write scholarly books and debate politics; they started a new periodical, *Christianity Today;* and Ockenga himself played a central role in founding Fuller Seminary, a major center of evangelical intellectual inquiry and theological innovation, in 1947.

The central hallmark of the new movement was the formation of the National Association of Evangelicals (NAE) in 1942. Though billed as a conservative alternative to the Federal Council of Churches, the NAE promised far more than a simple reaction to liberalism. For one thing, it encompassed a broad unity across a variety of conservative denominations, from Mennonite to pentecostal, Dutch Reformed to fundamentalist. The NAE also sponsored an energetic program of revival that, its members hoped, would bring the United States back to its spiritual roots. Though the campaign for the nation's soul faltered in the years ahead, the NAE itself laid down a formidable record of achievement. In the following decades, spurred by the unprecedented success of the young Billy Graham's evangelistic crusades, the NAE sat at the forefront of religious change in American society. By 1976, *Time* magazine's so-called year of the evangelical, the National Association of Evangelicals had helped lead a sea-change in Protestant identity, as the older, "mainline" denominations gave way before a surge of new membership into conservative churches.[42]

Park Street was at the center of the new movement. In 1943, the NAE settled into office space at the church, and in 1944 Ockenga became its executive secretary. But the new evangelical movement spurred activity at Park Street in other ways as well. In 1943, in concert with the Providence Bible Institute, Park Street Church opened an Evening School of the Bible, drawing thousands of students and young professionals from all around New England. In 1945, under the urging of Elizabeth Evans, Ockenga helped organize an evangelical Protestant day school, which eventually found its way to permanent quarters in suburban Lexington. During Ockenga's tenure, Boston also saw a regular round of visits from leading evangelists, including Charles Fuller in 1939 and Walter Meier in 1945.[43]

In a larger sense, however, the connection between the new evangelical movement and Park Street really goes back to J. Elwin Wright and the NEF. Wright played a central role at the NAE's first organizing meeting in 1942, helping a fractured conservative Protestant coalition find common ground by embracing revival. The language of interdenominational cooperation was of course familiar to him, from his years not just in the NEF but also growing up as the son of Joel Wright, who left the Free Methodists half a century before.

Clearly, the NAE owed much to New England's particular conservative Protestant culture. The aggressive separatism so often associated with the movement's national leadership—typified by controversialists like New York's John Roach Straton and the Minneapolis pastor William Bell Riley—gained relatively few adherents on the banks of the Charles River. On the whole, New England's conservative Protestants had a respect for religious institutions that served the larger evangelical movement well.

Common wisdom suggests that Boston was simply too literary and liberal for fundamentalism to survive, but that vast oversimplification hardly stands up to history. Over the past hundred years or more, Boston, like most American cities, has hosted a wide range of religious groups, including some of the largest and most influential conservative Protestant churches in the country. No only did fundamentalism take root in Boston, it also developed into a particular form that shaped the national movement's direction and purpose. During the 1940s and 1950s, the new evangelicalism's program of stepped-up cultural engagement owed much to the particular style of Boston's Protestant conservatism.

That style was generally moderate in tone. New England conservatives were heirs to an ancient, battle-tested denominational structure that, by the mid-twentieth century had survived more than three centuries of schismatic confrontation. Over the years, Unitarians and their more conservative Protestant cousins had learned to co-exist, nursing the memories of old conflicts—often visible in nearly identical white clapboard buildings facing each other in the public square—but steadfastly observing an outward civility. Whereas in less settled regions of the country the disgruntled few could move elsewhere, in Boston's close quarters, leaving an old and expensive church building was not always an attractive option.

Boston's particular religious mix also moderated the fundamentalist urge toward separatism. Protestant conservatives were supremely conscious of their minority status in a largely Catholic city, and perhaps more immediately understood the value of public solidarity. From the late nineteenth century through the 1950s, conservative church leaders never uttered public criticisms of their fellow combatants, or openly competed with them for converts. Long before J. Elwin Wright helped form the NAE, Boston's conservative Protestants learned to work together. The Catholic presence moderated fundamentalism in other ways as well. Though the overwhelming numerical superiority of Catholics was the initial source of Protestant militancy, over the years Catholic ownership of Boston seemed to mellow those angry conservatives a bit. At the very least, Boston's particular type of Catholic presence undercut the need for evangelicals to mount a moral purity campaign; on such issues, the city's Catholic authorities were renowned for their thoroughness and persistence. By the 1920s, when offensive literature and film were routinely banned in Boston, conservative Protestants had little reason to mount their own moral crusade.

Another reason for the relative quiet of fundamentalism in Boston has to do with the region's unique denominational profile. To begin with, of course, the liberal tradition was much more visible in Boston than in other parts of the country. Unitarians were not some nameless heterodox group but, to many Congregationalists, ecclesiastical cousins once or twice removed. Moreover, by the nineteenth century, individual churches in New England's largest denominations, the Congregationalists and the Baptists, had evolved a fair amount of independence from hierarchical control. Unlike Presbyterians and Methodists, who predominated in other parts of the country, they could ignore or appropriate influences from above if they so chose. The epic clashes in the Presbyterian General Assembly over creeds and statements of faith, where the denomination's theological future was in many ways at stake, did not occur among Congregationalists. And though Baptists certainly hosted their share of confrontations, as J. C. Massee's story illustrates, these did not have the depth or staying power of the Presbyterian division.

Moreover, by the 1920s, the dominating physical presence of both Tremont Temple and Park Street Church also played a role in shaping evangelical presence. To a large degree, both of these churches operated as quasi-denominational clearinghouses, providing any New Englander with access to a radio opportunities for theological training, access to orthodox literature, and trustworthy sources of spiritual inspiration. Though most of their congregants commuted in from suburban neighborhoods, both churches by choice remained firmly entrenched in Boston's old downtown. All but unassailable by virtue of their size and geographical reach, they offered conservative Protestants a constant visual reassurance that God was not yet done with the hardened sinners of Boston and New England.

Nowhere was that awareness deeper than at Park Street Church. Harold Ockenga was neither a New Englander or a Congregationalist when he arrived in Boston, but he soon developed a clear appreciation of Park Street's historic role in the city. His sermons often included references to his famous predecessors or to the church's influential past, specifically designed to inspire the congregation toward a more public, confrontational stance. In one typical flourish, Ockenga summoned his people to action "in the light of our history, in the light of our former accomplishments and in the light of the unchanging message of the Bible." Invoking Park Street's famous steeple, a "Puritan finger pointing to God," he reminded the congregation that God had long ago given them a mission to the city of Boston. "Our fathers caught the message from the Pilgrims and in their very words they encased it in the Park Street Church. While Brimstone Corner stands Boston cannot forget its origins."[44]

Almost instinctively, Ockenga carved a public role for Park Street along some old and familiar paths. His self-described "most thrilling moment" at Park Street was the decision in 1943 to terminate the commercial leases in the church basement and restore it to solely spiritual purposes. No longer burdened by pew rents or artificially buoyed by rental income, Park Street's parishioners learned, as Tremont Temple's had many years before, the power of uninterrupted sacred space in the city—as well as the challenge of a yearly budget regularly met by voluntary donations.[45]

Ockenga also honed his congregation's loyalty through political confrontation with Roman Catholics. In 1938, just a few years after his arrival in Boston, he published a historical overview entitled *Our Protestant Heritage*, tracing the story from Martin Luther through John Knox, Oliver Cromwell, and Roger Williams. Ockenga's purpose was to argue against the modern ecumenical movement by showing that "genius of Protestantism" had always championed individualism and freedom of thought. The prototype of error was the Roman Catholic Church, now being replicated in "modern church union movements" that, he believed, required a blind uniformity.[46] But Ockenga's opposition to Catholics was not just theoretical. In 1950 he led a movement to prevent tax funds from going to provide bus transportation for Catholic school students, denouncing it as a violation of the separation of church and state. He was not afraid to employ arguments that relied openly on conspiratorial speculation. "The price of liberty is eternal vigilance," he declared, noting that "most Americans condemned the German nation for following Hitler without much of a struggle. If we lose our great education system so precious to democracy we will stand condemned because we did not express ourselves when the original attacks on that system were made."[47]

To a degree, Ockenga was simply following local custom. Opposing Catholics had few disadvantages for Protestant leaders in Boston, and represented a well-worn path to unity. In fact, by the late 1940s, anti-Catholicism united rather than divided American Protestants. Though more elite Protestants shied away from the disreputable image of anti-Catholic movements in the 1880s, they shed their hesitation in the post–World War II era. Paul Blanshard's bestselling denunciation of Roman Catholicism, *American Freedom and Catholic Power*, was widely embraced by liberal intellectuals. In the late 1940s, Ockenga's opposition to Cardinal Spellman and to Catholic schools placed him squarely in the mainstream of educated opinion, along with the Harvard University president James Bryant Conant, who publicly denounced Spellman in 1952.[48]

HISTORIC CHURCH KEEPS EVANGELISM TO FORE
Outdoor Pulpit of Park Street Church in the Heart of Boston

FIGURE 9.8. Mayflower Pulpit. Front cover, *United Evangelical Action*, 15 August 1949.

Ockenga, like many of his predecessors, also felt a pull toward Boston Common. In 1943 he began holding regular meetings there, mostly for servicemen, until "Roman Catholic authorities," in time-honored fashion, denied him a preaching permit. Undaunted, Ockenga went out to the Common with an oak table to stand on and continued to preach, and to demand legal recognition. City authorities eventually granted him the proper paperwork, and for the next two years, Ockenga set up his preaching platform on the Common every Sunday evening after the regular church service. But in the face of "clerical pressure," to use biographer Harold Lindsell's phrase, the permit was revoked. Still resolute, Ockenga moved his meetings to his own church step, and the large crowds continued unabated, despite the constant din of the traffic on Tremont Street. The example of persistence eventually moved one of Park Street's parishioners to provide a permanent outdoor pulpit. In 1945, Charles Dooley, a wealthy businessman and a former Roman Catholic, donated funds for what came to be known as the Mayflower pulpit, a small exterior platform built over the front door of the Park Street Church, directly facing onto the busiest corner of Boston Common (see fig. 9.8).[49]

Subsequent events would show, however, that the heavily symbolic gesture was more regrouping than retreat. Ockenga still had his eye on the Common's public grounds and had plans bigger than city authorities would have imagined. The next, and perhaps most famous, evangelistic preacher to stake out turf on the Common would be Billy Graham. The story of his 1950 revival campaign in Boston and his remarkable meeting on the Common, an event set in motion many years earlier by A. J. Gordon, H. L. Hastings, and W. F. Davis, is told in the next and final chapter.

IO

Conclusion

Billy Graham in Boston, 1950

Over and over again the novelists and historians repeat that Boston is dead; and still the mummy rolls a bright and watchful eye.
—Katharine Simonds, "We Come to Bury Boston"

By the end of April 1950, almost everything about Billy Graham's visit to Boston seemed unprecedented. When the evangelist first arrived on New Year's Eve, 1949, no one would have dared to predict that famously skeptical New Englanders would surge forward by the weeping thousands, heeding a gospel invitation from a lanky southern preacher. Nor could they have imagined that Boston's greatest sports arena, Boston Garden, the home of famously rowdy hockey fans, would host one of the largest religious gatherings in the city's history.

But as the numbers of converts began to build, not just in Boston but all around New England, anything seemed possible. As Harold Ockenga reported excitedly, "when Billy Graham arrived in Boston and saw the holiday crowds walking the streets of the heart of the city past the doors of Park Street Church, he said, 'It seems impossible that anything could be done to stir these people.'" But within days, the Park Street pastor exulted, "those same people who seemed so indifferent, so intent upon their own interests, so impervious to anything of religion were the people who pounded upon the doors of Mechanics Hall attempting to get in," who "tried to pass the police barrier at the Opera House," and who "gathered in thousands outside the Boston Garden only to be turned away nearly an hour before the service began."[1]

The excitement lasted for months. Graham's New England campaign began on December 30, 1949, with an instantaneous wave of public enthusiasm. When other commitments forced Graham to leave Boston on January 17, his audiences already totaled 105,000 and his converts more than 3,000. He returned to Boston on March 27, this time for an epic journey across all six New England states. He finished with a momentous five-day crusade that brought tens of thousands more into Boston Garden. For his last public meeting, on April 23, 1950, Graham chose a spot that positively resonated with historical significance: Monument Hill in the heart of Boston Common. This was, as Harold Ockenga was well aware, the very same spot where evangelist George Whitefield had addressed revival crowds over two hundred years before. Contemporary accounts of A. J. Gordon's preaching in 1885 did not record his exact location, but it is not hard to imagine that on that day in April Graham shared physical as well as spiritual space with his largely unknown Baptist predecessor.

The successes and failures of the Graham crusade offer a revealing glimpse of Boston evangelicals at midcentury, and to a considerable degree the state of conservative Protestantism across the United States. Beyond any doubt, Graham's huge crowds demonstrated that the dramatic power of revival preaching had hardly lessened since the days of Billy Sunday. The hundreds of thousands who went to hear Graham night after night allayed all doubt that "the old-fashioned gospel" still had a place along the banks of the Charles. But other events of those revival months suggest that much had changed, including the role of conservative Protestants in the city of Boston. A smaller minority than ever before and geographically spread across a large metropolitan area, they had no pretensions of permanently affecting Boston's moral or political climate. Neither Graham nor his local allies were primarily interested in confronting local sin, nor did they hope to save this, or any other, American city. They had set their sights much higher.

The New Billy Sunday?

The comparisons were irresistible. Even in the first phase of the campaign, in January 1950, the Boston press began to describe the inexplicable new sensation from North Carolina as a "'smooth' edition of a Billy Sunday."[2] Like his namesake, the thirty-year-old Graham weaved and crouched across the platform, denouncing sin in vivid, unforgettable metaphors. He too seemed to have an endless capacity to quote lengthy Bible passages, punctuating them with a long accusatory finger aimed squarely at his quaking audience. Like Sunday, he denounced the lurid vices of a "sex-crazed" society; in one memorable performance he strutted across the stage as the decadent Babylonian king Belshazaar, his bravado suddenly turning to abject fear as an invisible hand traced his doom across the wall. Like the former Chicago White Stocking Billy Sunday, Graham was reportedly "crazy over baseball," to the point of considering a professional career. The comparisons went even further than that: the chair of his Boston campaign, Allan C. Emery, Jr., was the son and namesake of Sunday's local organizer in 1916. Graham even traveled with a musical sidekick, Cliff Barrows, who, like Homer Rodeheaver of years past, entertained the crowds with lusty trombone solos.[3]

Nudged by Graham's supporters, newspaper accounts soon fell into a common narrative. Early on, his press agent described him as "six feet, two inches of southern farm boy," a statistic that grew as the weeks passed.[4] As press attention began to build, Graham's physical stamina became an object of major curiosity. According to the Boston Post, the evangelist recovered from the strain of preaching with a rubdown and a "steak that would warm the heart of a stevedore." A "veteran of hundreds of thousands of air miles," Graham was also said to have several times "escaped death" in plane crashes. He prepared for the strain of preaching through a regimen of daily calisthenics, golf, tennis, and "orange juice vitamin pills."[5] Early press reports also noted that the handsome Graham, fresh from an immensely successful evangelistic crusade in Los Angeles, had been cast to star in a movie entitled "The Billy Sunday Story." He had turned it down, however, because, in his words, "'many of our movies, crime radio programs, comic and cheap books are being used to tear down the moral background of our country.'"[6]

In early 1950, Graham, by his own later admission, was not as polished as he would later become. "I did not know how to conduct myself in front of the reporters," he recalled in 1997. "Sometimes in my innocence I made statements on politics and foreign affairs that were outside my jurisdiction as a preacher."[7] According to press accounts, he certainly pulled few punches in front of his Boston audiences. During the January campaign he described heaven as "just as real a place as Los Angeles, London, Algiers, or Boston" and in fact exactly sixteen hundred miles long, sixteen hundred miles wide, and sixteen hundred miles high.[8] He assailed communism, warned of impending nuclear war, and charged that thousands of Bostonians were literally possessed by demons.[9] His oratory was so intense that on January 13, a woman collapsed during the sermon and had to be carried out on a stretcher, all of the time moaning for God to save her.[10] Graham even took on a Harvard professor, Ernest Hooten, who had supported the "mercy killing" of a terminal cancer patient. Even if this doctor's act had saved the patient "'just one minute's suffering,'" Graham charged, "he could not be forgiven by God, 'for in that one minute God could have healed the woman if such had been His will.'"[11]

Despite such remarks, Graham enjoyed an overwhelmingly supportive press. In January, editors of the leading papers recognized the revival's ratings appeal, and later that March they sent a drove of reporters along on the New England tour. After a week or two of nightly altar calls, a number of reporters had utterly succumbed to Graham's magnetic appeal. According to one account, when a skeptic in Concord, New Hampshire, expressed contempt for Billy's methods, an equally hard-bitten Boston reporter "drummed his fingers into the chest of the scoffer" and growled, "'Say listen, the most important thing in the world is to accept Christ, see?'"[12] The editor of the *Boston Post* (a "devout Roman Catholic") not only gave the campaign favorable press but helped Ockenga reserve Boston Garden for Graham's final meeting in January. The *Post* also ran feature stories about its own coverage, quoting at length letters of praise about the positive exposure given Graham.[13]

But Graham hardly needed such help. By the time he arrived in Boston for a second time on April 19, the attention of the city, as well as the entire region, was thoroughly riveted on the "dynamic preacher from Dixie."[14] Graham began his New England tour on March 27, with two meetings at Park Street Church, one to greet local clergy and another to shore up the faith of converts from his previous visit. From Park Street, he traveled north, then west and south in a huge arc, in a grueling tour that began in Portland, Maine, on March 28. From there Graham moved on to Waterville and Houlton, Maine, where he preached in a converted airplane hangar. By April 2, the evangelist and his entourage had reached Portsmouth, New Hampshire, only to move on in the next several days to Manchester and Concord, before heading west to Burlington, Vermont, on April 6. Over the course of the next week, the Graham team scheduled mass meetings in Springfield, Massachusetts; Bridgeport, Connecticut; and Fall River, Providence, Worcester, and Lowell, Massachusetts.

Every step of the way, reporters from all of the Boston newspapers sent back increasingly startled reports of enormous, fervent crowds, and of thousands more turned away for lack of space. Describing the flood of weeping converts at the front of the Portland auditorium, one reporter simply declared that this mass response had happened only "infrequently" in Graham's previous ministry "and never before in New England."[15] Not surprisingly, Graham struggled with illness and fatigue during those hectic weeks; by the time he reached Bridgeport he was physically unable to preach, and he was also forced to bring in a substitute the next day in Fall River. The illnesses were minor and, given the travel schedule, certainly understandable, but press accounts declared Graham perilously close to death.[16] The drama continued to mount as the evangelist circled ever closer to Boston. On April 15 he rode into Worcester, Massachusetts, in a huge motorcade, led by police and local dignitaries. A city council member met the "dashing dispenser of salvation" on the steps of the City Auditorium and presented him with the key to the city.[17] The next day, in Lowell, Massachusetts, Graham announced plans for a massive rally on Boston Common on April 23, an event he believed would bring in one hundred thousand people. By the time the "handsome chief of the modern 'sawdust trail'" made his second advent in Boston, excitement was at a fever pitch.[18]

Evangelicals and the "New Boston"

Graham arrived in Boston at an auspicious time, when old patterns no longer seemed to hold. Barely two months before his first appearance in December 1949, the city's famed "rascal king," the longtime mayor James Michael Curley, had been defeated by his mild-mannered city clerk, John B. Hynes. The election was hard fought and in the end very close, but Curley's defeat, after decades in office, carried momentous significance, promoting the *Boston Globe* to declare "the end of one era and the beginning of another."[19] A notorious machine politician—who had in fact served part of a previous term in a federal penitentiary—had been swept out of office by a reform candidate promising a more efficient, honest "New Boston."

The same was true in Boston's largest religious community. In 1945, Richard J. Cushing became leader of the city's Catholics, replacing Bishop John Henry O'Connell, who had died in April of the preceding year. Like Curley, O'Connell had presided over a city rife with political favors and tribal loyalties; he and Curley had been, in many ways, equally notorious for autocratic, often corrupt rule. Like Hynes, the genial Cushing promised a new era of openness and efficiency. He presided over a church brimming with confidence, free of its old immigrant stereotypes, and moving quickly into center of middle-class American culture.[20] By 1950, even some of the old animosities against Protestants had begun to dim. The extroverted Cushing, who considered any enemy of communism an ally of the Church, openly courted public ties with Protestant and Jewish leaders. Indeed, in January 1950, the *Pilot* ever endorsed the Graham crusade, albeit somewhat backhandedly. "If, as some people seem to think," the editor wrote, "the non-Catholic Christian congregations of New England are disintegrating, we are not such bigots as to rejoice therein. It is no comforting sight to see a handful of worshippers coming out of Protestant churches on Sunday morning." Decrying the drift of Protestant orthodoxy, the *Pilot* took up common cause with its old antagonists, declaring that "it is our fraternal prayer that they will once again address themselves to the 'four square Gospel,' 'the old time religion,' 'the rock of ages cleft for me,' and other positive subjects."[21]

In many ways, the *Pilot's* assessment was right: Boston's old-line Protestants were a somewhat demoralized lot at midcentury. A 1949 survey described them as "largely apathetic and disorganized," with only sporadic outbursts of social concern and certainly little capacity for long-range planning. In comparison to Boston's Catholics, who spoke with "assurance and with unanimity," "the voice of Protestantism sound[ed] confused and uncertain."[22] Already in the 1930s, surveys of Boston's neighborhoods by students from Boston University's School of Religious Education found Protestants far less connected to stable neighborhoods than the city's Catholics.[23] The 1949 survey confirmed that impression of confused detachment. Even the strongest Protestant urban churches existed mostly for show, the report lamented, with "no sense of responsibility for suburban missions or weak city churches. They tend to concentrate and absorb the best leadership in the institutions with the least problems."[24]

Of course, that pessimistic conclusion ignored a major shift in Boston's religious makeup. Beginning in the World War I era, city directories had begun listing ever larger numbers of churches that could not be categorized by denomination. The "various" group, which included thirty-seven congregations in 1915, and sixty-six by 1945, included growing numbers of Greek and Russian Orthodox, as well as a changing array of New Thought groups and Vedanta societies. Most of the increase, however, came from holiness and pentecostal churches, the majority of them located in the South End and rarely persisting in the record for more than a few years at a time. To a large degree, this new religious presence reflected Boston's changing racial demographics. In the nineteenth century, African Americans never made up more than 2 percent of Boston's total population; but from World War I through the 1940s, a steady influx of migrants from southern states, as well as the West Indies, helped solidify an African American community in the South End, and later further outward in Roxbury and Dorchester. During the World War II era, Boston's African American population more than doubled, reaching over forty thousand—over 5 percent of the total—by 1950.[25]

Perhaps it is not surprising that traditional religious survey methods missed these Protestant believers. Boston's minority communities were relatively small, especially compared to other northern cities, and were slow to achieve the "critical mass" necessary for political clout. Their churches were geographically isolated from white Protestant congregations, and they were poor. But their presence was certainly not inconsequential; by 1945, the directory listed at least forty-five holiness and pentecostal churches in the city of Boston—at least fifteen more than were listed as Congregational.[26]

In 1950, however, these potential allies did not factor into assessments of Boston's spiritual condition, at least partly because so few white evangelicals had remained behind to witness their arrival. By then, most of the major conservative Protestant institutions, like the Gordon Bible Institute and Rumney campground, were outside the city, in suburban or even rural locations. Park Street Church had become a sort of shorthand for evangelical presence, even though, like Tremont Temple, it was heavily dependent on Boston's subway system to fill its pews on Sunday mornings.

Saving New England

The crusade for New England's soul began at Brimstone Corner. Park Street Church provided the original setting for Graham's evangelistic campaign, which began quietly, without much public fanfare, on December 30. When the New Year's Eve meeting, across the way in Mechanics Hall, turned into an unexpected success, Ockenga scrambled to locate a larger venue, and ended up ferrying the evangelist from Mechanics Hall to the Opera House and then back again. "Before it was over," Ockenga reported in a February press release, "Park Street Church . . . found itself the center of a New England revival, with more than 75 Boston area Churches co-operating actively in the rallies." "Without banners, fanfare or planning, a single church meeting for evangelism expanded in eighteen days to become the greatest thing spiritually which has hit this conservative, cultured, intellectual center in half a century."[27] In late March, Graham launched the second phase of the revival with meetings again at Park Street, and when he became ill in Fall River, Ockenga, often described as Graham's sponsor, filled in for him. Though churches from all around the Boston metropolitan area cooperated in the revival, they did not own it equally. Even requests for reserved seats in Boston Garden had to be cleared through the Park Street "headquarters."

The rest of the city of Boston functioned mostly as a backdrop to the Graham crusade. Eager to demonstrate the magnitude of his success, the evangelist's supporters often described the city as essentially pagan, or at the very least heavily Catholic. Thus, a Baptist paper found the crusade "nothing short of a miracle in a city where Romanism boasts of a seventy-five per cent 'possession' of the population," with most of the other 25 percent devoted to "Christian Scientism," "philosophic cults [and] Judaism" and a small minority of Protestant churches divided between liberal and conservative.[28]

Boston provided the Graham campaign with a variety of publicity motifs. The evangelist began his second set of meetings on April 19, during the city's Patriots' Day observance commemorating the "shot heard round the world" in 1775. Patriots' Day was an auspicious time, a city holiday created for Protestants as an alternative to the Catholic celebration of St. Patrick's Day. It included a dawn reenactment of Minutemen confronting redcoats on Lexington Green, as well as the running of the Boston Marathon and, in 1950, an early season showdown between the Red Sox and the New York Yankees. (Boston's home opener was the day before, a game they lost to the Bronx Bombers, 10–15.) Not surprisingly, Graham told a noon press meeting that America needed "a spiritual Paul Revere" and "Minute Men to stand in the gap while we get ready to fight the onslaught of enemies." He also admitted to following the Red Sox between speaking engagements, and wisely commiserated with the local press on the opening day loss. "'Man, O man, those Red Sox were 9 to 0 and then the next time I saw a paper they'd been slaughtered.'"[29]

But Boston itself was not the primary objective. Throughout the campaign, press accounts and Graham's own commentary constructed the revival as a campaign for all of New England's soul. Every night local organizers reserved five thousand seats in Boston Garden for delegations arriving from more than fifty miles away. As the campaign chairman, Allan Emery, Jr., explained, "we want to give these people preference if possible." Each night, the meetings featured a different New England delegation, beginning with Rhode Island on April 19, followed by Connecticut the next, and then western Massachusetts and Cape Code, Maine, New Hampshire, and Vermont.[30]

Regional stereotypes abounded. Most descriptions of "the dashing preacher from Dixie" commented on his southern roots—one newspaper sidebar solemnly explained why Billy referred to his audience as "you all"—and the improbability of this simple North Carolina farm boy (who was at the time a college president and director of a national organization, Youth for Christ) leading stoic Maine Yankees, tweed-jacketed intellectuals, or cultured Back Bay matrons down the sawdust trail.[31] Steeped in regional clichés, Graham's Boston campaign lacked the specificity of Chapman's call for civic virtue or the political urgency of Sunday's attacks on the local liquor trade; in 1950, however, evangelicals had set their sights not on a city but on a cultural ideal.

By the mid–twentieth century, New England was more than just a geographic region of the country or a tourist spot famous for its historical significance. In a society fast being overtaken by faceless suburban tract homes and anonymous superhighways, it symbolized an older, more authentic communal order. If the Hollywood stars converted in Graham's Los Angeles crusade signified artificiality and empty pleasure, the mythic no-nonsense Yankee, with his famous accent and dry, canny wit, represented the ancient values of hearth and home. To the surprise of many, Graham got along well with his Yankee audiences. "'I was told that New Englanders were conservative and stand-offish,'" he declared at the end of the campaign. Instead he had found them uniformly "warm and kind." "When they shake hands, you know they mean it."[32]

In some ways, Graham's strong southern identity was the point of connection. As the historian Joseph Conforti has observed, in the early twentieth century Yankee New England became a "historical analogue to the Old South of the defeated Confederacy." New England had not been defeated in battle but by midcentury certainly resonated with a broader sense of historical loss. Once the epicenter of white Protestant high culture, its regional identity had been fundamentally transformed under a flood of immigration. By 1940, even after the imposition of strict quotas, New England had more foreign-born inhabitants than any other region in the United States, about twice the national average. That statistic moved one critic to declare that mythic New England was no more than a "handful of native storekeepers, come-outers, schoolteachers or inventors, surrounded by thousands upon thousands of recently arrived strangers." Not only were Yankees beset by South Boston Irish, North End Italians, French-Canadians, and eastern Europeans but even "our motels are filled with tourists from the Bronx."[33]

The sense of loss also reflected an economic decline. While the rest of the country climbed out of the Great Depression into postwar prosperity, New England never seemed to recover. In the decade after World War II, the region's textile industry faltered badly, as the number of workers fell from 280,000 to 170,000 and industries moved steadily south. Once a financial capital, Boston became more and more of a second-tier city, falling to tenth in population by 1965. As the historian Lawrence Kennedy observes, "although the core problem was economic, an attitude of depression infected Boston like a plague and the city was dismissed as a 'shabby, brokendown, bluestocking, politically corrupt city and the subject of satire and ridicule.'" Contemporary critics agreed. Writing in the *New England Quarterly*, Stewart Holbrook declared the Yankee "the most set-upon, the most abused, the most caricatured American of all."[34]

Evangelicals leaders knew that Graham's upbeat piety would to be a hard sell in cold, cynical New England. One of Graham's most widely reported feats was a meeting he held for students at the Rockwell Cage Gymnasium at the Massachusetts Institute of Technology. Rumors circulated that a few students planned to interrupt the service by hobbling forward on crutches, throwing them down, and shouting "I'm healed, I'm healed!" But Graham headed them off, whispering to Ockenga to "'give me the most intellectual introduction you've ever given anybody.'" The Park Street pastor followed through admirably, silencing the unruly students with a lengthy peroration on "the major philosophical and intellectual trends of the day" that concluded with praise for MIT's centennial observance "and the school's tradition of objective scientific inquiry."[35]

Taking New England meant something. The battle over local sin in Boston was quickly overshadowed by the prospect of a larger national transformation, beginning with a section of the country that was presumed to be its cultural and spiritual core. Just days into his first visit to Boston, as the surprising momentum began to grow, Graham announced that "New England is a crucial spot in this revival," for if it "breaks out here, it will sweep across the nation. The country is waiting for New England to set off the revival wave."[36] As Ockenga told his fellow evangelicals, "if Boston and New England can receive such a shaking of God . . . we believe that God is ready to shake America to its foundations in revival."[37] From the beginning, then, the crusade was not just for a few northeastern states but for the entire nation, and the world itself.

Graham's success encouraged evangelical leaders to plan boldly. In early January, they launched a nationwide prayer campaign, calling on Christians everywhere to commit half an hour a day to petitioning for success. Volunteers from Graham's New England audiences agreed to send postcards to friends in each of the other forty-eight states, asking them to pray for the Boston revival.[38] The evangelist's second arrival in Boston also came amid rumors that he was to meet with President Harry Truman at the close of the crusade.[39] Indeed, in those heady days, nothing seemed impossible. On Saturday, April 22, Graham and a few of his organizers met on Boston Common for prayer. John Bolten, a business executive who had been converted in the January revival, took the evangelist aside. "'Billy,' he said, 'I believe God's telling me you are going to preach in the great stadiums of every capital city of the world the Gospel of our crucified Lord. I believe the world is ripe and ready to listen.'"[40]

The Common, Yet Again

Graham's Boston crusade ended on the Common. As the "amazing wavy-haired, ex–dairy farmer from North Carolina" set off on his whirlwind tour of New England on March 28, Ockenga announced plans for a giant rally to be held on Sunday afternoon, April 23. The Park Street pastor cited a "strong historical precedent" for the event, recalling that the famous evangelist George Whitefield had preached there during the First Great Awakening; in fact the sermon title for Billy's talk, "Shall God Reign in New England?" was reportedly the same as that of the eighteenth-century revivalist two centuries earlier.[41] But Graham's supporters fully expected him to equal, if not surpass, Whitefield's success. Weeks before the event they began to pray for good weather, and confidently predicted a turnout of one hundred thousand.[42]

Graham and his supporters also chose a strong contemporary theme. The rally was to be a "Prayer for Peace," giving explicit recognition to the Cold War fears that had gripped the country in earnest by 1950. Barely a year before, the Soviets announced their successful detonation of a nuclear warhead; by June 1950, Americans would be headed off to war in Korea. Graham announced his intention to open the rally, described in the press as "one of the greatest peace demonstrations ever held in the world," with a prayer for an end to world conflict; he asked attendees to bring white handkerchiefs to wave aloft, symbolizing "their great desire for a lasting peace minus the dangers of a cold war." But in the meantime he was not going to promise much. As he promoted the rally on April 19, Graham reportedly swept the crowd with "blazing eyes" and dropped his voice to a "low throbbing tone," warning them that God would "'get angry'" if the nation refused to repent. He declared his conviction that "unless God intervenes within two or three years, it will be 'all over for this nation.'" And then he "roared out" that God might well use the Soviet Union to "invade and destroy America in punishment." "'I thank God I am an American,' the energetic preacher declared, as he lunged across the rostrum and pounded his chest. 'But I fear for this nation. I love to see our flag unfurled. But that great flag is in more danger today than ever before in history.'"[43]

On Sunday, April 23, Bostonians woke to gray skies and a cold, drenching rain. As the 3:30 starting time approached, worried organizers considered moving the proceedings inside, but as ever larger crowds began to gather on the Common, they soon decided otherwise. Pouring out of subways and rented buses, armed with umbrellas and picnic lunches, enthusiastic hordes of people started assembling by noon. For hours they endured the forty-six-degree drizzle, filling up the lawn around the Soldiers and Sailors Monument, singing revival hymns, and sitting through a performance by a Salvation Army band. The one hundred thousand that Graham's organizers hoped for did not materialize, but the forty thousand people who did (some estimates said fifty thousand) made the rally the largest ever held on the Common.

At 3:30 Graham ascended the platform. The skies were gray and threatening, but the rain had finally stopped, and as the evangelist faced his audience, a small, dramatic patch of blue appeared overhead. He beamed, and gave credit to the quick prayer he had whispered just a moment before. "'I said the Lord wouldn't let it!' he exulted, 'and it isn't—there's even a little patch of sun up yonder!'" The crowd yelled back an enthusiastic "a-a-a-men!"[44] And then Graham began to preach. Despite the previously announced title, his sermon brushed aside New England's sin rather lightly, focusing instead on the national revival necessary for "Peace in Our Time." Calling on President Truman to proclaim a national "R-Day" of repentance, he read the text of a telegram sent to the White House: "Fifty thousand gathered in the rain on Boston Common for a nation-wide peace offensive through repentance and prayer. Suggest on their behalf you set aside a day of prayer for peace that God may defer the impending catastrophe of war."[45] Graham also announced his own Five-Point Program to ensure world peace: a strong military defense, strengthening the FBI and CIA, economic security, national unity, and moral and spiritual regeneration.

Despite the dire predictions of a world on the brink, Boston's evangelicals had good reason to believe that Boston Common would be the starting place for a worldwide revival. Cooperative city authorities had installed microphones in the trees, and these carried Graham's voice some quarter of a mile, from the brownstones on Beacon Street to the expensive hotels bordering the Public Garden. A portable generator and transmitter in a nearby car also carried Graham's message to a station in Minneapolis, and from there it was broadcast across the Midwest. In marked contrast to their behavior on a spring Sunday sixty-five years earlier, Boston's police proved immensely helpful to the open-air meeting, shuffling traffic along efficiently and shepherding crowds across busy streets. Unaware of the historical irony, Ockenga paused during the proceedings to publicly thank Boston city officials for their assistance in making the peace rally a success.[46]

Graham left the next afternoon for Washington, D.C., eagerly anticipating a meeting with President Truman. Evangelicals in Boston no doubt spent the day considering the events of the past winter and spring, wondering what else the future might have in store. Graham's meeting with a grouchy, truculent president on the verge of war did not go well; Truman found the fervent young evangelist unduly presumptuous and banned him from the Oval Office. Graham would not return until the Nixon administration. Evangelicals, however, saw their stock rise steadily across New England and the rest of the country, with Boston-based leaders like Harold Ockenga and J. Elwin Wright becoming recognized spokesmen for the new evangelical cause.

But in the years and decades ahead, lasting success was elusive. New England was not saved by Billy Graham, any more than it had been by J. Wilbur Chapman or Billy Sunday before him. While conservative churches prospered across the nation, New England continued to lag; by 1980, according to one study, the region had the country's lowest proportion of self-proclaimed evangelicals, at 2 percent—this compared to 45 percent of respondents in the South and about 15 percent in the upper Midwest.[47] Even into the late 1990s, Roman Catholics continued to account for well over half of religious adherents in Massachusetts, but by then even Christianity was apparently on the decline. In 1990, Massachusetts listed more "neo-pagans" than Southern Baptists, more Buddhists than Assemblies of God.[48] And in one survey, more people claimed to have "no religion" (16 percent) than were Congregational (3), Episcopal (3), and Baptist (4) combined.[49] Part of the reason is the confusing language often used in religious definitions: many conservative Protestants in New England might not have recognized terminology familiar to people in Wheaton, Illinois, or Grand Rapids, Michigan. But behind this complexity is the general absence of institutional forms broadly typical of modern evangelicals. The megachurch phenomenon, for example, has largely skipped New England. Four of the nine states without any congregation consistently drawing over two thousand people were New Hampshire, Rhode Island, Vermont, and Maine. Massachusetts and Connecticut ranked thirty-sixth and thirty-ninth in the national tally.[50]

Why has evangelical Protestantism fared so poorly? Part of the answer to that difficult question has to do in part with the religious history of Boston and New England, and the rest, I think, with the nature of conservative Protestant faith. Obviously, over the past hundred and fifty years, the region's primary story is the remarkable success of Roman Catholicism and the consequent decline in the numeric strength and social power of all Protestant groups, not just conservative ones. The stereotype of Massachusetts as a bastion of elite liberal Protestants simply doesn't measure up to demographic fact; for the past century or more, most of the people in Boston, in Massachusetts, and in New England have been Catholics.

But demographics only tell part of the story. In a sense, Boston proved itself not too liberal, but too conservative to fully accommodate fundamentalism. In the late nineteenth century, the city's denominational institutions were already centuries old and its public spaces highly regulated; despite its reputation for religious diversity, Boston provided relatively few open spaces where upstart new movements could challenge older, established ones.

Conservative evangelicalism, on the other hand, seeks a vacuum. It found its true stride in New England once it broke out of Boston's narrow confines, establishing outposts on the city's north shore and gathering converts in the under-churched small towns of Vermont and New Hampshire. Today in New England, the newest churches tend to be the most conservative; that quaint white clapboard building nestled against the town green is far more likely to be socially and theologically liberal than the steel and Plexiglas auditorium down by the interstate. In recent years, evangelicalism has enjoyed its greatest growth in the new settlements of the southern and western sunbelt states; it has always been an attractive faith among immigrants, who perhaps share the classic evangelical mix of moral suspicion and patriotic awe toward their adopted home. Over the past half century conservative evangelicalism has emerged as a highly nimble movement, constantly seeking out new cultural spaces and constructing new moral opponents as needed along the way. In many ways, the "conservative" label is fundamentally misleading.

Never once while I was writing this book was I completely sure whether it was a story of success or failure. To be sure, fundamentalism found a home in Boston, but, on the whole, it is not surprising that it has remained relatively invisible to the city's many historians. For all the many people who passed through their doors over the years, conservative Protestant churches made relatively little impact on the city's social and political institutions. They resisted the pull of the suburbs for only so long before succumbing to the inevitable in the early twentieth century, abandoning even the fairly narrow political agenda they had managed to build in the 1880s and 1890s. Boston's fundamentalists were not even particularly outrageous, especially compared to the goings on in John Roach Straton's New York, J. Frank Norris's Detroit, or Aimee Semple McPherson's Los Angeles. By a variety of different measurements, Boston's fundamentalists did not emerge as winners; they are perhaps somewhat rightfully a forgotten group.

But there are other ways of thinking about religious winners and losers. From my office window in downtown Boston, a stone's throw from Brimstone Corner, the view is mostly of old brownstones set against a solid wall of glass and concrete skyscrapers. I hear and see jets flying overhead every ten minutes or so, and in the summer even with the window shut, I can't escape the regular rant of historical impersonators entertaining tourists in the old burial ground below. Few of the people I talk to have ever heard of Tremont Temple, much less walked inside, though they pass it on the street every day. Park Street Church is most familiar to local people as a stop along Boston's historical Freedom Trail.

But every day, on the quarter hour, the bells at Park Street Church toll the time of day and sound a gospel hymn, a Christmas carol, or a familiar chorus. Sometimes I listen and even hum along (usually against my will), and I often complain, especially when the bells are out of key or I just can't stand to hear any more Christmas music. But it's not worth raising a fuss; that music will play on whether or not I'm enjoying it or even paying attention. In an oddly similar way, fundamentalism was not a dramatic, disruptive event in Boston's daily life, at least not enough to win a permanent spot in the city's complex sense of its own history. Instead, the story of fundamentalism in Boston demonstrates the remarkable durability of religious institutions, even in the midst of constant disruption and change. Fundamentalism did not happen easily. It is important to remember that behind any obstreperous new religious movement is a complex welter of painful disruptions: congregational conflicts, sagging church budgets, jobs lost and personal relationships forever fractured. Religious change is rarely pleasant or purposeful to those living through it; our retelling of these events should reflect that human reality.

Notes

CHAPTER I

I. The best single study of fundamentalism is George Marsden, *Fundamentalism and American Culture: The Shaping of Twentieth-Century Evangelicalism, 1875–1925* (New York: Oxford University Press, 1980), which built off of Ernest Sandeen, *The Roots of Fundamentalism: British and American Millenarianism, 1800–1930* (Chicago: University of Chicago Press, 1970). The best study of mid-twentieth-century fundamentalism is Joel Carpenter, *Revive Us Again: The Reawakening of American Fundamentalism* (New York: Oxford University Press, 1997). All of these books, including my own, *Fundamentalism and Gender, 1875 to the Present* (New Haven: Yale University Press, 1993), deal with the movement primarily on a national level, and emphasize the importance of theology. Important biographical studies include William Vance Trollinger, Jr., *God's Empire: William Bell Riley and Midwestern Fundamentalism* (Madison: University of Wisconsin Press, 1990); Dale E. Soden, *The Reverend Mark Matthews: An Activist in the Progressive Era* (Seattle: University of Washington Press, 2001); Barry Hankins, *God's Rascal: J. Frank Norris and the Beginnings of Southern Fundamentalism* (Lexington: University Press of Kentucky, 1996).

2. Historical studies of fundamentalist congregations include Walter Ellis, "Social and Religious Factors in the Fundamentalist-Modernist Schisms among Baptists in North America, 1895–1934" (Ph.D. diss., University of Pittsburgh, 1974); Barbara Dobschuetz, "Fundamentalism and American Urban Culture: Community and Religious Identity in Dwight L. Moody's Chicago, 1864–1914" (Ph.D diss., University of Illinois, Chicago, 2002); Douglas James Curlew, "'They Ceased Not to Preach: Fundamentalism, Culture, and the Revivalist Imperative at the Temple Baptist Church of Detroit" (Ph.D. diss., University of Michigan, 2001). Trollinger, *God's Empire,*

is one of the only studies to deal with fundamentalism as a regional movement, in this case, the upper Midwest.

3. Although the literature on urbanization and secularization is vast, few studies have dealt directly with American fundamentalism as an urban movement. Some exceptions are Gregory H. Singleton, "Fundamentalism and Urbanization: A Quantitative Critique of Impressionistic Interpretations," in *The New Urban History: Quantitative Explorations by American Historians,* ed. Leo F. Schnore (Princeton, N.J.: Princeton University Press, 1975), 205–227; Darren Dochuk, "'Praying for a Wicked City': Congregation, Community, and the Suburbanization of Fundamentalism," *Religion and American Culture* 13 (2003): 167–203.

4. Emmanuel Sivan, "The Enclave Culture," in *Fundamentalisms Comprehended,* ed. Martin Marty and R. Scott Appleby (Chicago: University of Chicago Press, 1995), 11–68.

5. See, for example, Steve Bruce, *Fundamentalism* (Oxford: Blackwell, 2000), 10, 66.

6. Bendroth, *Fundamentalism and Gender;* Betty DeBerg, *Ungodly Women: Gender and the First Wave of American Fundamentalism* (Minneapolis: Fortress Press, 1990); John S. Hawley and Wayne Proudfoot, eds., *Fundamentalism and Gender* (New York: Oxford University Press, 1993).

CHAPTER 2

1. Moses King, ed., *King's Handbook of Boston* (Boston: Rand, Avery, 1885), 206.

2. Arthur M. Schlesinger, Sr., "A Critical Period in American Religion," *Massachusetts Historical Society Proceedings* 64 (October 1930–June 1932): 532–546; Aaron Abell, *Urban Impact on American Protestantism, 1865–1900* (Cambridge: Harvard University Press, 1943); Henry F. May, *Protestant Churches and Industrial America* (New York: Harper, 1949).

3. Kevin J. Christiano, *Religious Diversity and Social Change: American Cities, 1890–1906* (Cambridge, England: Cambridge University Press, 1987); John M. Giggie and Diane Winston, eds., *Faith in the Market: Religion and the Rise of Urban Commercial Culture* (New Brunswick, N.J.: Rutgers University Press, 2002), 1.

4. Alan Lupo, *Liberty's Chosen Home: The Politics of Violence in Boston* (Boston: Beacon Press, 1977; reprint, 1988), xiii–xiv.

5. *Illustrated Boston, the Metropolis of New England* (New York: American Publishing and Engraving, 1889), 48. Boston's first subway was built in 1897.

6. *Report on Statistics of Churches in the United States at the Eleventh Census: 1890* (Washington, D.C.: Government Printing Office, 1894), 91.

7. Frank E. Frothingham, *The Boston Fire, November 9th and 10th 1872. Its History, Together with the Losses in Detail of Both Real and Personal Estate* (Boston: Lee and Shepard, 1873), 5–15.

8. "Trade Centers," in Richard Herndon, comp., *Boston of Today: A Glance at Its History and Characteristics* (Boston: Boston Post, 1892), 8–9.

9. Table based on Massachusetts census, in Albert Benedict Wolfe, *The Lodging House Problem in Boston* (Boston: Houghton Mifflin, 1906), 188. Italian and Jewish immigration were only just beginning in the 1880s.

10. Thomas H. O'Connor, *The Boston Irish: A Political History* (Boston: Northeastern University Press, 1995), 128–133.

11. Charles Zueblin, *American Municipal Progress* (New York: Macmillan, 1916), 393.

12. Roger Lane, *Policing the City: Boston 1882–1885* (Cambridge: Harvard University Press, 1967), 199–219.

13. Gerald Gamm, *Urban Exodus: Why the Jews Left Boston and the Catholics Stayed* (Cambridge: Harvard University Press, 1999).

14. Stephan Thernstrom, *The Other Bostonians: Poverty and Progress in the American Metropolis, 1880–1970* (Cambridge: Harvard University Press, 1973), 19.

15. John Von Rohr, *The Shaping of American Congregationalism, 1620–1957* (Cleveland: Pilgrim Press, 1992), 252; Paul Kemeny, "Power, Ridicule, and the Destruction of Religious Moral Reform Politics in the 1920s," in Christian Smith, ed., *The Secularization of American Public Life* (Berkeley: University of California Press, 2003), 133–152. See also "A Legend of Brimstone Corner," by M. A. DeWolfe Howe, reprinted in H. Crosby Englizian, *Brimstone Corner: Park Street Church, Boston* (Chicago: Moody Press, 1968), 14. Some sources argue that the real reason for the "Brimstone Corner" appellation was the fact that during the War of 1812, munitions were stored in the Park Street Church basement. See "One Hundred Years in the Heart of Boston," *Congregationalist and Christian World*, 13 March 1909, 343.

16. Membership figures from *Year-Book of the Congregational Church* (Boston: Congregational Publishing Society, 1886), 130.

17. "The Story of Park Street Church," *Congregationalist and Christian World*, 7 February 1903, 196.

18. Henry James, *The American Scene* (London: Chapman and Hall, 1907), 233, 234.

19. *Boston and Its Suburbs: A Guide Book* (Boston: Press of Stanley and Usher, 1888), 61.

20. Description in King, *King's Handbook of Boston*, 201–202; *Report on Statistics of Churches in the United States at the Eleventh Census: 1890*, 98.

21. Andrew Peabody, "The Unitarians in Boston," in *Memorial History of Boston*, vol. 3, ed. Justin Windsor (Boston: James R. Osgood, 1881), 479; *Report of Statistics of Churches in the United States at the Eleventh Census: 1890*, 95, 97, 99. See also observations in Wendte, "Why Do Not People Go to Church?" *Christian Register*, 7 May 1885, 296.

22. *The Education of Henry Adams: An Autobiography*, ed. D. W. Brogan (Boston: Houghton Mifflin, 1961), 27, 34.

23. George Santayana, *The Last Puritan: A Memoir in the Form of a Novel* (New York: Scribner's, 1936), 19.

24. King, *King's Handbook of Boston*, 170–171; *Boston and Its Suburbs*, 44–45; George Francis Marlowe, *Churches of Old New England: Their Architecture and Their Architects, Their Pastors and Their People* (New York: Macmillan, 1947), 18–36.

25. King, *King's Handbook of Boston*, 301–311.

26. Herndon, *Boston of Today*, 8. During the 1880s, Boston was in the middle of a strong upswing in foreign shipping trade. See W. H. Bunting, *Portrait of a Port: Boston, 1852–1914* (Cambridge: Harvard University Press, 1971), 13.

27. "The Soul of the City," in King, *King's Handbook of Boston*, 68–170; Marlowe, *Churches of Old New England*, 10–18.

28. *Illustrated Boston*, 64.

29. *Report of Statistics of Churches in the United States at the Eleventh Census: 1890*, 96–97. Thirty Congregational edifices were valued at $2,318,000. Unitarians had thirty churches, valued at $2,477,500.

30. *Report of Statistics of Churches in the United States at the Eleventh Census: 1890,* 97, 99; James Mudge, "A Brief Historical Sketch of Boston Methodism," in *Boston Methodism Survey* (Boston: Taylor Press, 1914), 5–11; King, *King's Handbook of Boston,* 202; John Winthrop Platner and William W. Fenn, *The Religious History of New England* (Cambridge: Harvard University Press, 1917), 251–294.

31. *Report of Statistics of Churches in the United States at the Eleventh Census: 1890,* 97, 99.

32. In 1885, the Boston city directory listed thirty-one Roman Catholic churches, located in a fringe around Beacon Hill and the business district, and spreading out into the new suburban areas, from Winthrop to Dorchester. The directory also listed eight Jewish congregations, all in the North and South Ends. See *The Boston Directory, Containing the City Record, Directory of the Citizens, and Business Directory, No. 81, For the Year Commencing July 1, 1885* (Boston: Sampson, Murdock, 1885), 1426–1427.

33. Herndon, *Boston of Today,* 54.

34. King, *King's Handbook of Boston,* 201. See also Winthrop and Fenn, *Religious History of New England,* 325–347.

35. Thomas H. O'Connor, *Bibles, Brahmins, and Bosses: A Short History of Boston,* 3rd ed. (Boston: Trustees of the Public Library, 1991), 121–122, 213–214; William H. Hester, *One Hundred and Five Years by Faith: A History of the Twelfth Baptist Church* (Boston, 1946). See also Arthur E. Paris, *Black Pentecostalism: Southern Religion in an Urban World* (Amherst: University of Massachusetts Press, 1982).

36. *Boston and Its Suburbs,* 68; *Dr. Cullis and His Work. Twenty Years of Blessing in Answer to Prayer,* ed. W. H. Daniels (Boston: Willard Tract Repository, n.d.; reprint, New York: Garland, 1985). On faith healing, see James Opp, "Healing Hands, Healthy Bodies: Protestant Women and Faith Healing in Canada and the United States, 1880–1930," in *Women and Twentieth-Century Protestantism,* ed. Margaret Bendroth and Virginia Brereton (Urbana: University of Illinois Press, 2002), 236–256.

37. "The Army Arrested," *Boston Globe,* 30 May 1885, 1. One other large holiness group in New England was established by Frank Sanford in Shiloh, Maine, in 1882 as a community for believers that specialized in care for orphans. His increasingly authoritarian role in the community is described by Shirley Nelson, *Fair, Clear, and Terrible: The Story of Shiloh, Maine* (Latham, N.Y.: British American, 1989).

38. "They Jump and Shout, Great Enthusiasm at the Park Street Revival," *Boston Globe,* 9 December 1901, 1, 3. For the full story, see chapter 8.

39. Katherine McCarthy, "Psychotherapy and Religion: The Emmanuel Movement," *Journal of Religion and Health* 23 (summer 1984): 92–105. Figures for Christian Science from Sidney Ahlstrom, *A Religious History of the American People* (New Haven: Yale University Press, 1972), 1022–1023.

40. "Christian Science," *Congregationalist,* 30 April 1885, 149. The address was subsequently published: Stacy Fowler, "Christian Science," *Homiletic Review* 10 (August 1885): 134–141. On Unitarians, see Raymond J. Cunningham, "The Impact of Christian Science on the American Churches, 1880–1910," *American Historical Review* 72 (April 1967): 887.

41. Cook's brief remarks are found in "Joseph Cook's Lecture," *Congregationalist,* 19 March 1885, 151. See also Townsend, *"Faith-Work," "Christian Science," and Other Cures* (Boston: W. A. Wilde, 1885), and Gordon, "Christian Science," *Watchman,* 5 March 1885, n.p.

42. *Boston and Its Suburbs*, 41–42; "Letter from Boston," *Congregationalist*, 16 April 1885, 138.

43. Robert W. Snyder, *The Voice of the City: Vaudeville and Popular Culture in New York* (New York: Oxford University Press, 1989), 26.

44. "The Social Side of the City," in King, *King's Handbook of Boston*, 247–251; "The Theaters," in Herndon, *Boston of Today*, 90–100.

45. David Kruh, *Always Something Doing: Boston's Infamous Scollay Square*, rev. ed. (Boston: Northeastern University Press, 1999).

46. Edward Stanwood, "Topography and Landmarks of the Last Hundred Years," in *Memorial History of Boston*, ed. Justin Windsor, vol. 1 (Boston: J. R. Osgood, 1880–81), 53.

47. Editorial, *Converted Catholic* 4 (May 1887): 130.

48. Santayana, *Last Puritan*, 32.

49. *Illustrated Boston*, 88.

50. Walter Muir Whitehill, *Boston: A Topographical History*, 2nd ed. (Cambridge: Harvard University Press, 1968), 156; *Illustrated Boston*, 85. The state spent $1,750,000 on land reclamation but brought in $4,625,000 in land sales.

51. Whitehill, *Boston*, 159.

52. Arthur Warren Smith, *Special Report to the Committee of Seven upon the Baptist Situation in Boston Proper: A Survey of Historical and Present Conditions* (Boston: Griffith-Stillings Press, 1912), 65–67.

53. A. R. Willard, "Recent Church Architecture in Boston," *New England Magazine* (February 1890): 641–662.

54. Robert H. Lord, John E. Sexton, and Edward T. Harrington, *History of the Archdiocese of Boston in the Various Stages of Its Development 1604 to 1943 in Three Volumes*, vol. 3 (New York: Sheed and Ward, 1944), 242–243.

55. Whitehill, *Boston*, 164.

56. Whitehill, *Boston*, 168.

57. *Boston and Its Suburbs*, 13.

58. Hamilton Andrews Hill, *History of the Old South Church (Third Church) Boston 1669–1884*, vol. 2 (Boston: Houghton Mifflin, 1890), 551–580. The aggressive questioning by Withrow and Plumb was, of course, problematic for Congregationalists, whose institutional structure placed primary emphasis on the individual congregation's primary right to call and ordain their own pastors.

59. Cook cited in Sharon Taylor, "That Obnoxious Dogma: Future Probation and the Struggle to Construct an American Congregationalist Identity" (Ph.D. diss., Boston College, 2004).

60. C. H. Blackall, "Boston Sketches—The Churches," *Inland Architect and News Record* 12 (December 1888), 77.

61. *Boston and Its Suburbs*, 3–18.

62. "Letter from Boston," *Congregationalist*, 18 March 1886, 96.

63. *Illustrated Boston*, 89; King, *King's Handbook of Boston*, 178; *Boston of Today*, 70. (Historical information is also provided at the First Spiritual Temple website, available online at: www.fst.org. Consulted January 24, 2003.)

64. The count included both evening services at Protestant churches and the four or five Sunday Masses offered to Catholics. "Church Attendance in Boston,"

Congregationalist, 26 April 1882, 4. The highest proportion of evening church attenders among Protestants were Methodists (66 percent) and Baptists (54 percent), followed by Episcopalians (39 percent), Congregationalists (38 percent), and Unitarians (17 percent).

65. Daniel Dorchester, *Christianity in the United States* (New York: Phillips and Hunt, 1888), 747.

66. *The Boston Directory Containing the City Record: A Directory of the Citizens, Business Directory, and Street Directory with Map for the Year Commencing 1885; The Boston Directory Containing the City Record, A Directory of the Citizens, Business Directory and Street Directory with Map, No. 111, For the Year Commencing July 1, 1915* (Boston: Sampson and Murdock, 1915), 101–105; *Boston City Directory for the Year Commencing July, 1935* (Boston: Sampson, Murdock, and Company, 1935), 2539–2540, 2542–2544.

67. *Boston and Its Suburbs*, 87.

68. Albert Wolfe, *The Lodging-House Problem in Boston* (Boston: 1906), 14.

69. Lord, Sexton, and Harrington, *History of the Archdiocese of Boston*, 247.

70. *Illustrated Boston*, 61; King, *King's Handbook of Boston*, 181–183.

71. A German congregation, the Church of the Holy Trinity, was also in the South End, on Shawmut Avenue. See *Boston Directory, 1885*, 1427.

72. Ellen Smith, "'Israelites in Boston,' 1840–1880," in *The Jews of Boston*, ed. Jonathan D. Sarna and Ellen Smith (Boston: Combined Jewish Philanthropies of Greater Boston, 1995), 49–67; William A. Braverman, "The Emergence of a Unified Community, 1880–1917," in Sarna and Smith, *The Jews of Boston*, 71–90; Solomon Schindler, *Israelites in Boston: A Tale Describing the Development of Judaism in Boston, Preceded by the Jewish Calendar for the Next Decade* (Boston: Berwick and Smith, 1889); *Boston Directory, 1885*, 204–205; Gamm, *Urban Exodus*, 104.

73. On Reformed Episcopalians, see Allen C. Guelzo, *For the Union of Evangelical Christendom: The Irony of the Reformed Episcopalians* (University Park: Pennsylvania State University Press, 1994); Charles Edward Cheney, *What Do Reformed Episcopalians Believe?* (Philadelphia: Reformed Episcopal Publication Society, 1888). Gray met Dwight Moody in 1893, at the Northfield conferences. He was also fond of controversy, publically denouncing Boston's three great sins, "yellow journalism, rum, and the pagan doctrine of Christian Science." See Helen Dixon, *A. C. Dixon: A Romance of Preaching* (New York: Putnam, 1931; reprint, New York: Garland, 1988), 145–156.

74. "A Blessing to Boston: The Ruggles Street Baptist Church and Its Work," *Watchman*, 2 May 1901, 10–12.

75. See Dixon, *A. C. Dixon*, 145–156.

76. Curtis Lee Laws, "Ruggles Street Church, Boston," *Watchman-Examiner*, 20 April 1916, 489–492.

77. For description, see King, *King's Handbook of Boston*, 195–196. The city directory listed two "First" Universalist Churches, one in Charlestown and the other in the Roxbury area (1427).

78. *Report of Statistics of Churches in the United States at the Eleventh Census: 1890*, 95. The census also listed eight Universalist churches in Boston, with assets at $396,000; 97, 99. The city directory for 1885 listed ten Universalist churches, including two in the South End, and the rest in East and South Boston, and in outlying sections of the city (1427).

79. On the classification scheme, see Dorchester, *Christianity in the United States,* 750–751.

80. On Miner, see David Robinson, *The Unitarians and the Universalists* (Westport, Conn.: Greenwood Press, 1985), 296. On his anti-Catholicism, see George H. Emerson, *Life of Alonzo Ames Miner* (Boston: Universalist, 1896), 465; Lord, Sexton, and Harrington, *History of the Archdiocese of Boston,* 107.

81. Emerson, *Life of Alonzo Ames Miner,* 230–231, 235–236, 238.

82. Census listed assets at 220,000. On Plan of Union, see Von Rohr, *The Shaping of American Congregationalism, 1620–1957,* 262–65.

83. Gary Burrill, *Maritimers in Massachusetts, Ontario, and Alberta: An Oral History of Leaving Home* (Montreal: McGill-Queen's University Press, 1992), 98–106.

84. *Boston and Its Suburbs,* 89; King, *King's Handbook of Boston,* 187, 194.

85. Jonathan Dorn, " 'Our Best Gospel Appliances': Institutional Churches and the Emergence of Social Christianity in the South End of Boston, 1880–1920" (Ph.D diss., Harvard University, 1994), 51.

86. Ernest R. Gordon, *Adoniram Judson Gordon: A Biography* (New York: Fleming H. Revell, 1896; reprint, New York: Garland, 1984), 103, 106.

87. Figures taken from *Minutes of Boston South Baptist Association, 1885* (Boston, 1885).

88. Dorn, " 'Our Best Gospel Appliances,' " 218–220, 313–322.

89. Jack Tager, *Boston Riots: Three Centuries of Social Violence* (Boston: Northeastern University Press, 2001), 4.

CHAPTER 3

1. "Preaching on the Common," *Boston Evening Transcript,* 21 May 1885, 1.

2. H. L. Hastings, "A Proud Day for Boston," *Safeguard* 20 (July 1885): 2.

3. "Preaching on the Common."

4. Hastings, "A Proud Day for Boston"; "Clergymen in Court," *Boston Globe,* 21 May 1885, 1.

5. *Report of Proceedings of the City Council of Boston, for the Municipal Year 1885* (Boston: Rockwell and Churchill, 1886), 429.

6. Geoffrey Blodgett, "Frederick Law Olmsted: Landscape Architecture as Conservative Reform," *Journal of American History* 62 (March 1976): 869–889.

7. Harry S. Stout, *Divine Dramatist: George Whitefield and the Rise of Modern Evangelicalism* (Grand Rapids, Mich.: Eerdmans, 1991), 119–123; "After Fifty Years," *Zion's Herald,* 11 October 1916, 1289.

8. The *Boston Evening Record* printed a map of the gambling establishments on the Common on 27 May 1885.

9. See description in *Illustrated Boston: The Metropolis of New England* (New York: American Publishing and Engraving, 1889), 40–47.

10. See also Roy Rosenzweig, "Middle-Class Parks and Working-Class Play: The Struggle over Recreational Space in Worcester, Massachusetts, 1870–1910," *Radical History Review* 21 (fall 1979): 31–46.

11. Stephen Hardy, *How Boston Played: Sport, Recreation and Community, 1865–1915* (Boston: Northeastern University Press, 1982), 82–83.

12. "Letter from Boston," *Congregationalist*, 13 May 1886, 168; James R. Green and Hugh Carter Donahue, *Boston's Workers: A Labor History* (Boston: Trustees of the Public Library, 1979), 36–40.

13. Hardy, *How Boston Played*, 80.

14. Thomas W. Lawson, *The Krank: His Language and What It Means* (Boston: Rand Avery, 1888).

15. C. Allyn Russell, "Adoniram Judson Gordon: Nineteenth-Century Fundamentalist," *American Baptist Quarterly* 4 (1985): 61–89.

16. See Hastings's account in "An Unlooked-for Honor," *Safeguard* 20 (July 1885): 3.

17. "William F. Davis: The Story of His Life," *British-American Citizen*, 15 September 1888, 3.

18. The elder Davis's obituary and a quotation from some of his writings on holiness were cited in Elizabeth E. Flagg, "New England Letter," *Christian Cynosure*, 3 October 1889, 4–5.

19. "Mr. Davis in Music Hall," *British-American Citizen*, 15 September 1888, 3.

20. If Hastings's figures are correct, he was right as far as Protestant papers were concerned. The Roman Catholic *Pilot* had a circulation of seventy thousand, but among Protestants the *Christian* was well in the lead, even approaching figures for secular newspaper dailies. In 1885, the *Congregationalist* was the most widely read religious periodical (21,000), followed by the Baptist *Watchman* (17,500) and the Methodist *Zion's Herald* (16,000). The Spiritualist *Banner of Light* reported 18,400. The *Boston Globe* (Democratic) reported a morning and evening circulation of fifty-five thousand and the *Boston Journal* (Republican) forty-eight thousand. Boston's most popular newspaper was the independent *Herald*, with a morning and evening circulation of 102,500. See figures in N. W. Ayer and Son's *American Newspaper Annual* (Philadelphia: N. W. Ayer, 1885), 29–32.

21. See, e.g., Albert Johnson, *A Concise Narrative of the Origin and Progress, Doctrine and Work of This Body of Believers* (Boston: Advent Christian Publication Society, 1918), 398–400. Hastings's career is also documented in his wife Harriet's popular *Pebbles from the Path of a Pilgrim* (Boston: H. L. Hastings, 1885). The *Christian* was a monthly bound together with several other small papers that Hastings published, including the *Armory*, the *Safeguard*, and the *Common People*.

22. Accounts mentioned Abijah Hall, Cyrus Peckham, and O. Peterson, as well as the Salvationists William Dean, Anne Shirley, and Lizzie Lothian.

23. See, e.g., "The Army Arrested," *Boston Globe*, 30 May 1885, 1. The article quoted a Salvation Army captain's wife vowing that "she would commit murder if her conscience told her she was doing her Master's will."

24. Thomas H. O'Connor, *The Boston Irish: A Political History* (Boston: Northeastern University Press, 1995), 128–132.

25. Blodgett, "Yankee Leadership in a Divided City, 1860–1919," in *Boston, 1700–1980: The Evolution of Urban Politics*, ed. Ronald P. Formisano and Constance K. Burns (Westport, Conn.: Greenwood Press, 1984), 88, 98.

26. Blodgett, "Yankee Leadership in a Divided City," 132.

27. "Letter from Boston," *Congregationalist*, 16 July 1885, 244.

28. Robert H. Lord, John E. Sexton, and Edward T. Harrington, *History of the Archdiocese of Boston*, vol. 3 (New York: Sheed and Ward, 1944), 87.

29. Lord, Sexton, and Harrington, *History of the Archdiocese of Boston*, 141.

30. "The Amendment Defeated in Massachusetts, April 22," *Union Signal,* 2 May 1889, 4.

31. Richard Harmond, "Troubles of Massachusetts Republicans During the 1880s," *Mid-America* 56 (April 1974): 91–93.

32. In 1888, Boston had forty-seven Total Abstinence Societies with a membership of 3,742. See "C.T.A.U. of America," *Pilot,* 11 August 1888, 1. By 1909, the over two hundred total abstinence societies had formed in the Boston archdiocese. See Maurice Dinneen, *The Catholic Total Abstinence Movement in the Archdiocese of Boston* (Boston: Grimes, 1908), n.p. See also John F. Quinn, "Father Mathew's Disciples: American Catholic Support for Temperance, 1840–1920," *Church History* 65 (December 1996): 624–640.

33. Blodgett, "Yankee Leadership in a Divided City," 97.

34. Roger Lane, *Policing the City: Boston, 1822–1885* (Cambridge: Harvard University Press, 1967), 211. The measure in question was the ratio of arrests for drunkenness measured against city population.

35. *Standard Encyclopedia of the Alcohol Problem,* vol. 1 (Westerville, Ohio: American Issue, 1925), 377–378.

36. Lane, *Policing the City,* 214–215.

37. "Robbing Boston of Her Rights," *Republic,* 16 March 1884.

38. In the long run, the takeover of Boston's municipal services by outsiders was successful. By the turn of the century, Boston had a metropolitan police force, though it was one of the last large cities in the country to do so, as well as a state-appointed metropolitan water and sewage board and a park system administered by the governor. The state also administered Boston's street railways, gas and electric utilities, liquor licensing, and civil service commissions. But the changes did not proceed without conflict. The regular presence of the state legislature in the city of Boston, as well as "the absence of any constitutional limitations restricting [its] power and authority . . . over cities in Massachusetts," one city planner observed in 1910, "has subjected Boston to a greater degree of central control by the legislature and the state administration than is found elsewhere in the United States." See Delos F. Wilcox, *Great Cities in America: Their Problems and Their Government* (New York: Macmillan, 1910), 347. See also Charles Zueblin, *American Municipal Progress* (New York: Macmillan, 1916), 393–394.

39. "Review of the Week: Disgraceful Proceedings," *Watchman,* 18 June 1885, 8.

40. "A Fable for Boston," *Pilot,* 30 May 1885, 1.

41. "Short-Sighted Partisans," *Republic,* 16 May 1885, 4.

42. Editorials, *Pilot,* 30 May 1885, 4. See also "Preaching on the Common," *Boston Globe,* 22 May 1885, 2; "What People Talk About," *Boston Globe,* 28 May 1885, 4.

43. "Rev. A. J. Gordon," *Boston Evening Transcript,* 25 May 1885, 4; "The City's Public Grounds," *Herald Supplement,* 18 May 1885, 1.

44. "Brevities," *Christian Register,* 9 July 1885, 435.

45. Lucius Beebe, *Boston and the Boston Legend* (New York: Appleton-Century, 1936), 163.

46. "The Out-Door Exhorters," *Boston Globe,* 27 May 1885, 4.

47. "Clergymen in Court," *Boston Globe,* 28 May 1885, 1.

48. "Clergymen Not Relenting," *Boston Globe Supplement,* 26 May 1885, 2.

49. *Report of Proceedings of the City Council of Boston, for the Municipal Year 1885* (Boston: Rockwell and Churchill, 1886), 379.

50. "Boston Ministers' Meeting," *Boston Globe Supplement*, 18 June 1885, 209.

51. "Preaching on Boston Common," *Congregationalist*, 4 June 1885, 190 (partial reprint of *New York Independent*).

52. C., "Permits to Preach on the Common," *Boston Evening Transcript*, 28 May 1885, 6.

53. W. H. Davis, *Christian Liberties in Boston: A Sketch of Recent Attempts to Destroy Them Through the Device of a Gag-By-Law for Gospel Preachers* (Chelsea, Mass., 1887), 25.

54. Davis, *Christian Liberties in Boston*, 33.

55. Editorial, *Watchman*, 18 June 1885; see "City and Suburbs. About Town," *Boston Daily Advertiser*, 4 August 1884, 8.

56. "To the Members of the Legislature of Massachusetts," *Safeguard* 21 (June 1886): 2. Hastings detailed the story of his arrest in "In Jail for Preaching," *Christian* 21 (May 1886): 3.

57. "What Has Been Gained?" *Safeguard* 21 (June 1886): 3.

58. Davis, *Christian Liberties in Boston*, 38.

59. Davis, *Christian Liberties in Boston*, 46. At the annual meeting of the Massachusetts Woman Suffrage Association in Boston, Reverend L. B. Bates, a friend of Gordon from East Boston, publicly applauded the Protestant martyrs. Bates's list, however, included Gordon, Hastings, and the YMCA secretary M. R. Deming, who was not arrested, and omitted Davis. "Woman Suffragists," *Boston Globe*, 27 May 1885, 3.

60. The move was apparently also controversial within the YMCA. See letter to the editor, "Preaching on the Common," *Boston Evening Transcript*, 13 June 1885, 11. Eventually the Salvation Army and the "Brethren" also received permits from the city.

61. "The Common, Not Common," *Boston Globe* 30 May 1885, 4.

62. "Boston Shaking Herself," *Safeguard* 24 (January 1889): 3.

63. *Inaugural Address of Hugh O'Brien, Mayor of Boston, Before the City Council, January 2, 1888* (Boston: Rockwell and Churchill, 1888), 29. John Boyle O'Reilly described Hastings and Davis in similar term, dismissing them angrily as "political reptiles . . . stirring up the slime of religious hatred in Boston of late." "Preaching in Boston Common," *Pilot*, 7 January 1888, 1.

64. *Inaugural Address of Hugh O'Brien*, 32.

65. "Liberty of Speech in Boston," *Watchman*, 8 March 1888, 6.

66. "Music Hall Meetings," *Woman's Voice and Public School Champion*, 30 October 1890, 1.

CHAPTER 4

1. Mark S. Massa, *Anti-Catholicism in America: The Last Acceptable Prejudice* (New York: Crossroad, 2003), 18–19; John Higham, *Strangers in the Land: Patterns of American Nativism, 1860–1925* (New York: Athenaeum, 1965); Les Wallace, *The Rhetoric of Anti-Catholicism: The American Protective Association, 1887–1911* (New York: Garland, 1990); Richard Hofstadter, *The Paranoid Style in American Politics, and Other Essays* (New York: Knopf, 1965), and *Anti-Intellectualism in American Life* (New York: Knopf, 1963).

2. On the school controversy, see John McGreevy, *Catholicism and American Freedom: A History* (New York: Norton, 2003), 112–126. On the Boston controversy, see Lawrence W. Kennedy, "Pulpits and Politics: Anti-Catholicism in Boston in the 1880s and 1890s," *Historical Journal of Massachusetts* 28 (winter 2000): 23–55; Polly Welts Kaufman, *Boston Women and City School Politics, 1872–1905* (New York: Garland, 1994); Robert H. Lord, John E. Sexton, and Edward T. Harrington, *History of the Archdiocese of Boston in the Various Stages of Its Development 1604–1943*, vol. 3 (New York: Sheed and Ward, 1944), 75–159.

3. "News from the Field. Massachusetts," *Union Signal*, 10 November 1887, 11.

4. See, e.g., Martin Marty and Scott Appleby, eds., *Fundamentalisms and the State: Remaking Politics, Economies, and Militance* (Chicago: University of Chicago Press, 1993).

5. "Grand Rally Held by the Independent Women Voters," *Woman's Voice and Public School Champion*, 25 September 1890, 1.

6. John Wolffe, "Anti-Catholicism and Evangelical Identity in Britain and the United States, 1830–1860," in *Evangelicalism: Comparative Studies of Popular Protestantism in North America, the British Isles, and Beyond, 1700–1990*, ed. Mark A. Noll, David W. Bebbington, and George A. Rawlyk (New York: Oxford University Press, 1994), 179–197.

7. McGreevy, *Catholicism and American Freedom*.

8. "Review of the Week: A New Movement," *Watchman*, 17 September 1885, 8; Editorial, *Congregationalist*, 17 September 1885, 309; "The Boston School Committee," *Woman's Journal*, 12 September 1885, 292.

9. Kaufman, *Boston Women and City School Politics*, 102.

10. Lois Bannister Merk, "Boston's Historic Public School Crisis," *New England Quarterly* 31 (June 1958): 176.

11. *Minutes of the Eleventh Annual Meeting of the Massachusetts WCTU, Held in the Methodist Episcopal Church, Somerville, October 8 and 9, 1884* (Malden, Mass., 1884), 15. Mary Hunt, director of Scientific Temperance Education for the national WCTU, lived in Boston.

12. "Review of the Week: Registration of Women," *Watchman*, 24 September 1885, 8.

13. *Minutes of the Fourteenth Annual Meeting of the WCTU, Held in Tremont Temple, Boston* (Boston, 1887), 21, 26.

14. Nathan R. Wood, *A School of Christ* (Boston: Halliday Lithograph, 1953), 33–34. Clara C. Chapin, ed., *Thumb Nail Sketches of White Ribbon Women* (Chicago: Woman's Temperance Publishing Association, 1895), 113.

15. John Beauregard, ed., *Journal of Our Journey: By Maria Hale Gordon and Adoniram Judson Gordon* (Wenham, Mass.: Gordon College Archives, 1989), 106.

16. Dolan, "Catholic Attitudes Toward Protestants," in *Uncivil Religion: Interreligious Hostility in America*, ed. Robert Bellah and Frederick Greenspahn (New York: Crossroad, 1987), 76.

17. McGreevy, *Catholicism and American Freedom*, 117; Lord, Sexton, and Harrington, *History of the Archdiocese of Boston*, 79–85.

18. "School Suffrage Symposium," *Woman's Journal*, 10 October 1885, 329.

19. "Review of the Week: A New Movement," *Watchman*, 17 September 1885, 8.

20. Editorial, *Woman's Journal*, 19 September 1885, 298.

21. Editorial, *Woman's Journal*, 12 September 1885, 289.

22. Kaufman, *Boston Women and City School Politics*, 130–131; "Women Voters a Power in Boston," *Woman's Journal*, 26 December 1885.

23. "Women in Public Life," *Boston Herald*, 24 October 1887, 5.

24. "In the Lap of Rome," *British-American Citizen*, 8 September 1888, 6.

25. Wylie, "Popery, Rescusitated and Consumated Paganism," *Watchword* 10 (October 1888): 178.

26. Justin Dewey Fulton, *How to Win Romanists* (Somerville, Mass.: Pauline Propaganda, 1898), 297–298.

27. Jonathan M. Butler, "Adventism and the American Experience," in *The Rise of Adventism: Religion and Society in Mid-Nineteenth-Century America*, ed. Edwin S. Gaustad (New York: Harper and Row, 1974), 186; Robert Fuller, *Naming the Antichrist: The History of an American Obsession* (New York: Oxford University Press, 1995), 103–107.

28. Ernest Sandeen, *The Roots of Fundamentalism: British and American Millenarianism, 1800–1930* (Chicago: University of Chicago Press, 1970), 76–78. Sandeen also cites evidence that, during his time in Boston, Darby may also have met with A. J. Gordon, who would later become another leader of the premillennial movement in America. Hastings's views on Darby are not known. In 1885, according to the city directory, there were only two Adventist congregations in Boston, one in the South End and the other on Boylston Place, most likely in the Back Bay. See also David T. Arthur, "Joshua V. Himes and the Cause of Adventism," in *The Disappointed: Millerism and Millenarianism in the Nineteenth Century*, ed. Ronald L. Numbers and Jonathan M. Butler (Bloomington: Indiana University Press, 1987), 36–58.

29. "The Warfare," *Christian* 17 (April 1882): 2.

30. "Running a Church," *Safeguard* 17 (June 1882): 3.

31. "The Hidden Hand," *Safeguard* 22 (November 1887): 3.

32. Ernest B. Gordon, *Adoniram Judson Gordon: A Biography* (New York: Fleming H. Revell, 1896; reprint, New York: Garland, 1984), 119.

33. Western Union telegram from Joseph Cook to A. J. Gordon, 23 May 1885, in Gordon Family Correspondence, 1830–1885, box 1 (1 D1 [G5]), A. J. Gordon Papers, Gordon College, Wenham, Mass.

34. On Gordon and Catholics before 1889, see Gordon, "Christ—The Light and the Glory," *Watchword* 5 (December 1882): 56; George Marsden, *Fundamentalism and American Culture, 1875–1920* (New York: Oxford University Press, 1980), 67.

35. Paul Boyer, *When Time Shall Be No More: Prophecy Belief in Modern American Culture* (Cambridge: Harvard University Press, 1992), 273–274.

36. A. J. Gordon, *Ecce Venit: Behold He Cometh* (New York: Fleming H. Revell, 1889), 136.

37. Gordon, *Ecce Venit*, 102, 104.

38. Scott Gibson, *A. J. Gordon: American Premillennialist* (Lanham, Md.: University Press of America, 2002), 33–36, 166; Timothy Weber, *Living in the Shadow of the Second Coming: American Premillennialism, 1875–1982* (Chicago: University of Chicago Press, 1987), 9–12. See Brookes, "What Is the Temple of God?" *Truth* 10 (December 1883): 17.

39. Gordon, *Ecce Venit*, 94, 121. In another sense, the pope and Catholic ritual were not the main issue. In Minneapolis, where Jews formed the main opposition to moralistic

evangelical politics of civic renewal, anti-Semitism substituted for anti-Catholicism. William Bell Riley, the leader of fundamentalists in Minneapolis, marshalled his followers around his own conspiracy theory linking Jews with New Deal communists and liberals. See William Vance Trollinger, *God's Empire: William Bell Riley and Midwestern Fundamentalism* (Madison: University of Wisconsin Press, 1990), 62–82.

40. Gordon, "My People Love to Have It So," *Watchword* 13 (March 1891): 71.

41. Gordon, "The Uplifted Gaze," *Watchword* 10 (October 1888): 173.

42. "Music Hall Meetings," *Woman's Voice and Public School Champion*, 30 October 1890, 1; "Music Hall Meetings," *Woman's Voice and Public School Champion*, 18 March 1893, 1,3.

43. "The Church of Rome in Prophecy and Politics," *British-American Citizen*, 14 July 1888, 2.

44. "Boston Aroused," *Converted Catholic* 5 (August 1888): 233.

45. William F. Davis, *Christian Liberties in Boston: A Sketch of Recent Attempts to Destroy Them Through the Device of a Gag-By-Law for Gospel Preachers* (Chelsea, Mass.: 1887), 18.

46. Davis, *Christian Liberties in Boston*, 9.

47. "Who Is at the Bottom of It?" *Safeguard* 20 (July 1885): 3.

48. Phelps, "Preaching on Boston Common," *Congregationalist*, 23 July 1885, 245.

49. Gerald W. McFarland, *Mugwumps, Morals and Politics: 1884–1920* (Amherst: University of Massachusetts Press, 1975), 28; "Music Hall Meetings," *Woman's Voice and Public School Citizen*, 16 October 1890, 3.

50. Editorial, *Pilot*, 21 July 1888, 4.

51. "The Evangelical Alliance," *British-American Citizen*, 15 September 1888, 1. For a similar impression, see "Work at Home," *Record of Christian Work* 11 (September 1892): 271.

52. Lord, Sexton, and Harrington, *History of the Archdiocese of Boston*, 104.

53. Lord, Sexton, and Harrington, *History of the Archdiocese of Boston*, 106.

54. "'The Converted Nun,'" *British-American Citizen*, 14 April 1888, 1.

55. In the 1880s, Boston housed 13,496 immigrants from Nova Scotia in Boston, 10,197 from England, 7,516 from New Brunswick, and 4,055 English Canadians. Most were concentrated in East Boston. See "The British-Americans," *Boston Herald*, 7 November 1887, 5.

56. Lord, Sexton, and Harrington, *History of the Archdiocese of Boston*, 101–102; D.G. Paz, *Popular Anti-Catholicism in Mid-Victorian England* (Stanford, Calif.: Stanford University Press, 1992); Wolffe, "Anti-Catholicism."

57. These are described in Beauregard, *Journal of Our Journey*.

58. "British Immigration," *British-American Citizen*, 7 April 1888, 1.

59. Boston: Arnold, 1890.

60. "Evangelist George C. Needham," *Converted Catholic* 3 (January 1886): 1–2. Elizabeth Needham was a published author in her own right, perhaps best known for *Woman's Ministry* (Chicago: Revell, 1880). She also wrote, on eschatology, *The Antichrist* (New York: C. C. Cook, 1881), and *Angels and Demons* (Chicago: Gospel, 1891), and on biblical interpretation, *Melchizedek and Aaron as Types of Christ the Royal Priest* (New York: C. C. Cook, 1904).

61. Editorial, *Congregationalist*, 30 June 1887, 228; British-American Association, *Faneuil Hall: Who Are Its Conservators?* (Boston, n.d.).

62. "British Immigration," *Safeguard* 23 (April 1888): 3.

63. Mark C. Carnes, *Secret Ritual and Manhood in Victorian America* (New Haven: Yale University Press, 1989), 69–90. Ironically, the leader of the anti-Catholic American Protective Association, Henry F. Bowers, was a devoted Mason; much of his support came from Masonic lodges, and he borrowed heavily from Masonic ritual in putting together the black-and-yellow regalia used in the Association's initiation ceremonies.

64. Marsden, *Fundamentalism and American Culture*, 30; Blanchard quoted in David Hackett, "The Church and the Lodge: Gender Tensions, Region, and Theology in Late Nineteenth Century Protestant Culture," unpublished paper, 5.

65. Carnes, *Secret Ritual and Manhood in Victorian America*.

66. "To the Pastors of New England and Their People," *Christian Cynosure*, 14 November 1889, 8; *Boston Directory Containing the City Record, Directory of the Citizens and Business Directory, for the Year Commencing July 1, 1885* (Boston: Sampson, Murdock, 1885), 1431–1436.

67. Elizabeth E. Flagg, "Address Before the New Hampshire Christian Association," *Christian Cynosure* 5 January 1888, 2–3.

68. "No Gospel on Boston Common," Christian Cynosure, 21 June 1888, 1; "The Voice from Suffolk Jail, Charles Street, Boston," *Christian Cynosure*, 31 May 1888, 2.

69. Mathews, "Our Boston Letter," *Christian Cynosure*, 5 April 1888, 4.

70. "The Boston Conference," *Christian Cynosure*, 5 December 1885, 8; Gordon, "Divided Allegiances," in *Danger Signals: Secret Societies Illuminated* (Boston: James H. Earle, 1894), 8–9.

71. "To the Pastors of New England and Their People," *Christian Cynosure*, 14 November 1889, 8; Gleason, "A Foe to Reformers," in *Danger Signals*, 37.

72. "A Timely Paper. Freemasons and the Church of Rome," *British-American Citizen*, 28 November 1889, 2; Davis, *Christian Liberties in Boston*, vii.

73. "Annual Convention of the New England Christian Association," *Woman's Voice and Public School Champion*, 10 December 1892, 1; and contributors to New England Christian Association, *Danger Signals*.

74. "The Boston Congress: Report of Proceedings," *Christian Cynosure*, 19 December 1889, 9.

75. "New England Letter," *Christian Cynosure*, 19 December 1889, 12.

76. Stephen Hardy, *How Boston Played* (Boston: Northeastern University Press, 1982), 168–175; Michael T. Isenberg, *John L. Sullivan and His America* (Urbana: University of Illinois Press, 1988), 202–203.

77. "How Boston Honors Prize-Fighters and Preachers!" *Safeguard* 22 (November 1887): 2; "Things to Be Remembered," *Safeguard* 24 (October 1889): 1.

78. "Women to the Front," *British-American Citizen*, 9 March 1889, 5.

79. John F. Kasson, *Houdini, Tarzan and the Perfect Man: The White Male Body and the Challenge of Modernity in America* (New York: Hill and Wang, 2001), 40–41.

80. "The Irish Athletes," *Pilot*, 6 October 1888, 1, 4. See also McDannell, "'True Men as We Need Them': Catholicism and the Irish-American Male," *American Studies* 26 (fall 1986): 19–36.

81. Gail Bederman, *Manliness and Civilization: A Cultural History of Gender and Race in the United States, 1880–1917* (Chicago: University of Chicago Press, 1995), 10–15.

82. "Home Rule in New Ireland," *Safeguard* 23 (March 1888): 1.

83. Fulton, *How to Win Romanists*, 239, 240. See also Marie Anne Pagliarini, "The Pure American Woman and the Wicked Catholic Priest: An Analysis of Anti-Catholic Literature in Antebellum America," *Religion and American Culture* 9 (winter 1999): 97–128.

84. Fulton, *How to Win Romanists*, 422, 423, 429, 430.

85. Elizabeth P. Gordon, "Municipal Election in Boston," *Union Signal*, 27 December 1888, 2.

86. Lord, Sexton, and Harrington, *History of the Archdiocese of Boston*, 120–123; Kennedy, "Pulpits and Politics," 62–63; Kaufman, *Boston Women and City School Politics*, 149–151.

87. "Women to the Front," 5; "The Converted Nun," *British-American Citizen*, 14 April 1888, 1.

88. "Women to the Front," 5. The article also noted that of the 73,666 men registered, only 63,548 (86 percent) voted. Kaufman, *Boston Women and City School Politics*, 158.

89. Kennedy, "Pulpits and Politics," 65.

90. "Private Schools," *Pilot*, 7 April 1888, 1.

91. "How Do You Read It?" *British-American Citizen*, 7 December 1889, 4.

92. Tensions were obvious in some older Protestant organizations. The national YMCA voted in 1868 to restrict office-holding and voting to members of "Evangelical" churches. In 1871 a local Unitarian minister unsuccessfully challenged the rule. In 1885, however, when the Boston YMCA took over new property on Boylston Street, it was bound by the conditions of a trust that would transfer title to the American Bible Society "if at any time hereafter the said Association shall cease to promote evangelical religion" or its Board of Managers include nonevangelicals. The move was supported by Joseph Cook, who argued that "evangelicals and unevangelicals are so at variance, that they should be represented by different ecclesiastical organizations." "The Monday Lecture," *Woman's Voice and Public School Citizen*, 6 March 1890, 2. See also William B. Whiteside, *The Boston Y.M.C.A. and Community Need* (New York: Association Press, 1951), 87–89.

93. Jack Tager, *Boston Riots: Three Centuries of Social Violence* (Boston: Northeastern University Press, 2001), 108–119.

94. Henry Morgan, *Boston Inside Out! Sins of Great City! A Story of Real Life* (Boston: Shawmut, 1880), 205. Titus also rejoices in anti-Catholic persecution, because it promised to shock "tender Protestants" into a "revolution in public feelings." "We looked for it, longed, for it, prayed for it, and did everything to precipitate a massacre," he crows. "Would you believe it? Some of the most rapid agitators in the 'Know Nothing' counsels were secretly our agents; at heart the most fervid Catholics" (207).

95. *The Priest; A Tale of Modernism in New England. By the Author of Letters to His Holiness, Pope Pius X* (Boston: Sherman, French, 1911), 105. A handwritten note on the title page names the author as William Sullivan, an ex-priest teaching in a school of ethical culture.

96. Puritan, "No 'Halt' But 'Forward,'" *Woman's Voice and Public School Citizen*, 6 February 1890, 1; Puritan, "No 'Halt' But Forward," *Woman's Voice and Public School Citizen*, 13 February 1890, 1.

97. Puritan, "Illiberal Liberals, Papal Promoters and Sectarian Supporters," *Woman's Voice and Public School Citizen*, 20 March 1890, 4. Other anti-Catholics also viewed liberal elites as effeminate men and as women without natural affinities for children, increasing the irony of their involvement in public school politics. See "How Do You Read It?" *British-American Citizen*, 7 December 1889, 4.

98. Merk, "Boston's Historic Public School Crisis," 189–191; "Eliza Trask Hill," in *American Women: Fifteen Hundred Biographies with over 1,400 Portraits*, vol. 1, ed. Frances E. Willard and Mary A. Livermore (New York: Mast, Crowell and Kirkpatrick, 1897), 379–380.

99. "The Origin of the Work," *Woman's Voice and Public School Champion*, 9 January 1890, 2. Members of the King's Daughters wore a bow of purple or silver ribbon and a Maltese cross with the initials "I.H.N." Local branches existed in the Boston suburbs, including Newtonville, Cambridge, and Waltham.

100. "Music Hall Meetings," *Woman's Voice and Public School Champion*, 9 January 1890, 3–4.

101. Editorial, *Woman's Voice and Public School Champion*, 20 March 1890, 2.

102. A Woman, "Questions for the Stronger Sex to Answer," *Woman's Voice and Public School Champion*, 17 July 1890, 3.

103. "Ugly Boston Women," *Pilot*, 20 October 1888, 4.

104. "The 'Escaped Nun' in Trouble," *Pilot*, 16 May 1891, 5; "Not Friendly to Margaret. Mrs. Shepherd Hauled over the Coals by One of Her Own Sex," *Boston Herald* 18 May 1891, 10. See also Lord, Sexton, and Harrington, *History of the Archdiocese of Boston*, 107–109.

105. "Not Friendly to Margaret"; "Secular Summary," *Watchman*, 21 May 1891, n.p.

106. Quoted in editorial, *Pilot*, 23 May 1891, 4.

107. "Not Friendly to Margaret."

108. "Are Women Usurping Too Much Authority?" *Woman's Voice and Public School Champion*, 3 December 1892, 2.

109. "A Narrow Minded Reformer," *Woman's Voice and Public School Champion*, 2 November 1892, 2. Fulton had published his conservative views on women's rights in *Woman as God Made Her; The True Woman* in 1869, and they were very probably common knowledge by the 1890s.

110. William Byrne and William Leahy, eds., *History of the Catholic Church in the New England States*, vol. 2 (Boston: Hurd and Everts, 1899), 99. For another side of the story, though with essentially the same details, see "The Boston Riot," *Converted Catholic* 12 (August 1895): 235–236.

111. Byrne, *History of the Catholic Church in the New England States*, 100.

CHAPTER 5

1. "Preaching on Boston Common," *Watchman*, 4 June 1885, 1.

2. "Dr. Gordon's View. His Reasons for Speaking on the Common," unid. clipping, 1 D1 [A4] addresses, A. J. Gordon Papers, Gordon College, Wenham, Mass.

3. Quoted from description of sermon in Ernest Gordon, *Adoniram Judson Gordon: A Biography* (New York: Fleming H. Revell, 1896; reprint, New York: Garland, 1984), 120–122.

4. Robert A. Woods, ed., *The City Wilderness: A Settlement Study* (Boston: Houghton Mifflin, 1898), 208.

5. "Brief Locals," *Boston Evening Transcript*, 22 June 1885, 1.

6. "Still Preaching on the Common," *Christian* 20 (October 1885): 3.

7. "Other Denominations," *Congregationalist*, 11 June 1885, 201; "In Brief," *Congregationalist*, 30 May 1895, 832.

8. "Meddling with Politics," *Safeguard* 343 (July 1894): 3.

9. "Summer Work for the Unsaved," *Congregationalist*, 17 September 1885, 309.

10. "The Crescent Beach Bible Conference," *Congregationalist*, 27 August 1885, 285.

11. "Hints to Outdoor Preachers," *Common People* 341 (May 1894): 2.

12. "Good Work in Boston," *Converted Catholic* 4 (May 1887): 133. Many Protestants did, however, make inroads into Catholic territory. From the 1890s onward, evangelists regularly met immigrant ships at the docks, handing out tracts and offering food and shelter. They organized settlement houses and mission churches in Catholic neighborhoods and supported three missionary societies aimed at recruiting converts in Boston's neighborhoods. Catholics, of course, reciprocated with their own gospel wagons and roving evangelists, and managed to garner a respectable share of converts from the Protestant side. See Kristen Farmelant, "Trophies of Grace: Religious Conversion and Americanization in Boston's Immigrant Communities, 1890–1940" (Ph.D. diss., Brown University, 1992), 58–75.

13. *First Annual Report of the Evangelistic Association of New England, with Constitution and Rules and Regulations, May 31, 1888* (Lynn, Mass., 1888), n.p. For a history of the EANE, see Robert T. Rowlands, "Conservative Protestant Efforts to Institutionalize Revivalism as Seen in the Evangelistic Association of New England, 1887–1991" (M.A. thesis, Northeastern University, 1971). See also "New England Evangelicals Innovate and Grow," *Christianity Today*, 2 May 2001.

14. Hastings describes the efforts of the EANE to get a permit to preach in Marine Park in South Boston, and the denial of a permit by a "burly Irishman who manages that department of the city government." See "Open-Air Preaching," *Christian* 23 (September 1888): 3.

15. *Second Annual Report of the EANE, Presented at the Annual Meeting in the Bromfield Street Church, Thursday Evening, May 30, 1889* (Boston, 1889), 8, 10, 14, 19.

16. *Sixth Annual Report of the EANE, 1893* (Boston, 1893), 25.

17. Rowlands, "Conservative Protestant Efforts to Institutionalize Revivalism," 21–22.

18. "Reaching the Masses," *Congregationalist*, 5 November 1885, 372.

19. Phelps, "The Market Preachers of Philadelphia," *Congregationalist*, 11 June 1885, 197.

20. Editorial, *Congregationalist*, 24 March 1887, 100.

21. Dorn, "'Our Best Gospel Appliances,'" 179–180.

22. "A Blessing to Boston: The Ruggles Street Baptist Church and Its Work," *Watchman*, 2 May 1901, 10–12; "Problems of a Working-Class Church in Boston," in Helen Dixon, *A. C. Dixon: A Romance of Preaching* (New York: Putnam, 1931; reprint, New York: Garland, 1988), 145–156; Curtis Lee Laws, "Ruggles Street Church, Boston," *Watchman-Examiner*, 20 April 1916, 489–492.

23. Chapell, "The Secularization of the Church," *Watchword*, 13 May 1891, 117–118.

24. "A Hebrew Prophetess," *Watchword*, 13 August 1891, 212. The article described Mrs. E. L. Baeyertz as a "converted Jewess."

25. "Ministry of Woman," *Truth; or Testimony for Christ*, 21 (February 1895): 87–92; Arno C. Gaebelein, "Acts of the Apostles," *Our Hope*, 14 (August 1907): 320–321. See also Bendroth, *Fundamentalism and Gender, 1875 to the Present* (New Haven: Yale University Press, 1993), 41–47.

26. Leslie K. Andrews, "Restricted Freedom: A. B. Simpson's View of Women," in *Birth of a Vision*, ed. David F. Hartzfeld and Charles Nienkirchen (Regina, Saskatchewan: His Dominion, 1986), 231, 237.

27. *Minutes of the Fourteenth Annual Meeting of the WCTU Held in Tremont Temple, Boston* (Boston, 1887), 20–21.

28. See Scott M. Gibson, *A. J. Gordon: American Premillennialist* (Lanham, Md.: University Press of America, 2001), 101–114.

29. "Should Women Prophesy?" *Watchword* 8 (January 1887): 248–250. On Gordon's particular kind of dispensationalism, see, e.g., Gordon, "Not To Be Professed," *Watchword* 5 (August 1883): 242–243. Gordon did not believe, however, in the idea of spiritual perfection. In keeping with its Wesleyan roots, holiness theology taught that a believer who received a "second blessing" of grace after conversion could hope to reach a state in which willful sin was impossible. There were of course many variations on this idea, but Gordon rejected in principle the open-ended possibility of Christian sanctification.

30. Gordon, "The Ministry of Women," *Missionary Review of the World* 7 (December 1894): 910–921.

31. Mrs. A. J. Gordon, "Women as Evangelists," *Northfield Echoes* 1 (1894): 147–151. See also A. T. Pierson, "God's Word to Woman," *Northfield Echoes* 3 (1896): 252–263.

32. Maria Gordon to Children, 18 July 1893, Gordon Family Correspondence, Gordon College Archives, Wenham, Mass.

33. Beauregard, *Journal of Our Journey*, 230.

34. In a letter to her eldest son, Ernest, in 1898, she described her efforts to install James M. Gray as her husband's successor at Clarendon, and the countermoves by Allan Emery. The letter also discussed her differences with Gray's eschatology—she did not agree with him on the identity of the Antichrist—and her intention to publish a rebuttal in the next edition of the church newspaper. Maria Gordon to Ernest Gordon, 1 May 1898, Gordon Family Correspondence.

35. Maria Gordon to Haley Poteat, 24 October 1903, Gordon Family Correspondence. Haley's husband, Edwin McNeill Poteat, Sr., was president of Furman University from 1903 to 1918. Their son, Edwin McNeill Poteat, Jr., was president of Colgate-Rochester Seminary and a prominent liberal Protestant theologian.

36. Mrs. A. J. Gordon, "How We Celebrate," *Union Signal*, 2 July 1891, 4–5.

37. The school went through a series of name changes. Originally the Boston Missionary Institute and then the Boston Missionary Training School, after Gordon's death the name became the Gordon Bible and Missionary Training School.

38. Nathan Wood, *A School of Christ* (Boston: Halliday Lithograph, 1953), 12. While in the United States Guinness founded two other schools as well, in Kansas City and in Minneapolis. See Gibson, *A. J. Gordon*, 133. On anti-Catholicism, see Guiness,

Romanism and the Reformation; From the Standpoint of Prophecy (New York: A. C. Armstrong, 1887).

39. Wood, *School of Christ*, 15.

40. Wood, *School of Christ*, 33; Gibson, *A. J. Gordon*, 132–133.

41. Wood, *School of Christ*, 35.

42. Virginia Lieson Brereton, *Training God's Army: The American Bible School, 1880–1940* (Bloomington: Indiana University Press, 1990), 79.

43. Wood, *School of Christ*, 18.

44. Wood, *School of Christ*, 28.

45. See "Missionary Training Schools: Do Baptists Need Them?" *Baptist Quarterly Review* 12 (January 1890): 69–100, and Gordon's reply, "Short-Cut Methods," *Watchman*, 7 November 1889, 1.

46. Wood, *School of Christ*, 20, 16.

47. Gordon, *The Ministry of the Spirit* (Philadelphia: American Baptist Publishing Society, 1894), 165–166.

48. Chappell, "The Worker's Dispensational Environment," *Christian Alliance and Foreign Mission Weekly*, 20 March 1896, 274–275.

49. Ernest Gordon to Maria Gordon, 17 August 1891, Gordon Family Correspondence,. The letter was "typographically reproduced" for wider circulation. While at Clarendon, A. J. Gordon's annual salary was five thousand dollars, on the lower end for Boston pastors, and certainly not in the same range as Henry Ward Beecher's twenty thousand per annum. See Gibson, *A. J. Gordon*, 280 n. 56.

50. Wood, *School of Christ*, 39.

51. A. J. Gordon, *How Christ Came to Church: A Spiritual Autobiography* (Philadelphia: American Baptist Publication Society, 1895), 4–7.

52. Gordon, *Ministry of the Spirit*, 93–94.

53. "Gems Taken at Random from Dr. Gordon's Utterances," *Clarendon Light* 3 (January 1895): 8.

54. Gordon, "A Pastoral Letter," *Clarendon Light* 3 (January 1895): 7–8.

55. "Memorial Service, " *Watchman*, 28 March 1895, 413. See also "A Career Consecrated and Crowned," *Our Day* 14 (March 1895): 144–149.

56. Arthur Warren Smith, *The Baptist Situation in Boston Proper: A Survey of Historical and Present Conditions* (Boston: Griffith-Stillings Press, 1912), 5, 54–60. The committee also recommended merging Ruggles Street and Dudley Street, two South End churches also facing decline, and urged the Warren Avenue church to move in with First Baptist.

57. The proceedings are reproduced in Donald W. Dayton, ed., *The Prophecy Conference Movement*, vol. 3 (New York: Garland, 1988).

58. Allen Chesterfield, "From Day to Day," *Congregationalist and Christian World*, 21 December 1901, 994; "The International Prophetic Conference," *Congregationalist and Christian World*, 1013. See also William E. Barton, "Some Eschatological Fads," *Congregationalist and Christian World*, 30 November 1901, 840–841.

59. Chesterfield, "From Day to Day."

60. G. E. H., "The Prophetic Conference," *Watchman*, 19 December 1901, 13. See also "The Proportion of the Faith," *Watchman*, 5 September 1901, 7.

61. On the move from dispensationalism, see Wood, *School of Christ*, 55–56; bylaws required that twenty-four of the thirty-six trustees were to be Baptists, a move

deemed to be a "great safeguard of the evangelical character of the School," 200–201. In 1912, a Baptist survey reported that Clarendon Street's section of the South End was "overrun" by "colored people" and that this population's future movement was as yet unclear. See Smith, *Baptist Situation of Boston Proper*, 55–56.

62. Wood, *School of Christ*, 53.

63. Wood, *School of Christ*, 165–167.

64. *Gordon News-Letter* 10 (November 1925): 10.

65. *Gordon News-Letter* 22 (December 1929): 7.

66. *Gordon News-Letter* 21 (July 1929): 6. In December the *News-Letter* printed a correction, noting the previous ordination of Elida Frost Bascom (class of 1921) in Alstead, New Hampshire.

67. Nathan R. Wood, "Report of Recent Work of Gordon Students in Rural Fields," 12 May 1934, President's Office files, 1Dg3, Gordon College Archives.

68. President's Report, Minutes of the Board of Trustees, 12 June 1930, box 1, book 4, Gordon College Archives, 83; *Gordon News-Letter* 26 (November 1931): 1; Candace Waldron-Stains, "Evangelical Women: From Feminist Reform to Silent Femininity," *debarim* 3 (1978–79): 67–68.

CHAPTER 6

1. See, for example, E. F. Merriam, "The Strangers' Sabbath Home: Tremont Temple Baptist Church," *Watchman*, 9 May 1901, 10–12.

2. William Vance Trollinger, Jr., *God's Empire: William Bell Riley and Midwestern Fundamentalism* (Madison: University of Wisconsin Press, 1990), 16.

3. Barbara Dobschuetz, "Fundamentalism and American Urban Culture: Community and Religious Identity in Dwight L. Moody's Chicago, 1864–1914" (Ph.D diss., University of Illinois, Chicago, 2002); Trollinger, *God's Empire*; Dale E. Soden, *The Reverend Mark Matthews: An Activist in the Progressive Era* (Seattle: University of Washington Press, 2001); Barry Hankins, *God's Rascal: J. Frank Norris and the Beginnings of Southern Fundamentalism* (Lexington: University Press of Kentucky, 1996); Douglas James Curlew, " 'They Ceased Not to Preach': Fundamentalism, Culture, and the Revivalist Imperative at the Temple Baptist Church of Detroit" (Ph.D. diss., Ann Arbor: University of Michigan, 2001).

4. Curlew, " 'They Ceased Not to Preach,' " 283. On social class, see also Trollinger, *God's Empire*, 19–20; Dobschuetz, "Fundamentalism and American Urban Culture," 5.

5. Barth, *City People: The Rise of Modern City Culture in Nineteenth-Century America* (New York: Oxford University Press, 1980).

6. Guy Mitchell, "History of Tremont Temple," unpublished manuscript, n.d.; Edgar C. Lane, *A Brief History of Tremont Temple, 1839–1947* (Boston: Tremont Temple, 1947); *Tremont Temple Baptist Church: A Light in the City for 150 Years*, booklet (Boston: Tremont Temple Baptist Church, 1989).

7. George C. Lorimer, "The Strangers' Sabbath Home," in *Tremont Temple Sketch Book* (Boston: St. Botolph Press, 1896), n.p.

8. Lorimer, "Strangers' Sabbath Home," n.p.

9. The original members of the Society were drawn from Tremont Temple's leadership, including James W. Converse, Frederick Gould, Thomas Richardson, J. Warren Merrill, and George W. Chipman. The arrangement formally ended in 1925.

10. *The Work of God in Tremont Temple* (Boston: Union Temple Baptist Church, 1871), 12–13.

11. Lorimer, "Strangers' Sabbath Home," n.p.

12. Thomas H. O'Connor, *Civil War Boston: Home Front and Battlefield* (Boston: Northeastern University Press, 1997), 42–43.

13. Fulton quoted in Mitchell, "History of Tremont Temple," 96–100.

14. "Rant in the Pulpit," *Watchman-Examiner*, 10 August, 1926, 1037.

15. H. A. Bridgman, "Successful Churches: Tremont Temple, Boston," *Record of Christian Work* 20 (March 1901): 168–169. See also biographical note on Lorimer in *Tremont Temple Sketch Book*, n.p.

16. Bridgman, "Successful Churches," 169.

17. Mitchell, "History of Tremont Temple," 201–227.

18. Mitchell, "History of Tremont Temple," 219.

19. Bridgman, "Successful Churches," 167. See also Mitchell, "History of Tremont Temple," 106–107, and description in *Tremont Temple Baptist Church*, 81–82.

20. "Letter from the Pastor," in *Annual Report of the Tremont Temple Baptist Church, for the Year Ending April First, 1895* (Boston, 1895), 32. See also Mitchell, "History of Tremont Temple," 134–6.

21. Mitchell, "History of Tremont Temple," 130–136; *Annual Report of the Tremont Temple Baptist Church for the Year Ending April First, 1895*, 32–34. Tribute to Rhodes, who died in 1937, and George Lane, in *Annual Report of the Tremont Temple Baptist Church for the Year 1938* (Boston, 1938), 17. Tremont Temple changed its bylaws to allow women deacons in 1988.

22. Julia A. Bates, "Mrs. Amanda S. Ricker," *Temple Trumpet* 1 (November 1905): 147–149.

23. *Annual Report, Union Temple Baptist Church, 1888–1889*, 8–9.

24. *Annual Report of Tremont Temple Baptist Church for the Year Ending April 12th, 1904* (Boston, 1904), 10.

25. *Annual Report of Tremont Temple Baptist Church for the Year Ending April 21st, 1908* (Boston, 1908), 14.

26. Lorimer, "Strangers' Sabbath Home," n.p.

27. *Annual Report of the Tremont Temple Baptist Church for the Year Ending April First, 1893*, 22.

28. "Mason Active in Temple Work," *Boston Herald*, 20 January 1923, scrapbook clipping, J. C. Massee Papers, American Baptist Historical Society, Rochester, N.Y.

29. *Annual Report, Union Temple Baptist Church, 1888–1889*, 4.

30. "Men and Things in Boston," *Watchman*, 14 February 1901, 13.

31. "Men and Things in Boston," 13.

32. "Successful Churches," 168.

33. Lorimer, "Strangers' Sabbath Home," n.p.

34. *Annual Report of the Tremont Temple Baptist Church for the Year Ending April 21st, 1903* (Boston, 1903), 17.

35. Membership figures are drawn from annual reports, which includes a summary covering 1864–1911 in the annual report for 1912. From 1903 onward, church clerks also regularly "purged" the membership list of inactive members, so that it is possible to figure net losses and gains for each year.

36. Annual reports are available for 1888–1949, listing new members beginning in 1901; membership cards date back as far as 1865, and were surveyed up through 1949.

37. *Annual Report of Tremont Temple Baptist Church for the Year Ending April 1, 1912* (Boston, 1912), 24; "The Tremont Temple Brotherhood," *Watchman-Examiner*, 1 June 1916, 715; "Boston Notes," *Watchman-Examiner*, 20 July 1916, 939; *Annual Report of Tremont Temple Baptist Church for the Year Ending April 1, 1914* (Boston, 1914), 22.

38. *Annual Report of Tremont Temple Baptist Church for the Year Ending April 1, 1916* (Boston, 1916), 24–25; *Annual Report of Tremont Temple Baptist Church for the Year Ending April 1, 1917* (Boston 1917), 27–29.

39. Myers, *Why Men Do Not Go to Church* (New York: Funk and Wagnalls, 1899), 14.

40. See G. A. Rawlyk, *Champions of the Truth: Fundamentalism, Modernism, and the Maritime Baptists* (Montreal: McGill-Queen's University Press, 1990).

41. Studies of Canadian immigration to the United States include Marcus Lee Hansen, *The Mingling of the Canadian and American Peoples*, vol. 1, *Historical* (New Haven: Yale University Press, 1940); Alan A. Brookes, "Out-Migration from the Maritime Provinces, 1860–1900: Some Preliminary Considerations," *Acadiensis* 5 (1976): 26–55; W. G. Reeves, "Newfoundlanders in the 'Boston States': A Study in Early Twentieth-Century Community and Counterpoint," *Newfoundland Studies* 6 (1990): 34–55.

42. Gary Burrill, *Away: Maritimers in Massachusetts, Ontario, and Alberta: An Oral History of Leaving Home* (Montreal: McGill-Queen's University Press, 1992), 91–92.

43. John MacDougall, *Rural Life in Canada: Its Trends and Tasks* (Toronto: University of Toronto Press, 1913; reprint, 1973), 29.

44. Betsy Beattie, *Obligation and Opportunity: Single Maritime Women in Boston, 1870–1930* (Montreal: McGill-Queen's University Press, 2000), 13.

45. Beatty, *Obligation and Opportunity*, 108, 45.

46. See, e.g., Scott W. See, *Riots in New Brunswick: Orange Nativism and Social Violence in the 1840s* (Toronto: University of Toronto Press, 1993). Maritimers would also have recognized the infamous anti-Catholic agitator Father Chiniquy during his Tremont Temple days. In the 1850s he was known as the Canadian "apostle of temperance," until he quarreled with Catholic authorities and became a Presbyterian. See Hansen, *Mingling of the Canadian and American Peoples*, 129–130.

47. "The Bible Conference," *Watchman-Examiner*, 20 October 1927.

48. From church newsletters, 27 November 1938 (vol. 8, no. 48) and 12 March 1939 (vol. 9, no. 11). In 1938, thirteen members of the board of deacons were Knights Templar; the Executive Committee included six Knights Templars and two thirty-two-degree Masons. Massee, however, came out against fraternal organizations. See "Dr. Massee Attacks Secret Societies," unid. clipping, January 1923, scrapbook, box 9, Massee Papers.

49. Mitchell, "History of Tremont Temple," 236–239; *Annual Report*, 1926, 18.

50. The best source is still C. Allyn Russell, "J. C. Massee, Moderate Fundamentalist," in *Voices of American Fundamentalism: Seven Biographical Studies*, ed. C. Allyn Russell (Philadephia: Westminster Press, 1976), 107–134.

51. On Straton, see Russell, "John Roach Straton, Accusative Fundamentalist," in Russell, *Voices of American Fundamentalism*, 47–78. His antics are explored in J. Terry

Todd, "New York, the New Babylon? Fundamentalism and the Modern City in Reverend Straton's Jazz Age Crusade," in *Faith in the Market: Religion and the Rise of Urban Commercial Culture*, ed. John M. Giggie and Diane Winston (New Brunswick, N.J.: Rutgers University Press, 2002), 74–87.

52. On Riley, see Trollinger, *God's Empire*. Most of the important fundamentalist pulpiteers of the early twentieth century were southerners, including Riley, Massee, Mark Mathews, John Roach Straton, and J. Frank Norris.

53. Quoted in Russell, "John Roach Straton," 128–128.

54. W. J. Lhamon, "A Study in Fundamentalism," *Christian*, 4 November 1926, n.p. (A journal of "progressive religion," based in Kansas City).

55. Edward D. Cotton, "Interviews with Leaders of Religious Opinion—VI, Dr. Jasper C. Massee," *Zion's Herald*, 4 August 1926, 983.

56. "A Trampled World," *Christian Register*, 2 March 1922, 194; "The Religious Ku-Klux," *Christian Register*, 23 February 1922, 170.

57. Albert E. George, "Christ Is Coming to Boston with a Shout! How the Zealots Believe, How They Grow and Carry On," *Christian Register*, 16 March 1922, 245–6.

58. Organized by the Baptist layman and Boston city council president George W. Coleman in 1908, the Ford Hall Forum was funded by Daniel Sharpe Ford to promote Social Gospel work in Boston. Ford also gave a large bequest to the Ruggles Street Baptist Church. See George W. Coleman, "The Contribution of the Open Forum to Democracy in Religion," *Journal of Religion* 2 (January 1922): 1–15; Arthur S. Meyers, "A Bridge to the Future: From the Boston Baptist Social Union to the Beth El Open Forum," *American Baptist Quarterly* 14 (spring 1995): 225–240.

59. "Dr. Dieffenbach in Ford Hall," *Watchman-Examiner*, 13 April 1922, 454.

60. "Scores Creed. Christ to Wage War of Blood," *Boston Herald*, 13 March 1922, 1, 6.

61. "Modern Science Is Enemy of All True Religion, Says Dr. Massee, New Pastor of Tremont Temple," *Boston Herald*, 19 March 1922, 12; "The Religious Ku-Klux," *Boston Herald*, 10 March 1922, 18.

62. "Save the Churches!" *Christian Register*, 30 March 1922, 290.

63. "Ford Hall Forum and Dr. Dieffenbach," *Watchman-Examiner*, 20 April 1922, 488; see also Merriam, "An Attack on Baptists," *Watchman-Examiner*, 23 March 1922, 360; "The Boston Herald and Christian Register," *Watchman-Examiner*, 23 March 1922, 359.

64. Cotton, "Interviews with Leaders of Religious Opinion," 983.

65. "Damned by Doubt," sermon typescript, 26 January 1925, box 7, Massee Papers.

66. "Heaven Our Home," sermon typescript, 14 December 1924, box 7, Massee Papers.

67. "The Woman in the Home," sermon typescript, Sunday evening, 9 November 1924, box 7, Massee Papers; "My Mother's Legacy," undated typed manuscript, box 2, Massee Papers.

68. "The Man in the Home," sermon typescript, Sunday evening, 2 November 1924, box 7, Massee Papers.

69. "He Quit Beating 'Sallie' Drum and Became a College President," *Boston Post*, 1 January 1928, A-5.

70. Leo Rabbette, "'Men Afraid Girls Will Follow Their Example,' States Dr. Brown," *Boston Sunday Post*, 22 January 1928, B-4.

71. "Opens Revival Today at Tremont Temple," unid. clipping from scrapbook, box 9, Massee Papers.

72. "Says Devil Has a Throne Here; Chief One Is in New York, Declares Dr. Masse [*sic*] at Tremont Temple," *Traveller*, 6 April 1925; "Satan's Branch Office in Hub, Says Dr. Massee," unid. clipping, box 9, Massee Papers.

73. "Fruit of the Tremont Temple Meetings," unid. clipping from scrapbook, box 9, Massee Papers; "Radio Church Audience Big," unid. clipping, box 9, Massee Papers.

74. *Christian Register* Nov. 1923, clipping from scrapbook, box 9, Massee Papers.

75. "Tells Plans for Tremont Temple Radio," January 1924, box 9, Massee Papers.

76. "Should Girls Smoke?" sermon typescript, March 22, 1925, box 7, Massee Papers.

77. "Smoking Hot Topic," unid. clipping, box 8, Massee Papers; "Pauline Finds a Pipe Necessary," *Pittsburgh Press Daily Pictoral*, box 8, Massee Papers.

78. Paul Kemeny, "Power, Ridicule, and the Destruction of Religious Moral Reform Politics in the 1920s," in *The Secular Revolution: Power, Interests, and Conflict in the Secularization of American Public Life*, ed. Christian Smith (Berkeley: University of California Press, 2003).

79. In the early 1930s, according to figures gathered from membership cards, immigrants from Canada accounted for 23 percent of new members; ten years later, this had dropped to 14 percent.

CHAPTER 7

1. The most complete account of the revival is A. Z. Conrad, ed., *Boston's Awakening: A Complete Account of the Great Boston Revival Under the Leadership of J. Wilbur Chapman and Charles M. Alexander, January 26th to February 21st, 1909* (Boston: King's Business, 1909).

2. Quoted in "Revivals and Civic Cleansing," *Congregationalist and Christian World*, 6 March 1909, 301.

3. For a list of participating churches, see Conrad, *Boston's Awakening*, 227–235. "Dr. Johnson Preaches in Jewish Synagogue," *Boston Post*, 25 January 1909, 12.

4. "Spirituality for Coming Campaign," *Boston Globe*, 26 January 1909, 1.

5. "With Word to 334,000 Chapman Evangelists Open Revival Tomorrow," *Boston Globe*, 25 January 1909, 1, 7–8; "25,000 Attend Revival Services Last Night," *Boston Post*, 27 January 1909, 1, 12; "Revival Supplement," *Boston Post*, 20 February 1909; "After Day of Rest," *Boston Sunday Globe*, 7 February 1909, 2.

6. "After Day of Rest," *Boston Globe*, 2. See also description in "Simultaneous Evangelistic Campaign," *Zion's Herald*, 20 January 1909, 70–77.

7. "Churches Crowded to Doors at Chapman Revival Meetings," *Boston Post*, 29 January 1909, 1.

8. James J. Connolly, *The Triumph of Ethnic Progressivism: Urban Political Culture in Boston, 1900–1925* (Cambridge: Harvard University Press, 1998), 37, 13.

9. Connolly, *Triumph of Ethnic Progressivism*, 4.

10. Robert Wuthnow, *The Restructuring of American Religion* (Princeton, N.J.: Princeton University Press, 1988).

11. On remasculinization, see Gail Bederman, "'The Women Have Had Charge of the Church Long Enough': The Men and Religion Forward Movement of 1911–1912 and the Masculinization of Middle-Class Protestantism," *American Quarterly* 41 (1989): 432–465.

12. "Revivals and Civic Cleansing," *Congregationalist and Christian World*, 6 March 1909, 301; "A Revival of Christian Living," *Congregationalist and Christian World*, 6 February 1909, 169.

13. "Simultaneous Evangelistic Campaigns," *Zion's Herald*, 20 January 1909, 70–77.

14. Robert Cameron, "Chapman-Alexander Meetings," *Watchword and Truth* 31 (March 1909): 74–71.

15. "Boston Needs Evangelists," *Boston Post*, 20 January 1909, 4.

16. "The King's Business," *Boston Post*, 24 January 1909, 34, 35.

17. Constance K. Burns, "The Irony of Progressive Reform: Boston, 1898–1910," in *Boston, 1700–1980: The Evolution of Urban Politics*, ed. Ronald P. Formisano and Constance K. Burns (Westport, Conn.: Greenwood Press, 1984), 148–153.

18. "Intense Fervor, Big Crowds," *Boston Globe*, 1 Feburary 1909, 6.

19. Editorial in brief, *Congregationalist and Christian World*, 27 February 1909, 274.

20. "Notes on the Evangelistic Meetings," *Zion's Herald*, 3 February 1909, 160.

21. Lyle Dorsett, *Billy Sunday and the Redemption of Urban America* (Grand Rapids, Mich.: Eerdmans, 1991), 51.

22. Conrad, "Open Letter to 'Boston Transcript,'" Park Street Church Records, Congregational Historical Society, Boston (also reprinted in *Zion's Herald*, 11 November 1908).

23. George T. R. Davis, "Dr. Chapman's Life Story," *Zion's Herald*, 20 January 1909, 69–70; Dorsett, *Billy Sunday and the Redemption of Urban America*, 49–51.

24. Described in A. Z. Conrad, "Chapman-Alexander Campaign," *Congregationalist and Christian World*, 16 January 1909, 98; J. Wilbur Chapman, *Present-Day Evangelism* (New York: Baker and Taylor, 1903), 213.

25. Conrad, *Boston's Awakening*, 31.

26. "Remarkable Evangelistic meetings," *Zion's Herald*, 3 February 1909, 135.

27. "Dr. Daniel Steele's Column: The Factors in the Boston Revival," *Zion's Herald*, 10 March 1909, 293.

28. "Lawson Says Chapman Is a Bull on Human Uplift," *Boston Post*, 3 February 1909, 11.

29. Carol Srole, "'A Position That God Has Not Particularly Assigned to Men': The Feminization of Clerical Work, Boston, 1860–1915" (Ph.D. diss., University of California, Los Angeles, 1984), 119–120.

30. "Chapman's Morning Word to Boston People Through the Post," *Boston Post*, 1 February, 1909, 1.

31. Thomas H. O'Connor, *The Boston Irish: A Political History* (Boston: Little, Brown, 1995), 178.

32. Curley served terms as mayor in 1914–18, 1922–26, 1930–34, and 1945–49. Curley quoted in O'Connor, *Boston Irish*, 188; See also Thomas H. O'Connor, *Bibles, Brahmins, and Bosses: A Short History of Boston*, 3rd ed. (Boston: Trustees of the Public Library, 1991), 176–197.

33. See Paula Kane, *Separatism and Subculture: Boston Catholicism, 1900–1920* (Chapel Hill: University of North Carolina Press, 1994); James O'Toole, *Militant and Triumphant: William Henry O'Connell and the Catholic Church in Boston, 1859–1944* (Notre Dame, Ind.: University of Notre Dame Press, 1992).

34. "Chapman's Methods of Conducting Revival Meetings," *Boston Post*, 28 January 1909, 13.

35. "Chapman's Methods of Conducting Revival Meetings." Before his arrival in Boston, Chapman's advance men sent endorsements from clergy in towns he had already evangelized. See, e.g., "Permanent Gains from Chapman Campaigns: A Group of Testimonies from Different Cities," *Congregationalist and Christian World*, 23 January 1909, 113–114.

36. *Religious Bodies: 1906*, part 1, *Summary and General Tables* (Washington, D.C.: Government Printing Office, 1910), 416. According to census figures, 33 percent of Boston's Baptists were men, as were 37 percent of Episcopalians, 36 percent of white Methodists, 35 percent of Unitarians, and 31 percent of Congregationalists. The national figure (39.3 percent) is probably high, since it includes groups with relatively even sex ratios, like Roman Catholics, who reported numbers by parish, as well as Protestant denominations that reported only actual adult membership.

37. "Young Men and Religion," *Watchman*, 26 December 1901, 7.

38. On comparison of male and female conversion rates, see, e.g., "Preaches to 10,000," *Boston Sunday Globe*, 21 February 1909, 2; "Women Crowd Tremont Temple," *Boston Globe*, 11 February 1909, 1, 3. See also "Chapman's Way. How He Appeals to Men and Women," *Boston Sunday Globe*, 21 February 1909, 14.

39. "3000 Men at Temple," *Boston Post*, 1 February 1909, 2: "Every set of man was represented in this vast throng, from the well-groomed banker to the North End fisherman with his time-worn clothing. Any racial differences that may have existed were dispelled, as colored and white man, American and foreigner, stood shoulder to shoulder and accepted Christ as their Saviour."

40. "The Chapman Campaign in Boston," *Congregationalist and Christian World*, 6 February 1909, 181. See also the description in "Like a Tidal Wave Revival Is Sweeping over Greater Boston," *Boston Globe*, 2 February 1909, 7.

41. "3000 Men at Temple," 2.

42. "3,000 Men Take Pledge," *Boston Globe*, 12 February 1909, 11; "Men in Thousands Begin Holy Lives," *Boston Globe*, 13 February 1909, 1.

43. "Vast and Spellbound," *Boston Globe*, 4 February 1909, 1, 7.

44. "Solution of Labor Problems: 'Bear Ye One Another's Burdens.' 'Go Out and Live Christ,' Says Dr. Chapman," *Boston Globe*, 18 February 1909, 1, 5.

45. Conrad, *Boston's Awakening*, 28; "Campaign Opens in 24 Churches. Meetings Spirited, Yet Earnest, Devoid of Sensations," *Boston Globe*, 27 January 1909, 1; "Cameron, "Chapman-Alexander Meetings," *Watchword and Truth* 31 (March 1909): 74.

46. "25,000 Attend Revival Service Last Night," *Boston Post*, 27 January 1909, 12.

47. "Made Bright with Song," *Boston Globe*, 10 February, 1909, 1, 6.

48. "Churches Crowded to Doors at Chapman Revival Meetings," *Boston Post*, 29 January 1909, 3.

49. "Vast and Spellbound," 1.

50. "Preached to Aged Hearers," *Boston Globe*, 19 February, 1909, 5.

51. "The Hymn That Helps Most," *Boston Sunday Post*, 24 January 1909, 34.

52. "Chapman's Fervor Win's More Souls: His Picture of Home and Mother Moves Men to Tears and Repentance," *Boston Globe*, 2 February 1909, 1.

53. "Midnight Theater Meeting," *Boston Post*, 30 January 1909, 1; Conrad, *Boston's Awakening*, 140.

54. "Women's Share in Revivals," *Boston Globe*, 17 February 1909, 16. On Asher, see also "Observant Citizen," *Boston Post*, 1 February 1909, 6; "Moved Women to Tears," *Boston Post*, 2 February 1909, 2; "'In Neglected Fields': Mr. and Mrs. Asher, Saloon Evangelists, Called to Boston," *Boston Globe*, 26 January 1909, 1.

55. "Women's Share in Revivals."

56. Descriptions in "Women's Share in Revivals," 16.

57. "Religion or Selfishness—Which?" *Watchman*, 4 March 1909, 2. The Baptist report was in part a reprint of an article in the *Boston Journal* of 22 February 1909.

58. "Religion or Selfishness—Which?"

59. "Enthusiastic Song Service," *Boston Globe*, 9 February, 1909, 1, 5. See "Side Lights on Evangelism," *Watchman*, 25 February 1909, 6.

60. Samuel A. Eliot, "'Revivals,'" *Zion's Herald*, 3 March 1909, 288 (original in *Christian Register*, 25 February 1909); George S. Chadbourne, "Revival Critics," *Zion's Herald*, 31 March 1909, 397.

61. "The Real Effect of Revivals," *Springfield Republican*, 4 April, 1909.

62. "A Study of New England Revivals," *American Journal of Sociology* 15 (1909): 361–378. See response by L. T. Townsend, "Dr. Dike's Criticisms of Revivals," *Zion's Herald*, 14 April 1909, 462.

63. *Annual Report of Tremont Temple Baptist Church for the Year Ending April 1, 1909* (Boston, 1909), 17.

64. Arthur Warren Smith, "Historical Sketch of Baptist Consciousness in the Baptist Growth in Boston Proper," in *Baptist Situation in Boston Proper: A Survey of Historical and Present Conditions* (Boston: Griffith-Stillings Press, 1912), 15.

65. H. Crosby Englizian, *Brimstone Corner: Park Street Church Boston* (Chicago: Moody Press, 1968), 200–209. The other churches in the survey were the Maverick Church in East Boston, Phillips Church in South Boston, Winthrop Congregational in Charlestown, Shawmut Church in the South End, and Park Street. See also "Park Street Church and Its Problem," *Congregationalist and Christian World*, 2 July 1904, 8.

66. Waldron cited in Walter Leon Sawyer, "Overchurched Boston," *Zion's Herald*, 27 January 1909, 117.

67. James M. O'Toole, *Militant and Triumphant: William Henry O'Connell and the Catholic Church in Boston, 1859–1944* (Notre Dame, Ind.: University of Notre Dame Press, 1992), 121; Paula Kane, *Separatism and Subculture: Boston Catholicism, 1900–1920* (Chapel Hill: University of North Carolina Press, 1994).

68. All saw increases in Roman Catholic majorities between 1890 and 1906: Cambridge (from 68.9 percent to 72.8 percent Catholic), Somerville (58.3 percent to 67.4 percent), Lowell (74.5 percent to 81.4 percent), and Lynn (53.9 percent to 69.9 percent). See Kevin Christiano, *Religious Diversity and Social Change: American Cities, 1890–1906* (Cambridge, England: Cambridge University Press, 1987), 172–175.

69. *Religious Bodies: 1906*, part 1, *Summary and General Tables*, 80–81.

70. Conrad, *Boston's Awakening*, 13. Conrad's figure included members of Boston's Congregational, Methodist, Baptist, Episcopalian, and Presbyterian churches.

CHAPTER 8

1. George Marsden, *Fundamentalism and American Culture, 1875–1920* (New York: Oxford University Press, 1980), 141–153.

2. Wilfred T. Grenfell, M.D., "Billy Sunday—A First Impression," *Congregationalist and Christian World*, 7 December 1916, 762.

3. "Unity of the Faith—Differences of Opinion," *Watchman-Examiner*, 26 October 1916, 1382.

4. William G. McLoughlin, *Billy Sunday Was His Real Name* (Chicago: University of Chicago Press, 1955), 52–53.

5. "Getting Ready for Billy Sunday," *Watchman-Examiner*, 28 September 1916, 1254.

6. David A. Baldwin, "When Billy Sunday 'Saved' Colorado: That Old-Time Religion and the 1914 Prohibition Amendment," *Colorado Heritage* 2 (1990): 34–44.

7. "A New Opportunity," *Christian Register*, 14 September 1916, 860.

8. Samuel Eliot, "American Unitarian Association. The Revival in Boston," *Christian Register*, 16 November 1916, 1084–1975; "Getting Ready for Billy Sunday in Boston," *Watchman-Examiner*, 2 November 1916, 1414; McLoughlin, *Billy Sunday Was His Real Name*, 52–53.

9. "Making the Most of the Sunday Campaign," *Zion's Herald*, 18 October 1916, 1321.

10. Frederick T. Rouse, "Modern Theology and Billy Sunday," *Congregationalist and Christian World*, 2 November 1916, 581.

11. "Two Open Letters," *Congregationalist and Christian World*, 2 November 1916, 569.

12. "Boston Sunday Campaign," *Congregationalist and Christian World*, 26 October 1916, 550.

13. Curley quoted in "The Sunday Campaign in Boston," *Watchman-Examiner*, 9 November 1916, 1445–1446.

14. "Getting Ready for Billy Sunday in Boston."

15. "Boston Prepares for Mr. Sunday," *Watchman-Examiner*, 24 February 1916, 232; McLoughlin, *Billy Sunday Was His Real Name*, 67–68.

16. James A. Walker to Mrs. William A. Sunday, 28 September 1916, box 2–24, William A. Sunday Papers, Billy Graham Center Archives, Wheaton, Ill.

17. "The Sunday Campaign in Boston," *Watchman-Examiner*, 18 January 1917, 69–70.

18. "Plans for the Boston Campaign," *Congregationalist and Christian World*, 9 November, 1916, 611. The Sunday forces pushed through a special act of the state legislature to override the city ordinance and allow a wooden building, but the governor vetoed it.

19. "On the Eve of the Sunday Campaign," *Zion's Herald*, 8 November 1916, 1413; "At the Opening of the Boston Campaign," *Congregationalist and Christian World*, 16 November 1916, 646.

20. "On the Eve of the Sunday Campaign," 1413. See also "Plans for the Boston Campaign," 611.

21. Guy Mitchell, "History of Tremont Temple," unpublished manuscript, n.d., 201–227.

22. "Dr. Conrad's Body to Lie in State," unid. clipping, 24 January 1937, and "Tells Vigorous Steps He Would Take If He Were the President," unid. clipping, 24 March 1918, Park Street Church Records.

23. Herbert Achison Jump, "Four Acres of Folks Hear Billy Sunday," *Congregationalist and Christian World*, 23 November 1916, 677.

24. "The Sunday Campaign in Boston," *Watchman-Examiner*, 18 January 1917, 69–70.

25. "Revival Work for Businesswomen," *Boston Globe*, 6 January 1917, 6. On Miller as "female Billy Sunday," see "Reaching Boston Business Women," *Congregationalist and Christian World*, 18 January 1917, 73 and Grace M. Boynton, "The Women Behind Mr. Sunday," *Congregationalist and Christian World*, 7 December 1916, 763.

26. Quoted in "The Sunday Evangelistic Campaign," *Zion's Herald*, 22 November 1916, 1484.

27. Jump, "Four Acres of Folks Hear Billy Sunday," 677.

28. Jump, "Sunday Addresses the Unitarians," *Congregationalist and Christian World*, 23 November 1916, 678. See also "Mr. Sunday's Address to Unitarian Ministers," *Christian Register*, 21 December 1916, 1218–1219, an article printed "by demand" among local Unitarians.

29. "Sunday Evangelistic Campaign," *Zion's Herald*, 22 November, 1484.

30. James Huxtable, "Mr. Sunday and the Unitarian Ministers," letter to the editor, *Christian Register*, 23 November 1916, 1110.

31. "Unitarians Aroused," *Boston Evening Transcript*, 11 December 1916, 11.

32. "In and Around the Tabernacle," *Congregationalist and Christian World*, 30 November 1917, 736.

33. Joseph Edgar Chamberlain, "Trail-Hitting at the Tabernacle, Psychologically Considered," *Boston Evening Transcript*, 6 December 1916, 1.

34. "Boston," in *Standard Encyclopedia of the Alcohol Problem*, vol. 1 (Westerville, Ohio: American Issue, 1925), 379; Perry Duis, *The Saloon: Public Drinking in Chicago and Boston, 1880–1920* (Urbana: University of Illinois Press, 1983; reprint, 1999), 114–118.

35. Letter from William E. Smith to members of Hotel Men's Association, 17 November 1916, Sunday Papers, 1–26; Letter from Frances R. Bangs to members of Real Estate Exchange, 11 December 1916, Sunday Papers, 1–25.

36. "The Liquor Question," *Boston Globe*, 16 December 1916, 1.

37. "License Contest Most Vigorous in Years," *Boston Evening Transcript*, 12 December 1916, 10; "More on 'That Bunch,'" *Boston Evening Transcript*, 15 December 1916, 2; "A Challenge to Every Boston Voter," *Boston Evening Transcript*, December 17, 1916, 2.

38. "The Gains Against License," *Boston Evening Transcript*, 6 December 1916, 2.

39. "Billy Sunday in Boston," *Watchman-Examiner*, 30 November 1916, 1543–1544.

40. "Billy Sunday in Boston."

41. "Billy Sunday in Boston."

42. Sidney A. Weston, "Sunday's 'Booze' Sermon, The Highest Point in the Boston Campaign," *Congregationalist and Christian World*, 21 December 1916, 851. For

a complete text, see "Booze, or Get On the Water Wagon," *Zion's Herald*, 13 December 1916, 1586–1587.

43. Lawrence Winship, "Sunday, Angry, Makes Last Drive on 'Booze,'" *Boston Globe*, 19 December 1916, 1, 8.

44. "Sunday's Blood Is Up," *Boston Evening Transcript*, 18 December 1916, 2.

45. "Foss Hits Trail as 13,000 Cheer," *Boston Globe*, 18 December 1916, 1, 5.

46. "Billy Sunday and the Boston Saloons," *Watchman-Examiner*, 14 December 1916, 1613–1614.

47. "Big Victory for License," *Boston Evening Transcript*, 20 December 1916, 1, 9.

48. "Billy Sunday and the Boston Election," *Watchman-Examiner*, 28 December 1916, 1677–1678.

49. "Sunday a Good Loser," *Boston Evening Transcript*, 20 December 1916, 2.

50. "Myers Accuses Catholics," *Boston Evening Transcript*, 22 December 1916, 8.

51. "Billy Sunday and the Boston Election"; "Why Saloons Stay in Boston," *Congregationalist and Christian World*, 28 December 1916, 876. On suburbs, see Duis, *Saloon*, 212–213.

52. "Billy Sunday Audience Only 500. Ministers in Consternation," *Boston Globe*, 22 December 1916, 1.

53. "The Obduracy of Brookline," *Boston Evening Transcript*, 29 December 1916, 10.

54. "Billy Sunday Given $50,828; 60,000 Hear Goodly Sermons," *Boston Globe*, 22 January 1917, 1, 4.

55. "Statistics of Boston's Record-Breaking Revival," *Boston Globe*, 22 January 1917, 5.

56. "How Billy Sunday Felt About Boston Last Night," *Boston Globe*, 21 January 1917, 1.

57. Roger W. Babson, "Billy Sunday as an Investment," *Congregationalist and Christian World*, 4 January 1917, 31.

58. "Figures and the Sunday Campaign," *Watchman-Examiner*, 1 February 1917, 135; "Boston Trail Hitters," *Congregationalist and Christian World*, 1 February 1917, 149. The tally included a fairly large number of Episcopalians (6,195) and Catholics (1,513), and smaller numbers of Unitarians (296), Universalists (128), Friends (70), Lutherans (892), Christian Scientists (239), and "Hebrews" (177).

59. "Have We Been Fair?" *Congregationalist and Christian World*, 8 February 1917, 174.

60. "Boston Ministers on Billy Sunday," *Watchman-Examiner*, 25 January 1917, 105–108.

61. "Liberal Evangelism," *Christian Register*, 1 February 1917, 114–115.

62. "New England News," *Watchman-Examiner*, 18 January 1917, 89–90; "Liberal Evangelism," *Christian Register*, 25 January 1917, 90–91.

63. Eliot, "Opening Address at Symphony Hall, February 5, 1917," *Christian Register*, 15 February 1917, 152–153.

64. "The Symphony Hall Meeting," *Christian Register*, 15 February 1917, 162.

65. "New England News," *Watchman-Examiner*, 18 January 1917, 89–90.

66. "The Future of Unitarianism," *Christian Register*, 22 February 1917, 174; Frances Greenwood Peabody, "Preaching Power," *Christian Register*, 8 February 1917, 130–132. See also "The Positive Note Among Unitarians," *Congregationalist and Christian World*, 15 February 1917, 207–208.

CHAPTER 9

1. "Brimstone Corner" is in M. A. DeWolfe Howe, *Boston Common: Scenes from Four Centuries* (Boston: Houghton Mifflin, 1921), 44. Chauncey Brewer, "Park Street Church's One Hundred Years of Service," in *Commemorative Exercises at the One Hundredth Anniversary of the Organization of Park Street Church*, ed. A. Z. Conrad (Boston: Park Street Centennial Committee, 1909), 87–88. See also H. Crosby Englizian, *Brimstone Corner: Park Street Church, Boston* (Chicago: Moody Press, 1968), 28.

2. Quoted in Isaac Ogden Rankin, "The Story of Park Street Church," *Congregationalist and Christian World*, 7 February 1903, 195.

3. Rankin, "Story of Park Street Church," 196.

4. But not before they hid away the silver Communion set. See Roger Brand Hanson, *Dedham, Massachusetts 1635–1890* (Dedham, Mass.: Dedham Historical Society, 1976), 201–215.

5. Griffin quoted in Englizian, *Brimstone Corner*, 39. On the Unitarian controversy, see Brooks Holifield, *Theology in America: Christian Thought from the Age of the Puritans to the Civil War* (New Haven: Yale University Press, 2003), 197–217.

6. Conrad, "Park Street Church Centennial," in Conrad, *Commemorative Exercises at the One Hundredth Anniversary of the Organization of Park Street Church*, 20. Pew rents ranged from $100 to $460 on the main floor of the sanctuary and $100 to $300 in the balcony. Owners were also paid a quarterly tax that varied according to the church's financial condition. Englizian, *Brimstone Corner*, 43.

7. Englizian, *Brimstone Corner*, 55.

8. Robert Meredith, *The Politics of the Universe: Edward Beecher, Abolition, and Orthodoxy* (Nashville, Tenn.: Vanderbilt Press, 1968).

9. Englizian, *Brimstone Corner*, 12; Rankin, "The Story of Park Street Church," *Congregationalist and Christian World*, 195–198.

10. Brewer, "Park Street Church's One Hundred Years of Service," 102.

11. Brewer, "Park Street Church's One Hundred Years of Service," 1–2.

12. Murray, "The Moral Condition of Boston and How to Improve It," in *Music Hall Sermons* (Boston: Fields, Osgood, 1870), 250, 263–264, 268, and "The Power of Cities," in *Music Hall Sermons*, 238.

13. Englizian, *Brimstone Corner*, 167–170; *To The Members of the Committee Appointed by Park-Street Church and the Committee appointed by the Parish to Confer with the Pastor Touching an Associate Pastor* (Boston: Rand, Avery, 1874), 16–18. See also Charles L. Smith, Jr., "A History of Park Street Church with Special Emphasis on the Missionary Program" (B.D. thesis, Andover Newton Theological School, 1954), 9–10.

14. Englizian, *Brimstone Corner*, 175–177.

15. Englizian, *Brimstone Corner*, 190–209; "Shall the Downtown Church Stay?" *Congregationalist and Christian World*, 11 January 1902, n.p.

16. "They Jump and Shout. Great Enthusiasm at the Park Street Revival," *Boston Globe*, 9 December 1901, 1, 3; "Doors Closed Against Portsmouth Campmeeting Adherents," *Boston Globe*, 9 December 1901, 12; "Not Dismayed, Evangelists Secure a New Location," *Boston Globe*, 10 December 1901, 7; "Seek a Church," *Boston Globe*, 14 December 1901, 7.

17. "Strange Scenes at Park Street," *Congregationalist and Christian World*, 14 December 1901, 970.

18. Information on Park Street's membership is more difficult to systematize than Tremont Temple's. A cross-reference of new members (in ten-year cycles from 1880 to 1950) with city directories produced addresses and occupations for one-third to one-half of the names. Those not included in the list presumably lived and worked outside of Boston, or, particularly if female, were not listed because they were not primary breadwinners. Membership lists for Park Street Church are in the Park Street Church Records, Congregational Library, Boston.

19. "Park Street and Its Problem," *Congregationalist and Christian World*, 2 July 1904, 8–9.

20. "When Park Street Church Seemed Dying," *Boston Evening Transcript*, 20 April 1935, 3, 7.

21. *The Preservation of Park Street Church* (Boston: George H. Ellis, 1903), 17, 35.

22. "Dr. Conrad's Body to Lie in State," unid. clipping, Conrad file, Park Street Church Records; "When Park Street Church Seemed Dying," 3, 7.

23. Figures from National Council of the Congregational Churches in the United States, *Congregational Year-Book* (Boston: Congregational Publishing Society, 1885–1928); *The Year-Book of the Congregational and Christian Churches* (New York: Executive Committee of the Central Council of the Congregational and Christian Churches, 1929–1950).

24. "Tells Vigorous Steps He Would Take If He Were the President," unid. clipping, 24 March 1918, Conrad file, Park Street Church Records; "Rev. A.Z. Conrad Dies at 81; Won Fame at Park Street," unid. clipping, 23 January 1927, Park Street Church Records.

25. Conrad, "Eternal Vigilance the Price of Decency," *Christian Faith and Life* 40 (October 1934): 244; "'Son, Behold Thy Mother,' A Sermon by A. Z. Conrad at Park Street Church, May 12, 1935," Park Street Church Records, 7–12. Despite (or because of) this rhetoric, Conrad attracted some of the highest proportions of female members—and lowest proportions of men—in Park Street's history. The percentage of men was highest in the 1890s, reaching almost 39 percent by 1896, but plummeted in the following years, a time of stagnating and then declining membership. During the early years of Conrad's pastorate the percentage almost skimmed below one-quarter. During the World War I era and into the 1920s, a time of steady growth, men accounted for about 30 percent of Park Street's membership, though their proportion sagged again at the end of the 1920s and remaining relatively steady through the early years of the Depression.

26. Charles Angoff, "Boston Twilight," quoted in Edward H. Cotton, "Interviews with Leaders of Religious Opinion—II: Rev. A. Z. Conrad, D. D., Minister of Park Street Church, Boston," *Zion's Herald*, 7 July 1926, 854–855.

27. "Credo. What I Believe After 45 Years in the Christian Ministry. A Sermon Preached by the Rev. A. Z. Conrad, Ph.D., D.D., in Park Street Congregational Church on the 25th Anniversary of His Pastorate, November 23rd, 1930," Park Street Church Records, 5. See also "What Dr. Conrad Thinks of Modernism," *Boston Post*, 18 July 1926, B-7.

28. It's perhaps worth noting that, like Tremont Temple, Park Street did not directly benefit from either of these revivals. Church membership, already on an

upswing, grew in 1909 and 1917, but not sharply. In 1909, for example, the church took in seventy-five new members (growing from 533 to 608); but this was only slightly higher than the previous year (forty-eight) and exactly the same as in 1907. In 1917, Park Street took in 131 new members (growing from 1,025 to 1,156), but again, the increase was not substantially higher than growth at the time, and it was part of a general upswing in membership, beginning with the church's rescue in 1903.

29. Described in Robert Shackleton, *The Book of Boston* (Philadelphia: Penn, 1916; reprint, 1930), 106–107. At this point, the florist shop and tea room still occupied the ground floor, and would remain there until the mid-1940s.

30. See Stephen A. Marini, *Radical Sects of Revoutionary New England* (Cambridge: Harvard University Press, 1982).

31. Elizabeth Evans, *The Wright Vision: The Story of the New England Fellowship* (Lanham, Md.: University Press of America, 1991), 1–11; Kurt O. Berends, "A Mixed Harvest: The First Fruit Harvesters' Ministry in Rural New England," unpublished paper, 1994.

32. Described in "Sixteen Years Outside the Camp. Pentecostal Latter Rain with Signs Following," *Sheaf of the First Fruits* 12 (October 1914): 9–14.

33. Berends, "Mixed Harvest," 14–21.

34. See, e.g. Emily B. Harris, "Convention Notes," *Sheaf of the First Fruits* 12 (June-July 1914): 1–5; Evans, *Wright Vision*, 7; "Are the First Fruit Harvesters Pentecostal?" *Sheaf of the First Fruits* 23 (January 1925): 13–15.

35. "Constitution and By-Laws of the First Fruit Harvesters Association, Edition of 1927," privately published circular in author's possession, 14–15. The constitution did indicate the "special truths" of the Harvesters, including pentecostal baptism, miraculous healing, and the personal, premillennial coming of Christ (4–5).

36. H. N. Morse and Edmund DeS. Brunner, *The Town and Country Church in the United States* (New York: George H. Doran, 1923), 20, 49, 54, 98. Slow rates of church growth also reflected population loss. See also Charles Josiah Galpin, *Empty Churches: The Rural-Urban Dilemma* (New York: Century, 1925).

37. Elizabeth Evans interview, CN no. 279, Elizabeth Evans Papers, Billy Graham Center Archives, Wheaton, Ill., T-2, 6–7; Helen Evans interview, CN no. 445, Elizabeth Evans Papers, T-2.

38. Evans, *Wright Vision*, 54; Joel Carpenter, *Revive Us Again: The Reawakening of American Fundamentalism* (New York: Oxford University Press, 1997), 143.

39. Evans, *Wright Vision*, 86, 17; *Hitherto Hath the Lord Helped Us: Report of Activities During 1938* (New England Fellowship, Boston, Mass., 1938).

40. Evans, *Wright Vision*, 88–89.

41. Ockenga still lacks a scholarly biography, and at present the most comprehensive (though hardly objective) account is Harold Lindsell, *Park Street Prophet: A Life of Harold John Ockenga* (Wheaton, Ill.: Van Kampen Press, 1951; reprint, New York: Garland, 1988). The best accounts of his career as a "new evangelical" are George Marsden, *Reforming Fundamentalism: Fuller Seminary and the New Evangelicalism* (Grand Rapids, Mich.: Eerdmans, 1987), and Carpenter, *Revive Us Again*, 189–191, 146–152. See also Harold John Ockenga, " 'The New Evangelicalism,' Sermon Preached at Park Street Church December 8, 1957" (n.p., n.d.).

42. The standard treatment is James DeForest Murch, *Cooperation Without Compromise: A History of the National Association of Evangelicals* (Grand Rapids, Mich.: Eerdmans, 1956).

43. Evans, *Wright Vision*, 18, 47, 109, 84. See also descriptions in "News from the States: Massachusetts," *Watchman-Examiner*, 12 January 1950, 43; Elizabeth Evans, "New England Evangelicals Plan Christian Schools," *United Evangelical Action*, 15 November 1946, 3, 7.

44. "'The Unique and Unparalleled Position of Park Street Church in Boston's Religious History,' by Harold John Ockenga, Preached at Park Street Church, Boston, Mass.," (n.p., n.d.), 22.

45. "'The Most Thrilling Moment in My Boston Ministry,' by Harold John Ockenga, Preached at Park Street Church, Boston, Massachusetts, December 5, 1943," (n.d.).

46. Ockenga, *Our Protestant Heritage* (Grand Rapids, Mich.: Zondervan, 1938), v–vi.

47. "'What Cardinal Spellman Wants for the American Schools,' by Harold John Ockenga, Sermon Preached at Park Street Church, Boston, Massachusetts, September 16, 1949," 7. See also Lindsell, *Park Street Prophet*, 84–85.

48. John McGreevy, *Catholicism and American Freedom: A History*, 187–188.

49. Lindsell, *Park Street Prophet*, 76. See also accounts in Englizian, *Brimstone Corner*, 236–237; Carpenter, *Revive Us Again*, 189–190.

CHAPTER 10

1. Katherine Simonds's article is in *New England Quarterly* 21 (June 1948): 161. Ockenga, "Revival Is Here!" *Youth for Christ Magazine* 7 (April 1950): 8–9.

2. "Denounces 'Jellyfish' Christians," *Boston Post*, 3 January 1950. Clippings from the 1950 Graham campaign in Boston and New England, all in no. 360, scrapbooks 12 and 13, Billy Graham Evangelistic Association Collection, Billy Graham Center Archives, Wheaton, Ill.

3. For comparisons, see "Evangelist Calls City to Week of Repentance," *Boston Herald*, 2 January 1950, 1; "7500 Hear Dr. Graham in Crusade," *Boston Post*, 2 January 1950, 1; Bill Cunningham, "Billy Graham Great but Not a Sunday," *Boston Herald*, 15 January 1950. On Belshazaar, see "Graham Recalls Wicked Babylon in Rousing Sermon," *Boston Globe*, January 6, 1950; on baseball, see "Billy Graham's Life a Fascinating Story," *Boston Post Souvenir Edition*, CN 360, scrapbook 12, Billy Graham Evangelistic Association Collection, 3.

4. "Evangelist Graham Draws 6000 from 'Eve' Celebration," *Boston Herald*, 1 January 1950, 1.

5. "Gruelling Life Led by Preacher. Eats 4 Meals a Day, Keeps in Trim Like Prize Fighter," *Boston Post*, 8 January 1950; "Billy Graham Feels Like Wet Dishrag After Sermon," *Boston Globe*, 8 January 1950, 15.

6. "Evangelist Sees Return of Christ in 10–15 Years," *Boston Globe*, 30 December 1949; "Evangelist Could Make Hollywood," *Boston Post Souvenir Edition*, 2.

7. Billy Graham, *Just As I Am* (San Francisco: Harper and Row, 1997), 164.

8. "Billy Hits Red Anti-Religion," *Boston Advertiser*, 6 January, 1950; "Revivalist Gives Talk on Heaven," *Boston Post*, 16 January 1950, 1.

9. "Thousands in Boston Are Possessed of Demons, Charges Billy Graham," *Boston Herald*, 15 January 1950, 1.

10. "Revival Mounting in Fervor," *Boston Post*, 14 January 1950.

11. "Graham Raps Hooton's 'Mercy Killing' Defense," *Boston Globe*, 7 January 1950.

12. *Revival in Our Time: The Story of the Billy Graham Evangelistic Campaigns* (Wheaton, Ill.: Van Kampen Press, 1950), 61.

13. John Pollock, *Twenty Years with Billy Graham* (Minneapolis: World Wide, 1966), 73; "Post Lauded for Revival Stories," *Boston Post*, 7 January 1950, 12; "Post Lauded for Revival Stories," *Boston Post*, 15 January 1950, 1.

14. "Hub Series of Revivals On Tonight," *Boston Post*, 19 April 1950, 30.

15. "Throngs Again Pack Portland Hall as Billy Graham Inspires Converts," *Boston Globe*, 30 March 1950, 1.

16. "Billy Carries Gospel Despite Death Peril," *Boston Traveler*, 30 March, 1950, 1; "Strain Fells Graham in Bridgeport," *Boston Globe*, 11 April 1950, 1.

17. "8000 Hear Dr. Graham Hit Money," *Boston Post*, 15 April, 1950, 6.

18. "Graham Sees Boston Rally Biggest in U.S. Expects 100,000 on Common Sunday, 60,000 at Garden," *Boston Herald*, 18 April, 1950, 1; "8000 Hear Dr. Graham Hit Money," 1.

19. Quoted in Thomas H. O'Connor, *The Hub: Boston Past and Present* (Boston: Northeastern University Press, 2001), 211.

20. Thomas H. O'Connor, *Boston Catholics: A History of the Church and Its People* (Boston: Northeastern University Press, 1998), 239–282.

21. "Bravo Billy!" *Pilot*, 21 January 1950, 4. Later on, the *Pilot* gave a more guarded endorsement, allowing that though Catholics might support the revival, they should not attend it, reasoning that "if the Catholic Church is right, all forms of Protestantism are wrong." "Questions and Answers," *Pilot* 15 April 1950, 4.

22. *Boston Conference on the Urban Church* (Boston: Department of Research and Strategy, Massachusetts Council of Churches, 1949), 9, 13.

23. Boston University School of Religious Education and Social Service, *Sections of Boston: A Partial Religious Survey of Selected Urban Areas; South Boston, the North End, the West End, the Back Bay, 1933–1934* (Boston: Boston Federation of Churches and Department of Social Services in the School of Religious Education and Social Service of Boston University, 1934), 14.

24. *Boston Conference on the Urban Church*, 3.

25. O'Connor, *Hub*, 232–236.

26. Polk's Boston City Directory, 1945, vol. 141 (Boston: R. L. Polk & Co., 1945), 1893–4; Arthur E. Paris, *Black Pentecostalism: Southern Religion in an Urban World* (Amherst: University of Massachusetts Press, 1982).

27. "Billy Graham," *Southern Presbyterian Journal*, 15 February 1950, 2, 3.

28. Richard K. Mercer, "God Comes to Boston-Town," *Watchman-Examiner*, 23 March 1950, 282. Ockenga's press release gave the figures as 75 percent Catholic and 15 percent Unitarian.

29. "Graham Back in Boston, Ready for Giant Rally," *Boston Globe*, 19 April, 1950, 1, 6.

30. "To Reserve Seats for Revivals," *Boston Post*, 17 April 1950, 1. The plan somewhat backfired, since a small turnout from a delegation meant highly visible rows

of empty seats. On the first night, some confusion about the buses from Rhode Island gave the appearance of a thin turnout.

31. "Scoffers Lashed by Dr. Graham," *Boston Post*, 10 April 1950, 16; "Explains Why He Uses 'You All,'" *Boston Post*, 15 April 1950, 6.

32. Joseph Conforti, *Imagining New England: Explorations of Regional Identity from the Pilgrims to the Mid–Twentieth Century* (Chapel Hill: University of North Carolina Press, 2001), 205; "Warm Hearts and Kindly People Here," *Boston Post Souvenir Edition*, 2.

33. George Wilson Pierson, "The Obstinate Concept of New England: A Study in Denudation," *New England Quarterly* 28 (March 1955): 4, 12.

34. Lawrence W. Kennedy, *Planning the City upon a Hill: Boston Since 1630* (Amherst: University of Massachusetts Press, 1992), 132, 158; Holbrook, "There She Stands . . ." *New England Quarterly* 23 (March 1950): 11.

35. Graham, *Just As I Am*, 168.

36. "Denounces 'Jellyfish' Christians," *Boston Post*, 3 January 1950, 1.

37. Ockenga, "Boston Stirred by Revival," *United Evangelical Action*, 15 January 1950, 4.

38. "'Prayer Chain' to Convert N. E.," *Boston Traveler*, 3 January 1950, 11; "Week of Prayer in Boston Asked by Evangelist Graham," *Boston Globe*, 5 January 1950, 1, 21.

39. "Graham Back in Boston," 6.

40. Pollock, *Twenty Years with Billy Graham*, 82.

41. "Revival Climax Set for Common," *Boston Post*, 28 March 1950, 1, 10.

42. "Scoffers Lashed by Dr. Graham," 16; "Graham Sees Boston Rally Biggest in U.S.," *Boston Herald*, 18 April 1950, 1.

43. "9000 at Hub Revival of Dr. Billy Graham," *Boston Post*, 20 April 1950, 1, 18.

44. "50,000 Hear Graham Finale," *Boston Herald*, 24 April 1950, 1.

45. "Graham Asks Truman for Day of Prayer," *Boston Globe*, 24 April 1950, 1.

46. "40,000 Hear Billy Graham at Big Rally on Boston Common," *Boston Post*, 24 April 1950, 1, 8.

47. James Davison Hunter, *American Evangelicals: Conservative Religion and the Quandary of Modernity* (New Brunswick, N.J.: Rutgers University Press, 1983), 51–52. The survey was based on a combination of responses to theological questions about biblical inerrancy and salvation, and religious experience.

48. "Massachusetts," available online at: www.adherents.com. Consulted February 19, 2004.

49. Exhibit 15, American Religious Identification Survey, Graduate Center of the City University of New York, "State by State Distribution of Selected Religious Groups," available online at: www.gc.cuny.edu. Consulted February 19, 2004.

50. Statistics drawn from the Hartford Institute for Religion Research website, available online at: hirr.hartsem.edu. Consulted February 19, 2004.

Selected Bibliography

Abell, Aaron. *The Urban Impact on American Protestantism, 1865–1900.* Cambridge: Harvard University Press, 1943.

Adams, Henry. *The Education of Henry Adams: An Autobiography.* Ed. D. W. Brogan. Boston: Houghton Mifflin, 1961.

Andrews, Leslie K. "Restricted Freedom: A. B. Simpson's View of Women." In *Birth of a Vision,* ed. David F. Hartzfeld and Charles Nienkirchen. Regina, Saskatchewan: His Dominion, 1986.

Arthur, David T. "Joshua V. Himes and the Cause of Adventism." In *The Disappointed: Millerism and Millenarianism in the Nineteenth Century,* ed. Ronald L. Numbers and Jonathan M. Butler. Bloomington: Indiana University Press, 1987, 36–58.

Baldwin, David A. "When Billy Sunday 'Saved' Colorado: That Old-Time Religion and the 1914 Prohibition Amendment." *Colorado Heritage* 2 (1990): 34–44.

Barth, Gunther. *City People: The Rise of Modern City Culture in Nineteenth-Century America.* New York: Oxford University Press, 1980.

Beattie, Betsy. *Obligation and Opportunity: Single Maritime Women in Boston, 1870–1930.* Montreal: McGill-Queen's University Press, 2000.

Beauregard, John, ed. *Journal of Our Journey: By Maria Hale Gordon and Adoniram Judson Gordon.* Wenham, Mass.: Gordon College Archives, 1989.

Bederman, Gail. *Manliness and Civilization: A Cultural History of Gender and Race in the United States, 1880–1917.* Chicago: University of Chicago Press, 1995.

———. "'The Women Have Had Charge of the Church Work Long Enough': The Men and Religion Forward Movement of 1911–1912 and the Masculization of Middle-Class Protestantism." *American Quarterly* 41 (1989): 432–465.

Beebe, Lucius. *Boston and the Boston Legend.* New York: Appleton-Century, 1936.

Bellah, Robert, and Frederick Greenspahn, eds. *Uncivil Religion: Interreligious Hostility in America.* New York: Crossroad, 1987.

Bendroth, Margaret. "Billy Sunday and the Unitarians, 1916–1917." *Mid-America* 82 (fall 2001): 273–294.

———. *Fundamentalism and Gender, 1875 to the Present.* New Haven: Yale University Press, 1993.

———. "Men, Masculinity and Urban Revivalism: J. Wilbur Chapman's Boston Crusade, 1909." *Journal of Presbyterian History* 75 (winter 1997): 235–246.

———. "Rum, Romanism and Evangelism: Catholics and Protestants in Late Nineteenth-Century Boston, Massachusetts." *Church History* 68 (September 1999): 627–647.

Berends, Kurt O. "A Mixed Harvest: The First Fruit Harvesters' Ministry in Rural New England." Unpublished paper, 1994.

Blackall, C. H. "Boston Sketches—The Churches." *Inland Architect and News Record* 12 (December 1888): 77–78.

"A Blessing to Boston: The Ruggles Street Baptist Church and Its Work." *Watchman,* 2 May 1901, 10–12.

Boston and Its Suburbs: A Guide Book. Boston: Press of Stanley and Usher, 1888.

Boston Conference on the Urban Church. Boston: Department of Research and Strategy, Massachusetts Council of Churches, 1949.

The Boston Directory Containing the City Record, A Directory of the Citizens, Business Directory and Street Directory with Map. Boston: Sampson and Murdock, 1885–1950.

Boston University School of Religious Education and Social Service. *Sections of Boston: A Partial Religious Survey of Selected Urban Areas; South Boston, the North End, the West End, the Back Bay, 1933–1934.* Boston: Boston Federation of Churches and Department of Social Services in the School of Religious Education and Social Service of Boston University, 1934.

Boyer, Paul. *When Time Shall Be No More: Prophecy Belief in Modern American Culture.* Cambridge: Harvard University Press, 1992.

Brereton, Virginia Lieson. *Training God's Army: The American Bible School, 1880–1940.* Bloomington: Indiana University Press, 1990.

Bridgman, H. A. "Successful Churches: Tremont Temple, Boston." *Record of Christian Work* 20 (March 1901): 168–169.

British-American Association. *Faneuil Hall: Who Are Its Conservators?* Boston, n.d.

Brookes, Alan A. "Out-Migration from the Maritime Provinces, 1860–1900: Some Preliminary Considerations." *Acadiensis* 5 (1976): 26–55.

Bunting, W. H. *Portrait of a Port: Boston, 1852–1914.* Cambridge: Harvard University Press, 1971.

Burrill, Gary. *Maritimers in Massachusetts, Ontario, and Alberta: An Oral History of Leaving Home.* Montreal: McGill-Queen's University Press, 1992.

Butler, Jonathan M. "Adventism and the American Experience." In *The Rise of Adventism: Religion and Society in Mid-Nineteenth-Century America.* Ed. Edwin S. Gaustad. New York: Harper and Row, 1974.

Byrne, William, and William Leahy, eds. *History of the Catholic Church in the New England States.* Vol. 2. Boston: Hurd and Everts, 1899.

Carnes, Mark C. *Secret Ritual and Manhood in Victorian America*. New Haven: Yale University Press, 1989.

Carpenter, Joel. *Revive Us Again: The Reawakening of American Fundamentalism*. New York: Oxford University Press, 1997.

Chapman, J. Wilbur. *Present-Day Evangelism*. New York: Baker and Taylor, 1903.

Cheape, Charles W. *Moving the Masses: Urban Public Transit in New York, Boston, and Philadelphia, 1880–1912*. Cambridge: Harvard University Press, 1980.

Christiano, Kevin J. *Religious Diversity and Social Change: American Cities, 1890–1906*. Cambridge, England: Cambridge University Press, 1987.

"Church Attendance in Boston." *Congregationalist*, 26 April 1882, 4.

Coleman, George W. "The Contribution of the Open Forum to Democracy in Religion." *Journal of Religion* 2 (January 1922): 1–15.

Commemorative Exercises at the One Hundredth Anniversary of the Organization of Park Street Church. Ed. A. Z. Conrad. Boston: Park Street Centennial Committee, 1909.

Conforti, Joseph. *Imagining New England: Explorations of Regional Identity from the Pilgrims to the Mid–Twentieth Century*. Chapel Hill: University of North Carolina Press, 2001.

Connolly, James J. "Reconstituting Ethnic Politics: Boston, 1909–1925." *Social Science History* 19 (winter 1995): 479–509.

———. *The Triumph of Ethnic Progressivism: Urban Political Culture in Boston, 1900–1925*. Cambridge: Harvard University Press, 1998.

Conrad, A. Z., ed. *Boston's Awakening: A Complete Account of the Great Boston Revival Under the Leadership of J. Wilbur Chapman and Charles M. Alexander, January 26th to February 21st, 1909*. Boston: King's Business, 1909.

Cunningham, Raymond J. "The Impact of Christian Science on the American Churches, 1880–1910." *American Historical Review* 72 (April 1967): 885–905.

Curlew, Douglas James. " 'They Ceased Not to Preach': Fundamentalism, Culture, and the Revivalist Imperative at the Temple Baptist Church of Detroit." Ph.D. diss., Ann Arbor: University of Michigan, 2001.

Davis, William F. *Christian Liberties in Boston: A Sketch of Recent Attempts to Destroy Them Through the Device of a Gag-By-Law for Gospel Preachers*. Chelsea, Mass., 1887.

Dike, Samuel. "A Study of New England Revivals." *American Journal of Sociology* 15 (1909): 361–378.

Dinneen, Maurice. *The Catholic Total Abstinence Movement in the Archdiocese of Boston*. Boston: E. L. Grimes, 1908.

Dixon, Helen. *A. C. Dixon: A Romance of Preaching*. New York: Putnam, 1931; reprint, New York: Garland, 1988.

Dobschuetz, Barbara. "Fundamentalism and American Urban Culture: Community and Religious Identity in Dwight L. Moody's Chicago, 1864–1914." Ph.D. diss., University of Illinois, Chicago, 2002.

Dorchester, Daniel. *Christianity in the United States*. New York: Phillips and Hunt, 1888.

Dorn, Jonathan. " 'Our Best Gospel Appliances': Institutional Churches and the Emergence of Social Christianity in the South End of Boston, 1880–1920." Ph.D. diss., Harvard University, 1994.

Dorsett, Lyle. *Billy Sunday and the Redemption of Urban America*. Grand Rapids, Mich.: Eerdmans, 1991.

Dr. Cullis and His Work. Twenty Years of Blessing in Answer to Prayer. Ed. W. H. Daniels. Boston: Willard Tract Repository, n.d.; reprint, New York: Garland, 1985.

Englizian, H. Crosby. *Brimstone Corner: Park Street Church, Boston.* Chicago: Moody Press, 1968.

Evangelistic Association of New England. *Annual Reports,* 1888–1893.

Evans, Elizabeth. *The Wright Vision: The Story of the New England Fellowship.* Lanham, Md.: University Press of America, 1991.

Farmelant, Kristen. "Trophies of Grace: Religious Conversion and Americanization in Boston's Immigrant Communities, 1890–1940." Ph.D. diss., Brown University, 1992.

Formisano, Ronald P., and Constance K. Burns, eds. *Boston, 1700–1980: The Evolution of Urban Politics.* Westport, Conn.: Greenwood Press, 1984.

Fowler, Stacy. "Christian Science." *Homiletic Review* 10 (August 1885): 134–141.

Frothingham, Frank E. *The Boston Fire, November 9th and 10th 1872. Its History, Together with the Losses in Detail of Both Real and Personal Estate.* Boston: Lee and Shepard, 1873.

Fuller, Robert. *Naming the Antichrist: The History of an American Obsession.* New York: Oxford University Press, 1995.

Fulton, Justin Dewey. *How to Win Romanists.* Somerville, Mass.: Pauline Propaganda, 1898.

Galpin, Charles Josiah. *Empty Churches: The Rural-Urban Dilemma.* New York: Century, 1925.

Gamm, Gerald. *Urban Exodus: Why the Jews Left Boston and the Catholics Stayed.* Cambridge: Harvard University Press, 1999.

Gibson, Scott M. *A. J. Gordon: American Premillennialist.* Lanham, Md.: University Press of America, 2001.

Giggie, John M., and Diane Winston, eds. *Faith in the Market: Religion and the Rise of Urban Commercial Culture.* New Brunswick, N.J.: Rutgers University Press, 2002.

Gordon, A. J. *Ecce Venit: Behold He Cometh.* New York: Fleming H. Revell, 1889.

———. *How Christ Came to Church: A Spiritual Autobiography.* Philadelphia: American Baptist Publication Society, 1895.

———. *The Ministry of the Spirit.* Philadelphia: American Baptist Publication Society, 1894.

———. "The Ministry of Women." *Missionary Review of the World* 7 (December 1894): 910–921.

———. "My People Love to Have It So." *Watchword* 13 (March 1891): 71.

———. "Short-Cut Methods." *Watchman,* 7 November 1889, 1.

———. "A Pastoral Letter." *Clarendon Light* 3 (January 1895): 7–8.

———. "The Uplifted Gaze." *Watchword* 10 (October 1888): 173.

Gordon, Ernest R. *Adoniram Judson Gordon: A Biography.* New York: Fleming H. Revell, 1896; reprint, New York: Garland, 1984.

Gordon, Maria. "Women as Evangelists." *Northfield Echoes* 1 (1894): 147–151.

Graham, William A. *Just As I Am.* San Francisco: Harper and Row, 1997.

Green, James R., and Hugh Carter Donahue. *Boston's Workers: A Labor History.* Boston: Trustees of the Public Library, 1979.

Guiness, H. Grattan. *Romanism and the Reformation; From the Standpoint of Prophecy.* New York: A. C. Armstrong, 1887.

Hackett, David. "The Church and the Lodge: Gender Tensions, Region, and Theology in Late Nineteenth Century Protestant Culture." Unpublished paper, 1993.

Hankins, Barry. *God's Rascal: J. Frank Norris and the Beginnings of Southern Fundamentalism*. Lexington: University Press of Kentucky, 1996.

Hansen, Marcus Lee. *The Mingling of the Canadian and American Peoples*, Vol. 1. *Historical*. New Haven: Yale University Press, 1940.

Hardy, Stephen. *How Boston Played: Sport, Recreation and Community, 1865–1915*. Boston: Northeastern University Press, 1982.

Harmond, Richard. "Troubles of Massachusetts Republicans During the 1880s." *Mid-America* 56 (April 1974): 91–93.

Hastings, Harriet. *Pebbles from the Path of a Pilgrim*. Boston: H. L. Hastings, 1885.

Herndon, Richard, ed. *Boston of Today: A Glance at Its History and Characteristics*. Boston: Boston Post, 1892.

Hester, William H. *One Hundred and Five Years by Faith: A History of the Twelfth Baptist Church*. Boston, 1946.

Higham, John. *Strangers in the Land: Patterns of American Nativism, 1860–1925*. New York: Atheneum, 1965.

Hill, Hamilton Andrews. *History of the Old South Church (Third Church) Boston 1669–1884*. Vol. 2. Boston: Houghton Mifflin, 1890.

Hofstadter, Richard. *The Paranoid Style in American Politics, and Other Essays*. New York: Knopf, 1965.

Howe, M. A. DeWolfe. *Boston Common: Scenes from Four Centuries*. Boston: Houghton Mifflin, 1921.

Howells, William Dean. *The Rise of Silas Lapham*. 1885; reprint, New York: Signet Classics, 1963.

Hunter, James Davison. *American Evangelicals: Conservative Religion and the Quandary of Modernity*. New Brunswick, N.J.: Rutgers University Press, 1983.

Illustrated Boston, the Metropolis of New England. New York: American Publishing and Engraving, 1889.

Inaugural Address of Hugh O'Brien, Mayor of Boston, Before the City Council, January 2, 1888. Boston: Rockwell and Churchill, 1888.

Isenberg, Michael T. *John L. Sullivan and His America*. Urbana: University of Illinois Press, 1988.

James, Henry. *The American Scene*. London: Chapman and Hall, 1907.

Johnson, Albert. *A Concise Narrative of the Origin and Progress, Doctrine and Work of This Body of Believers*. Boston: Advent Christian Publication Society, 1918.

Kane, Paula. *Separatism and Subculture: Boston Catholicism, 1900–1920*. Chapel Hill: University of North Carolina Press, 1994.

Kasson, John F. *Houdini, Tarzan and the Perfect Man: The White Male Body and the Challenge of Modernity in America*. New York: Hill and Wang, 2001.

Kaufman, Polly Welts. *Boston Women and City School Politics, 1872–1905*. New York: Garland, 1994.

Kennedy, Lawrence W. *Planning the City upon a Hill: Boston Since 1630*. Amherst: University of Massachusetts Press, 1992.

———. "Pulpits and Politics: Anti-Catholicism in Boston in the 1880s and 1890s." *Historical Journal of Massachusetts* 28 (winter 2000): 23–55.

King, Moses, ed. *King's Handbook of Boston*. Boston: Rand, Avery, 1885.

Kruh, David. *Always Something Doing: Boston's Infamous Scollay Square*. Rev. ed. Boston: Northeastern University Press, 1999.

Lane, Edgar C. *A Brief History of Tremont Temple, 1839–1947*. Boston: Tremont Temple, 1947.

Lane, Roger. *Policing the City: Boston 1882–1885*. Cambridge: Harvard University Press, 1967.

Laws, Curtis Lee. "Ruggles Street Church, Boston." *Watchman-Examiner*, 20 April 1916, 489–492.

Lawson, Thomas W. *The Krank: His Language and What It Means*. Boston: Rand Avery, 1888.

Lhamon, W. J. "A Study in Fundamentalism." *Christian*, 4 November 1926, n.p.

Lindsell, Harold. *Park Street Prophet: A Life of Harold John Ockenga*. Wheaton, Ill.: Van Kampen Press, 1951; reprint, New York: Garland, 1988.

Lord, Robert H., John E. Sexton, and Edward T. Harrington. *History of the Archdiocese of Boston In the Various Stages of Its Development 1604 to 1943 In Three Volumes*. Vol. 3. New York: Sheed and Ward, 1944.

Lupo, Alan. *Liberty's Chosen Home: The Politics of Violence in Boston*. Boston: Beacon Press, 1977; reprint, 1988.

MacDougall, John. *Rural Life in Canada: Its Trends and Tasks*. Toronto: University of Toronto Press, 1913; reprint, 1973.

Marini, Stephen A. *Radical Sects of Revolutionary New England*. Cambridge: Harvard University Press, 1982.

Marlowe, George Francis. *Churches of Old New England: Their Architecture and Their Architects, Their Pastors and Their People*. New York: Macmillan, 1947.

Marsden, George. *Fundamentalism and American Culture, 1875–1920*. New York: Oxford University Press, 1980.

———. *Reforming Fundamentalism: Fuller Seminary and the New Evangelicalism*. Grand Rapids, Mich.: Eerdmans, 1987.

Marty, Martin, and R. Scott Appleby, eds. *Fundamentalisms and the State: Remaking Politics, Economies, and Militance*. Chicago: University of Chicago Press, 1993.

Massa, Mark S. *Anti-Catholicism in America: The Last Acceptable Prejudice*. New York: Crossroad, 2003.

Massachusetts Woman's Christian Temperance Union. *Golden Jubilee Magazine, 1924*. Boston, Massachusetts WCTU, 1924.

———. *Minutes of the Eleventh Annual Meeting of the Massachusetts WCTU, Held in the Methodist Episcopal Church, Somerville, October 8 and 9, 1884*. Malden, Mass., 1884.

———. *Minutes of the Fourteenth Annual Meeting of the WCTU Held in Tremont Temple, Boston*. Boston, 1887.

May, Henry F. *Protestant Churches and Industrial America*. New York: Harper, 1949.

McCarthy, Katherine. "Psychotherapy and Religion: The Emmanuel Movement." *Journal of Religion and Health* 23 (summer 1984): 92–105.

McDannell, Colleen. " 'True Men as We Need Them': Catholicism and the Irish-American Male." *American Studies* 26 (fall 1986): 19–36.

McFarland, Gerald W. *Mugwumps, Morals and Politics: 1884–1920*. Amherst: University of Massachusetts Press, 1975.

McGreevy, John. *Catholicism and American Freedom: A History*. New York: Norton, 2003.

McLoughlin, William G. *Billy Sunday Was His Real Name*. Chicago: University of Chicago Press, 1955.

Merk, Lois Bannister. "Boston's Historic Public School Crisis." *New England Quarterly* 31 (June 1958): 176.

Merriam, E. F. "The Strangers' Sabbath Home: Tremont Temple Baptist Church." *Watchman*, 9 May 1901, 10–12.

Meyers, Arthur S. "A Bridge to the Future: From the Boston Baptist Social Union to the Beth El Open Forum." *American Baptist Quarterly* 14 (spring 1995): 225–240.

"Missionary Training Schools: Do Baptists Need Them?" *Baptist Quarterly Review* 12 (January 1890): 69–100.

Mitchell, Guy. "History of Tremont Temple." Unpublished manuscript, n.d.

Morgan, Henry. *Boston Inside Out! Sins of Great City! A Story of Real Life*. Boston: Shawmut, 1880.

Morse, H. N., and Edmund DeS. Brunner. *The Town and Country Church in the United States*. New York: George H. Doran, 1923.

Mudge, James. "A Brief Historical Sketch of Boston Methodism." In *Boston Methodism Survey*. Boston: Taylor Press, 1914.

Murch, James DeForest. *Cooperation Without Compromise: A History of the National Association of Evangelicals*. Grand Rapids, Mich.: Eerdmans, 1956.

Murray, William Henry Harrison. *Music Hall Sermons*. Boston: Fields, Osgood, 1870.

Myers, Cortland. *Why Men Do Not Go to Church*. New York: Funk and Wagnalls, 1899.

National Council of the Congregational Churches in the United States. *Congregational Year-Book*. Boston: Congregational Publishing Society, 1885–1928.

Nelson, Shirley. *Fair, Clear, and Terrible: The Story of Shiloh, Maine*. Latham, N.Y.: British American, 1989.

New England Christian Association. *Danger Signals: Secret Societies Illuminated*. Boston: James H. Earle, 1894.

N. W. Ayer and Son's American Newspaper Annual. Philadelphia: N. W. Ayer, 1885.

O'Connor, Thomas H. *Bibles, Brahmins, and Bosses: A Short History of Boston*. 3rd ed. Boston: Trustees of the Public Library, 1991.

———. *Boston Catholics: A History of the Church and Its People*. Boston: Northeastern University Press, 1998.

———. *The Boston Irish: A Political History*. Boston: Northeastern University Press, 1995.

———. *The Hub: Boston Past and Present*. Boston: Northeastern University Press, 2001.

Ockenga, Harold John. "*The Most Thrilling Moment in My Boston Ministry, by Harold John Ockenga, Preached at Park Street Church, Boston, Massachusetts, December 5, 1943.*" Gordon-Connell Theological Seminary Archives, South Hampton, Massachusetts.

———. "'The New Evangelicalism,' Sermon Preached at Park Street Church December 8, 1957," *Park Street* 3 (February 1958): 2–7.

———. *Our Protestant Heritage*. Grand Rapids, Mich.: Zondervan, 1938.

———. "*The Unique and Unparalleled Position of Park Street Church in Boston's Religious History, by Harold John Ockenga, Preached at Park Street Church, Boston, Mass.*" Gordon-Connell Theological Seminary Archives, South Hampton, Massachusetts.

————. "'What Cardinal Spellman Wants for the American Schools,' by Harold John Ockenga, Sermon Preached at Park Street Church, Boston, Massachusetts, September 16, 1949."

"One Hundred Years in the Heart of Boston." *Congregationalist and Christian World*, 13 March 1909, 343.

O'Toole, James M. *Militant and Triumphant: William Henry O'Connell and the Catholic Church in Boston, 1859–1944.* Notre Dame, Ind.: University of Notre Dame Press, 1992.

Paris, Arthur E. *Black Pentecostalism: Southern Religion in an Urban World.* Amherst: University of Massachusetts Press, 1982.

Paz, D. G. *Popular Anti-Catholicism in Mid-Victorian England.* Stanford, Calif.: Stanford University Press, 1992.

Pointer, Stephen R. *Joseph Cook: Boston Lecturer and Evangelical Apologist.* Lewiston, N.Y.: Edwin Mellen, 1991.

Pollock, John. *Twenty Years with Billy Graham.* Minneapolis: World Wide, 1966.

The Preservation of Park Street Church. Boston: George H. Ellis, 1903.

The Priest; A Tale of Modernism in New England. By the Author of Letters to His Holiness, Pope Pius X. Boston: Sherman, French, 1911.

The Prophecy Conference Movement. Vol. 3. Ed. Donald W. Dayton. New York: Garland, 1988.

Quinn, John F. "Father Mathew's Disciples: American Catholic Support for Temperance, 1840–1920." *Church History* 65 (December 1996): 624–640.

Rankin, Isaac Ogden. "The Story of Park Street Church." *Congregationalist and Christian World*, 7 February 1903, 195.

Rawlyk, George A. *Champions of the Truth: Fundamentalism, Modernism, and the Maritime Baptists.* Montreal: McGill-Queen's University Press, 1990.

"The Real Effect of Revivals." *Springfield Republican*, 4 April 1909.

Reeves, W. G. "Newfoundlanders in the 'Boston States': A Study in Early Twentieth-Century Community and Counterpoint." *Newfoundland Studies* 6 (1990): 34–55.

Religious Bodies: 1906, part 1, *Summary and General Tables.* Washington, D.C.: Government Printing Office, 1910.

Report of Proceedings of the City Council of Boston, for the Municipal Year 1885. Boston: Rockwell and Churchill, 1886.

Report on Statistics of Churches in the United States at the Eleventh Census: 1890. Washington, D.C.: Government Printing Office, 1894.

Revival in Our Time: The Story of the Billy Graham Evangelistic Campaigns. Wheaton, Ill.: Van Kampen Press, 1950.

Rosenzweig, Roy. "Middle-Class Parks and Working Class Play: The Struggle over Recreational Space in Worcester, Massachusetts, 1870–1910." *Radical History Review* 21 (fall 1979): 31–46.

Rowlands, Robert T. "Conservative Protestant Efforts to Institutionalize Revivalism as Seen in the Evangelistic Association of New England, 1887–1991." M.A. thesis, Northeastern University, 1971.

Russell, C. Allyn. "Adoniram Judson Gordon: Nineteenth-Century Fundamentalist." *American Baptist Quarterly* 4 (1985): 61–89.

————. *Voices of American Fundamentalism: Seven Biographical Studies.* Philadephia: Westminster Press, 1976, 107–134.

Sandeen, Ernest. *The Roots of Fundamentalism: British and American Millenarianism, 1800–1930.* Chicago: University of Chicago Press, 1970.

Santayana, George. *The Last Puritan: A Memoir in the Form of a Novel.* New York: Scribner's, 1936.

Sarna, Jonathan, and Ellen Smith, eds. *The Jews of Boston.* Boston: Combined Jewish Philanthropies of Greater Boston, 1995.

Sawyer, Walter Leon. "Overchurched Boston." *Zion's Herald,* 27 January 1909, 117.

Schindler, Solomon. *Israelites in Boston: A Tale Describing the Development of Judaism in Boston, Preceded by the Jewish Calendar for the Next Decade.* Boston: Berwick and Smith, 1889.

Schlesinger, Arthur M., Sr. "A Critical Period in American Religion." *Massachusetts Historical Society Proceedings* 64 (October 1930–June 1932): 532–546.

See, Scott W. *Riots in New Brunswick: Orange Nativism and Social Violence in the 1840s.* Toronto: University of Toronto Press, 1993.

Shackleton, Robert. *The Book of Boston.* Philadelphia: Penn, 1916; reprint, 1930.

Smith, Arthur Warren. *Special Report to the Committee of Seven upon the Baptist Situation in Boston Proper: A Survey of Historical and Present Conditions.* Boston: Griffith-Stillings Press, 1912.

Smith, Charles L., Jr. "A History of Park Street Church with Special Emphasis on the Missionary Program." B.D. thesis, Andover Newton Theological School, 1954.

Snyder, Robert W. *The Voice of the City: Vaudeville and Popular Culture in New York.* New York: Oxford University Press, 1989.

Soden, Dale E. *The Reverend Mark Matthews: An Activist in the Progressive Era.* Seattle: University of Washington Press, 2001.

Srole, Carol. "'A Position That God Has Not Particularly Assigned to Men': The Feminization of Clerical Work, Boston, 1860–1915." Ph.D. diss., University of California, Los Angeles, 1984.

Standard Encyclopedia of the Alcohol Problem. Vol. 1. Westerville, Ohio: American Issue, 1925.

"The Story of Park Street Church." *Congregationalist and Christian World,* 7 February 1903, 196.

Stout, Harry S. *Divine Dramatist: George Whitefield and the Rise of Modern Evangelicalism.* Grand Rapids, Mich.: Eerdmans, 1991.

Tager, Jack. *Boston Riots: Three Centuries of Social Violence.* Boston: Northeastern University Press, 2001.

Taylor, Sharon. "That Obnoxious Dogma: Future Probation and the Struggle to Construct an American Congregationalist Identity." Ph.D. diss., Boston College, 2004.

Thernstrom, Stephan. *The Other Bostonians: Poverty and Progress in the American Metropolis, 1880–1970.* Cambridge: Harvard University Press, 1973.

To The Members of the Committee Appointed by Park-Street Church and the Committee Appointed by the Parish to Confer with the Pastor Touching an Associate Pastor. Boston: Rand, Avery, 1874.

Townsend, Luther T. *"Faith-Work," "Christian Science," and Other Cures.* Boston: W. A. Wilde, 1885.

Tremont Temple Baptist Church: A Light in the City for 150 Years. Commemorative booklet. Boston, Tremont Temple Baptist Church, 1989.

Tremont Temple Baptist Church. *Annual Reports.* 1888–1949.

Tremont Temple Sketch Book. Boston: St. Botolph Press, 1896.

Trollinger, William Vance, Jr. *God's Empire: William Bell Riley and Midwestern Fundamentalism.* Madison: University of Wisconsin Press, 1990.

Waldron-Stains, Candace. "Evangelical Women: From Feminist Reform to Silent Femininity." *debarim* 3 (1978–79): 57–73.

Wallace, Les. *The Rhetoric of Anti-Catholicism:The American Protective Association, 1887–1911.* New York: Garland, 1990.

Weber, Timothy. *Living in the Shadow of the Second Coming: American Premillennialism, 1875–1982.* Chicago: University of Chicago Press, 1987.

Whitehill, Walter Muir. *Boston: A Topographical History.* 2nd ed. Cambridge: Harvard University Press, 1968.

Whiteside, William B. *The Boston Y.M.C.A. and Community Need.* New York: Association Press, 1951.

Wilcox, Delos S. *Great Cities in America: Their Problems and Their Government.* New York: Macmillan, 1910.

Willard, A. R. "Recent Church Architecture in Boston." *New England Magazine* (February 1890): 641–662.

Windsor, Justin, ed. *Memorial History of Boston.* Vol. 3. Boston: James R. Osgood, 1881.

Wolfe, Alfred Benedict. *The Lodging House Problem in Boston.* Boston: Houghton Mifflin, 1906.

Wolffe, John. "Anti-Catholicism and Evangelical Identity in Britain and the United States, 1830–1860." In *Evangelicalism: Comparative Studies of Popular Protestantism in North America, the British Isles, and Beyond, 1700–1990,* ed. Mark A. Noll, David W. Bebbington, and George A. Rawlyk. New York: Oxford University Press, 1994, 179–197.

Wood, Nathan R. *A School of Christ.* Boston: Halliday Lithograph, 1953.

Woods, Robert A., ed. *The City Wilderness: A Settlement Study.* Boston: Houghton Mifflin, 1898.

The Work of God in Tremont Temple. Boston: Union Temple Baptist Church, 1871.

The Year-Book of the Congregational and Christian Churches. New York: Executive Committee of the Central Council of the Congregational and Christian Churches, 1929–1950.

Zueblin, Charles. *American Municipal Progress.* New York: Macmillan, 1916.

PERIODICALS

Boston Globe
Boston Herald
Boston Post
Boston Transcript
British-American Citizen
The Christian
Christian Cynosure
Christian Register
Common People

Congregationalist
Converted Catholic
New England Evangelist
Our Day
Pilot
The Republic
Safeguard
Sheaf of the First Fruits
Watchman
Watchword
Woman's Voice and Public School Champion
Union Signal
Zion's Herald

MANUSCRIPT COLLECTIONS

Elizabeth Evans Papers, Billy Graham Center Archives, Wheaton, Ill.
A. J. Gordon Papers, Gordon College, Wenham, Mass.
Gordon College Archives, Gordon College, Wenham, Mass.
Billy Graham Evangelistic Association Collection, Billy Graham Center Archives, Wheaton, Ill.
J. C. Massee Papers, American Baptist Historical Society, Rochester, N.Y.
Park Street Church Records, Congregational Library, Boston
William A. Sunday Papers, Billy Graham Center Archives, Wheaton, Ill.
Tremont Temple Records, Boston, Tremont Street, Mass.
Nathan Wood Papers, Gordon College, Wenham, Mass.

Index